OLYMPIC GAMES, ASIAN GAMES, AFRO ASIAN GAMES AND COMMON WEALTH GAMES

D1881100

OLYMPIC GAMES, ASIAN GAMES, AFRO ASIAN GAMES AND COMMON WEALTH GAMES

By

SHAMSHAD AHMED

ISHA

© **Author**

All rights reserved. No part of this work may be reproduced, stored, adapted, or transmitted in any form or by any means, electronic, mechanical, photocopying, micro-filming, recording or otherwise, or translated in any language, without the prior written permission of the copyright owner and the publisher. The book is sold subject to the condition that it shall not, by way of trade or otherwise, be lent, resold, hired out, or otherwise circulated without the prior publisher's written consent in any form of binding or cover other than that in which it is published.

The views and opinions expressed in this book are author(s) own and the facts reported by them have been verified to the extent possible, and the publishers are not in any way liable for the same.

ISBN : 978-81-8205-244-4

Published, 2018

Published by

Isha Books
D-69, New Gupta Colony,
Near DDA Market
Delhi – 110009
Ph.: +91-9212142040

Contents

1

Games in the Ancient Period

Man's interest in games and sports is since time immemorial. It comes as natural as is the pleasure of playing by almost all animals. But, it is not clear how it was introduced. Nor is is very clear what the earliest form of sport was. We are only certain that the earliest forms of sports were different from the ones played these days. True, entertainment was regarded as one of main driving forces for indulging in sports activities. But even people used to entertain themselves with those activities that would sharpen their skill in practical life.

The cave paintings of the ancient men bear certain evidence of some form of sport activities. For instance, one such painting display a group of men dancing around a fictitious animal with javelins in their hands. Though a mode of hunting spree, it basically reveals the ancient people in their sporting mood. With little of farming activity these men at the dawn of human civilization were basically hunters. Thus their sports and games were also influenced by this hunting habit.

In ancient Egypt, pharaohs demonstrated their fitness to rule by prowess in the hunt and by exhibitions of strength and skill in archery. However, Egyptians, with less claim to divinity, jumped, wrestled, and engaged in ball games and stick fights of the sort that can still be observed in Egypt. The great epics of the world also anecdote the games of wrestling, chariot race, archery, hunting and the likes. Ancient Greece had all these. It is where sports had a significance unequaled anywhere before the rise of modern sports.

One such "sports report," is found in book 23 of Homer's Iliad in the form of funeral games for the dead Patroclus. These games were a part of cult and therefore, lacked the present days' spirit of sports. But the contests in the Odyssey are essentially secular. Odysseus was challenged by the Phaeacians to demonstrate his prowess as an athlete.

In general, Greek culture included both cultic sports, such as the Olympic Games honoring Zeus, and secular contests.

Deifining Games

A game is a recreational activity involving one or more players, defined by a) a goal that the players try to reach, and b) some set of rules that determines what the players can do. Games are played primarily for entertainment or enjoyment.

Games can involve one player acting alone, but more often involve competition among two or more players. Taking an action that falls outside the rules generally constitutes a foul or cheating.

All through human history, people have played games to entertain themselves and others, and there is an enormous variety of games types; for specific information about any type, see links at the end of this article.

Philosopher David Kelley, in his popular introductory reasoning text *The Art of Reasoning*, defines the concept "game" as "a form of recreation constituted by a set of rules that specify an object to be attained and the permissible means of attaining it." This covers most cases well, but does not quite fit with things like war games and sports that are often done not for entertainment but to build skills for later use. In *Philosophical Investigations*, philosopher Ludwig Wittgenstein argued that the concept "game" could not be contained by any single definition, but that games must be looked at as a series of definitions that share a "family resemblance" to one another. In a different context, Stephen Linhart said, "People say you have to choose between games and real life. We think this claim that there's a dichotomy is very dangerous."

Many technical fields are often applied to the study of games, including probability, statistics, economics, ethnomathematics, and game theory.

Games of Ancient Period

Many of the games people played a long time ago, we still play today. Other games have now been completely forgotten. Most of them are fun to play, though.

Ball games have been known for thousands of years. People made balls out of leather stuffed with cloth scraps or wool, sewn together with leather thongs or string (like a football today). There are pictures of both boys and girls throwing balls to one another, and of boys in classical Athens playing a game like field hockey with curved sticks and a ball. (Unfortunately we don't know the rules). In this picture you can see a girl juggling three balls, on a vase from Athens in the 400's BC.

By this time, and possibly much earlier, people also played marbles, with small balls made out of clay (the crummy ones) and out of real marble (the good ones). (Glass marbles were not invented until much later. It is still possible, though not easy, to buy clay marbles, but we have not found a source for stone ones). Again we don't know the rules. But probably they played the same basic games of marbles that we know today: one version where you take turns tossing the marbles at a goal (another marble, a hole, or a wall), and another version where you take turns shooting the marbles within a circle drawn in the dirt, trying to get them out of the circle.

Another type of game was *played with wooden hoops and sticks*, either tossing the hoop up in the air and trying to keep it up in the air with the sticks (rather like a hula hoop), or rolling the hoop along the ground pushing it with the stick.

Many very simple games are also very old, like *running races and playing tag, or competing to see who can jump the highest or the farthest.* They also played hopscotch, which seems to have started out as a training exercise for the Roman army.

The Egyptians, Greeks, and Romans were also very fond of *board games* like backgammon and checkers. Archaeologists often find paving stones in houses and in public buildings and sidewalks which have had little hollows carved out of them to place stones in, to play board games. The hollows are made in different patterns for different games. Again we don't know the rules. These games may have been like the African game Mancala. Many times we find these boards in places where men were bored, like in the doorways of guardposts, where the men (maybe slaves) had to sit all day in case somebody came. Somewhere in China, chess was invented and became very popular, eventually making its way west to India, then the Islamic Empire, and finally to Europe.

Gambling games were also very popular, and dice have been found from very old houses. Dice were sometimes made out of stone, and sometimes carved from bone or ivory. They had the same six numbers on them as today's square dice, arranged in the same way. And, because they were used for gambling, we even find some dice which had been loaded: a little piece of lead was hidden inside to make the die heavier on one side so it would land on that side more often! Playing cards were completely unknown in the ancient world, though people did play cards in the middle ages.

People also played games with knucklebones. Knucklebones are the vertebrae (the backbone) of medium-sized animals like sheep or goats, and the games you play with them are like jacks (In fact you can still find jacks shaped like knucklebones some places).

Other toys have also been found. Children played with *dolls*: some are made of wood and some of clay and bone. Some have jointed legs and arms, so they can move them, and others are all in one piece. This jointed doll is from Tarragona in Spain. You have to be careful though. Some little figures which look like dolls or dolls' dishes are really religious objects meant to be put in people's tombs when they died. Children had wooden blocks that they could stack up and knock down.

Festival Games

Physical development was much prized in the ancient world and apart from the training in the gymnasia there were also ball games that the youth participated in and in Roman times special ball courts were built. Also equestrian and boat races were popular but the great Festival Games were by far the most popular. It may be coincidence that this happened along with religious events as the large crowds attracted to a festival provided the spectators for the athletic competitions. Any city with enough prize-money could and did mount games, where champions were given substantial monetary rewards, but at the religious festivals the prize was generally a simple wreath. However the home town of a winner would often shower him with gifts as it had brought them such prestige. Olympic winners paid no tax, were fed free for life and much was to be gained from becoming a hero.

The main circuit of panhellenic festivals were:

— *The Olympian games* in honour of Zeus in Olympia began in 776BC at which the only event may have been the stadion foot race. They continued until around 256AD but were officially banned in 391AD by the Christian Emperor Theodosius. They were held every four years, which became a dating system and lasted for five days with a truce being initiated for a period both before and after the contest. The athletic events were held in the stadium, except wrestling which may have been contested around the altar of Zeus. The straight track of the stadium was surrounded on three sides by a grass mound on which up to 45,000 spectators could sit or stand. The hippodrome was where the various horse, colt, donkey cart and chariot races were held as each came to or fell from favour. The prize was a wreath from a sacred olive tree believed to have been planted by Heracles.

— *The Pythian games* were held at Delphi in honour of Apollo in conjunction with a musical contest in honour of the god. These were held in the third Olympic year. The prize was a laurel wreath cut from the valley of Tempe.

— *The Isthmian games* on the Isthmus of Corinth in honour of Poseidon were celebrated during the first and third Olympic year. The prize was a wreath of dry wild celery or pine branches. Some say they were founded by Theseus but the came into existence around 580.

— *The Nemean games* were held in the sanctuary of Zeus at Nemea and were said to have been founded by Heracles or the Seven against Thebes. Begun around 573 and held in the second and fourth Olympic year. The prize was a crown of fresh wild celery.

The Greek states and others were in a constant state of war over even the most minor causes, but or the Olympic festival, held every four years, a truce or 'ekecheiria', which means 'holding of hands' was announced before and during the games. Messangers were sent out as far away as France to the Baltic Sea. This armistice (eventually deified) allowed visitors and competitors to travel safely to Olympia.

A bronze inscription describing the truce was displayed at Olympia. Wars were suspended, armies were prohibited from entering Elis or threatening the Games, and legal disputes and the carrying out of death penalties were forbidden. Elis had restarted the Games after a visit to the oracle at Delphi and the city itself, just north of Olympia acted as the Olympic village prior to the Games with, but during the Games all travelled to the sanctuary of Olympia which contained the great temple of Zeus and also a temple to his wife Hera. (The athletes entrance to the stadium at left and the stadium itself at right with the starting block visible.) Here the elite were housed in a huge Guest House while most slept out in the open.

The athletes themselves were more often than not soldiers and even though we are used to thinking of the games as a time of peace, some events like the pancration and boxing could end in death. Violent as these two events were there were strict rules which forbad cheating as well as bringing hatred to the competition.

The most common myth surrounding the origin of the Olympic Games was that of Pelops, a prince from Lydia in Asia Minor who wished to marry the daughter of King Oinomaos.

To do so any suitor must compete against the King in a Chariot race and if he lost he would be beheaded. Pelops replaced a pin with wax in the chariot of the King who was then killed. Pelops married Hippodamia and founded the Olympic games to celebrate his victory. A different version says they were funeral games in the memory of Oinomaos. The Delphi Charioteer right and if you ever get the chance to see it up close you will be stunned to see the fine eyelashes on the statue - left.

Another myth comes from the Tenth Olympian Ode (one of may variations) of the poet Pindar who tells how in his fifth labour, Herakles had to clean the stables of King Augeas of Elis. After disagreements, broken promises etc. Herakles sacked the city of Elis and instituted the Olympic Games in honour of his father, Zeus. He is said to have taught men how to wrestle and measured out the stade, or the length of the footrace.

Games in Ancient Greece

The Greek's took games of all kinds very seriously, but especially physical athletic competition. The Greeks believed that their gods particularly loved to see strong, fit, graceful human bodies, especially boys' and men's bodies. So one way to get on the good side of the gods was to exercise, to eat right, to oil your skin, to create a beautiful body that the gods would love. Because of the Greek tendency to turn everything into an agon, a competition, this also meant that there were a lot of athletic competitions in Greece. The most famous of these is the Olympic Games, but there were other games held in other places as well, like the Isthmian Games at Corinth.

Young men (from richer families who didn't have to work) in most Greek cities spent a lot of their time training for these competitions, and the best of them were chosen to compete against the best young men from other cities. Then they would all meet, at the Olympic Games or the Isthmian Games or elsewhere, and compete for prizes and for the favor of the gods. Of course these games also served as good training for the army, because all these men would be soldiers as well. The events were the same kind as in the Olympics today: running, jumping, throwing a javelin, and throwing a discus. Only men could compete.

Greek boys also played games which were not part of the Olympic games, like field hockey. Greek boys usually played games without their clothes on (and so girls were not allowed to watch). Greek girls played games like throwing balls, though the Greeks were much less interested in physical activity for girls.

Greeks also played less active games like dice and marbles, and knucklebones, and checkers. This is a famous vase from the Vatican museum showing Achilles and Ajax playing checkers. Even in these games, though, the competition was very important, and there was a feeling that losing at games meant that the gods didn't like you.

Gymnasia

As mentioned the gymnasia took it's name from the Greek word 'gymnos' meaning naked. This was a state run centre for training where men and boys met and practiced athletics and the youth also followed intellectual training. Three gymnasia in Athens - the Lyceum, the Academy and the Cynosarges became great schools of philosophy. The physical training was in preparation for war. The complex consisted of an open courtyard for wrestling and the like, a running track, a grand colonnade (the stoa), which could also be used for training during inclement weather and an assortment of cloak rooms, oiling rooms, baths and lecture-rooms. The practice of being totally naked was peculiar to Greece and does not appear to be followed elsewhere. Training was done to the accompaniment of rhythmical music and as a high emphasis was placed on both physical strength and aesthetics, a student could be eliminated for lacking in either strength or beauty of appearance. It is known that there existed special diets to compliment the physical needs of different sports.

Palaestra

This was a much simpler and privately owned school for wrestling and gymnastics and consisted of a sand covered courtyard surrounded by changing rooms.

Athletics

Used as training in preparation for war, athletics date back to the time of Homer. Much prized in Greece and always totally nude, but less popular in Rome although the more educated classes did practice the Greek sports for leisure and relaxation. The Etruscans also followed the Greek games but were clothed. The main forms were:-

— *Wrestling*: Individuals challenged according to age not weight. It was the most popular sport. The contestants oiled themselves and some dusted themselves for better grip. Three falls of the shoulder or knees touching the ground designated the winner. Biting and genital holds were illegal, but breaking your opponent's fingers was permitted. It is known that Aristotle, Plato and Hypocrites were capable wrestlers.

— *Pancration*: A more violent form of wrestling where the opponent gave in at the point of strangulation or having a bone broken. Only biting and gouging an opponent's eyes, nose, or mouth with fingernails were banned. There were both men's and boys divisions of this sport which eventually became a highly admired.

— *Boxing*: A continuos match which ended in a knock-out or a raised hand of submission. They wore soft leather around the fist and knuckles and even ear guards during training, but these could inflict great damage to the opponent. A referee was armed with a stick for disciplining any offence. In gladiatorial Rome the gloves were weighted with metal or spikes. There were no weight classes within the mens' and boys' divisions, and opponents were chosen randomly.

— *Running*: A 200 metre rectangular track with starting lines, where the competitors traversed it once for a single foot race (stadion), turned and ran back for a double foot race (diaulos), or completed twelve circuits for the long distance. There was also a two to four-stadion (384 m. to 768 m.) race in armour. (the standard hoplite armour of helmet, shield, and greaves weighed about 50-60 lbs. In the 5th century BC there were even mechanical starting gates. The actual length of the stadion was said to be stepped out by Heracles who measured the 600 lengths of his rather large foot. Some festivals included a relay race where the runners ran through the streets and passed a lighted torch. Originally the goal of the race was the great altar of Zeus.

— *Long Jump*: A sport which is relatively unknown and which saw the contestant carrying weights (halteres). It may also have been from a standing position.

— *Discus*: Much like the modern equivalent. A lead, bronze, iron or stone circular plate thrown from an upward swing of a straight arm. they weighed around 7kilos but varied for men and boys. The longest throw won.

— *Javelin*: Also judged on distance thrown in the best of five but it had to hit the ground with it's point. They used a thong attached to fingers and the Javelin (a mans height) which added distance and spin.

— *Pentathlon*: Contestants entered five events - long jump, foot race, discus throwing, javelin and wrestling.

— *Chariot Race:* There were two and four horse chariot races, with separate races for chariots drawn by foals. Another race was between carts drawn by two mules. The course was twelve laps around the stadium track (nine miles) or hippodrome. The Chariot race was said to have been started by King Pelops whom myth said was buried near the Temple of Zeus.

— *Riding:* The course was six laps with separate races for full-grown horses and foals. Riders rode naked and without stirrups. As the training, equipment, and feed of both the jockey and the horses was so expensive, the owner received the olive wreath of victory instead of the rider.

Games in Ancient India

In the area of recreation and sports India had evolved a number of games. One would be surprised to know today that games like, Chess, Snakes and Ladders, Playing Cards, Polo,. the martial arts of Judo and Karate had originated in India and it was from here that these games were transmitted to foreign countries, where they were further developed. At times the changes made in the original nature of the Indian sport-forms were so many and so fundamental that the game lost all similarity with its original form in India.

Some Indian games were not transmitted abroad and remained confined to India. For instance we have Kabbadi, Kho-Kho, AtyaPatya, Malkhamb, Gulli-danda, etc., which are being played today exclusively in India. In this chapter we shall look into how the games like Chess and Ludo (Snakes and Ladders), the martial art of Karate, and Playing cards had existed in India for the past 2000 years and how in some cases the indigenous form of the game became totally extinct erasing the fact that- the game had ever been pl· yed in India.

Chess

A game very similar to modern Chess and Ludo was played in ancient India. In this game there used to be four participants due to which it was named Chaturanga meaning 'four bodies'. This four-bodied game was played with counters and a dice (aksha). Another name for this game was Astapada meaning 'eight steps'. This game was perhaps the progenitor of both modern day games of Chess and Ludo. There are instances in Indian history of this game being played.

One such instance is in the Mahabharata when Pandavas and Kauravas play this game. Yudhistira the eldest of the Pandavas places his bets on his kingdom, his wife Draupadi and all other material possessions. And by a malevolent trick he loses to the Kauravas everything that he had placed his bets on. Consequently to humiliate the Pandavas, Dushasana one of the evil Kaurava brothers takes hold of Draupadi whom Yudhisthira has lost to the Kauravas, and tries to disrobe her in front of the assembled court. The Pandavas though powerful are helpless as they have lost Draupadi and according to the rules of the game they have no claim on her anymore.

In distress, Draupadi invokes Lord Srikrishna to come to her rescue. And in answer to her prayers the lord appears and in a miracle sends a continuous stream of apparel to clothe Draupadi's body. The evil Dushasana tires himself out trying to tear away Draupadi's clothes but he is powerless against the divine strength of Lord Srikrishna. After hours of struggling to achieve his evil intention he falls unconscious to the floor. Draupadi's honour is saved. In deference to Lord Srikrishna's wishes, the Kauravas relinquish their claim to Draupadi. But in return the Pandavas are obliged to relinquish their kingdom for fourteen years and go into exile in forests, after which they return and regain their kingdom from the Kauravas, but not before a devastating war is fought between the two clans on the battlefield of Kurutshetra.

The Mahabharata story throws light on the fact that a game similar to Chess was played in ancient India. The Mahabharata is variously dated around 800 and 1100 B.C. Thus this game was known in India nearly 3000 years ago. It is the view of some historians that this game was also used in the allocation of land among different members of a clan when a new settlement was being established.

The Indian origin of the game of chess is supported even by the Encylopedia Britannica according to which, "About 1783-89 Sir. William Jones, in an essay published in the 2nd Vol. of Asiatic Researches, argued that Hindustan was the cradle of chess, the game having been known there from time immemorial by the name Chaturanga, that is, the four angas, or members of an army, which are said in the Amarakosha (an ancient Indian Dictionary - S.B.) to be elephants, horses, chariots and foot soldiers.

As applicable to real armies, the term Chaturanga is frequently used by the epic poets of India. Sir William Jones' essay is substantially a translation of the Bhawishya Purana, in which is given a description of a four-handed game of chess played with dice." "Sir William, however, grounds his opinions as to the Hindu origin of chess upon the testimony of the Persians and not upon the above manuscript," He lays it down that chess, under the Sanskrit name Chaturanga was exported from India into Persia in the 6th century of our era; that by a natural corruption, the old Persians changed the name into chatrang; but when their country was soon afterwards taken possession of by the Arabs, who had neither the initial nor the final letter of the word in their alphabet, they altered it further into Shatranj, which name found its way presently into modern Persian and ultimately into the dialects of India."

The Encyclopedia Britannica further says that Wander Linde, in his exhaustive work, Geschichte and Litteraturdes Schachspiels, has much to say of the origin-theories, nearly all of which he treats as so many myths. He agrees with those who consider that the Persians received the game from the Hindus. The outcome of his studies appears to be that chess certainly existed in Hindustan in the 8th century, and that probably that country is the land of its birth. He inclines to the idea that the game originated among the Buddhists, whose religion was prevalent in India from the 3rd to the 9th century. According to their ideas, war and slaying of one's own fellow-men, for any purpose whatever, is criminal, and the punishment of the warrior in the next world will be much worse than that of the simple murderer, hence chess was invented as a substitute for war.

According to the Encylopedia "Altogether, therefore, we find the best authorities agreeing that chess existed in India before it is known to have been played anywhere else. In this supposition they are strengthened by the names of the game and some of its pieces. Shatranj as Forbes has pointed out, is a foreign word among the Persians and the Arabians, whereas its natural derivation from the term Chaturanga is obvious. Again affix the Arabic name for the bishop, means the elephant, derived from alephhind, the Indian elephant." Even the word checkmate is derived from the Persian term Shah Mat which means 'the king is dead!'. The Sanskrit translation of this term would be Kshatra Mruta. Another term viz. 'the rooks' which is the name for one set of the counters used in chess, originated from the Persian term Roth which means a soldier.The Persian term according to the Encyclopedia is derived from the Indian term Rukh, which obviously seems to have originated in the

Sanskrit word Rakshak which means a soldier from Raksha which means 'to protect'.

About the introduction of this game into Persia, the Encylopedia says that "The Persian poet Firdousi, in his historical poem, the Shahnama, gives an account of the introduction of Shatranj into Persia in the reign of Chosroes I Anushirwan, to whom came ambassadors from the sovereign of Hind (India), with a chess-board and men asking him to solve the secrets of the game, if he could or pay tribute. The king asked for seven days grace, during which time the wise men vainly tried to discover the secret. Finally, the king's minister took the pieces home and discovered the secret in a day and a night."

The Encyclopedia Britannica concludes that "Other Persian and Arabian writers state that Shatranj came into Persia from India and there appears to be a concensus of opinion that may be considered to settle the question. Thus we have the game passing from the Hindus to the Persians and then to the Arabians, after the capture V of Persia by the Caliphs in the 7th century, and from them, directly or indirectly, to various parts of Europe, at a time which cannot be definitely fixed, but either in or before the 10th century. That the source of the European game is Arabic is clear enough, nor merely from the words "check" and "mate", which are evidently from Shah mat ("the king is dead"), but also from the names of some of the pieces"

Thus it was from India that the ancient Persians are said to have learnt this game, and from them it was transmitted to the Greco Roman world. The evidence of the Persians having borrowed this game from India is seen in the name the Persians gave to it. The Persian word for chess is Chatrang, which was later changed by the Arabs to Shatranj. As said in Encyclopedia Britannica, thig word is obviously a corruption of the Sanskrit original Chaturanga.

The other term Astapada meaning eight steps, which was also used to describe this game in ancient India, perhaps was a description for the eight steps (Squares) which the modern Chessboard, has. The modern Chessboard is chequered with 64 (8 x 8) squares in all, with eight squares on each side. The old English word for chess which is Esches, possibly stems from this eight squared aspect of the game as did the Sanskrit word Astapada.

Playing Cards

The game of playing cards was also one of the favourite pastimes of Indians in ancient times. This game was patronised especially by the royalty and nobility. This game was known in ancient times as Kridapatram, in the middle ages, it was known as Ganjifa. In medieval India Ganjifa cards were played in practically all royal courts. This game is recorded to have been played in Rajputana, Kashyapa Meru (Kashmir), Utkala (Orissa) the Deccan and even in Nepal. The Mughals also patronised this game, but the Mughal card-sets differ from those of the ancient Indian royal courts.

Some scholars are of the opinion that this game was in fact introduced into India by the Mughals. But according to Abul Fazal author of the Ain-e-Akbari, the game of cards was of Indian origin and that it was a very popular pastime in the Indian (Hindu) courts when the Muslims came into India. According to Abul Fazal's description of the game, the following cards were used. The first was Ashvapati which means 'lord of horses'. The Ashvapati which was the highest card in, the pack represented the picture of the king on horseback. The second highest card represented a General (Senapati) on horseback. After this card come ten other with pictures of horses from one to ten.

Another set of cards had the Gajapati (lord of elephants) which represented the king whose power lay in the number of elephants. The other eleven cards in this pack represented the Senapati and ten others with a soldier astride an elephant. Another pack has the Narpati, a king whose power lies in his infantry. We also had other cards known as the Dhanpati, the lord of treasures, Dalpati the lord of the squadron, Navapati, the lord of the navy, Surapati, the lord of divinities, Asrapati, lord of genii, Vanapati, the king of the forest and Ahipati, lord of snakes, etc.

On the authority of Abul Fazal we can say that the game of playing cards had been invented by sages in ancient times who took the number 12 as the basis and made a set of 12 cards. Every king had 11 followers, thus a pack had 144 cards. The Mughals retained 12 sets having 96 cards. These Mughal Ganjifa sets have representations of diverse trades like Nakkash painter, Mujallid book binder, Rangrez, dyer, etc., In addition there were also the Padishah-i-Qimash, king of the manufacturers and Padishah-izar-i-Safid, king of silver, etc.

The pre-Mughal origin of the game of cards is evident if we examine the pattern of painting the cards. We can find that despite the observation of Abul Fazal that Akbar introduced the pack with 8 sets, we find that even earlier, in Indian (Hindu) courts we have packs with 8, 9 and 10 sets apart from the usual 12. The numbers were derived from the eight cardinal directions Ashtadikpala, for the pack with 8 set, from the nine planets Navagraha for the one with 9 sets and from ten incarnations Dashavatara of Vishnu for the pack with 10 sets.

Themes from the Ramayana and Mahabharata are painted on these cards. The largest number of such cards are to be found in Orrisa. The largest number of such cards are to be found in Orissa. The painters from Orissa have represented various illustrations like the Navagunjara, a mythical birdhuman animal which was the form xassumed by Sri Krishna to test Arjuna's fidelity, il lustrations from the Dashavatata of Vishnu are also portrayed.

All these cards were hand-made and were painted in the traditional style. This required considerable patience and hard meticulous work. The kings usually commissioned painters to make cards as per their preference. The commoners got their cards made by local artists who were to be ; found in urban and rural areas. In order to -obtain the required thickness a number of sheets of pieces of cloth were glued together. The outlines of the rim were painted in black and then the figures were filled with colours.

As cards were played by members all strata of society we find different types of cards. Some cards were also made of ivory, tortoise shell, mother of pearl, inlaid or enamelled with precious metals. The cards were of different shapes; they were circular, oval rectangular, but the circular cards were more common.

The cards were usually kept in a wooden box with a lid painted with mythological figures. This art of handmade, hand painted cards which had survived for hundreds of years. gradually feel into decay and became extinct with the introduction of printed paper cards by the Europeans in the 17-18th centuries. With the extinction of the art of making and painting cards also was erased the memory that Indians ever had played the game of cards with their own specific representations of the Narapati, Gajapati and Ashvapati.

Karate and Judo

Many eyebrows would be raised when an Indian lays claim to the martial arts of Judo and Karate. Such askance is understandable. Everybody the world over knowns that it was the countries of the far-east China, Korea and Japan who have given these arts to us. The finest exponents of Karate, Judo come from these countries, schools like Shaolin and Ninja that have nurtured these arts are from the far-east. But in the distant corner of India a dying martial art exists which comes significantly close to Karate. This art from is called Kalaripayate. The practitioners of Kalaripayate have to develop acrobatic capabilities and use swords or knives to attack an opponent. Even an unarmed exponent of Kalaripayate presents an invincible adversary.

This art from seems to have travelled from India to the countries of the far-east alongwith the Buddhist religion. Buddhists monks who travelled barefoot and unarmed to spread the gospel of Buddha seem to have accepted this art with alterations suitable to the philosophy of nonviolence. Such a technique of defence would have been necessary for them as they travelled individually or in small groups in foreign lands during which they were exposed to dangers from bandits and fanatics from other religions. Buddhist monks seem to have tempered the originally violent character of this art. The violent and exterminative nature of Kalaripayate is evient from the daggers and knives that are used. Unlike Kalaripayate, Judo and Karate do not allow the use of lethal weapons.

The aim of a Karate practitioner is mainly to disarm and disable his opponent without mortally wounding him. This can be looked upon as a reflection of the Buddhist attitude towards life. Further both Judo and Karate are deeply interwoven with meditation unlike other martial arts like boxing, wrestling, fencing, etc. The concentration aspect in Judo and Karate perhaps stems from this. Both Judo and Karate are sought to be kept as arts to be used for just purposes for pro tection of the weak, etc.

The oath that every student of these disciplines has to take is evidence of this. A teacher of Judo or Karate traditionally commands deep respect of students and a lesson always starts with a bow of the students to the teacher. The teacher here is not looked upon only as a coach as in western martial arts like boxing and fencing. This relationship between a teacher and student in Judo and Karate could have its roots in the Guru-Shishya tradition of India.

Thus it is quite possible that these martial art forms originated in southern India and were transmitted to China, Korea and Japan by Buddhist monks. But it has to be conceded that they were neglected in India where like Buddhism they atrophied and today the world considers them to be a legacy bequeated by the countries of the far-east.

Ancient Games of Egyptians

The Egyptians engaged in many sports and honoured the body. There is also evidence of sports like bull-leaping, acrobatics, wrestling, and boxing, in Minoan Crete found on relief vases, wall frescoes, seals, and in figurines. The "Boxer Vase" from Hagia Triada in Crete has several bands of relief depicting wrestling, bull-leaping, and boxing. Leaping and somersaulting over bulls appears as early as 2000 BC. Boxing also appears and the figures show a clenched fist, and sometimes wear hand-coverings or ancient boxing gloves. The four major Minoan Palaces of Knossos, Phaestos, Mallia, and Zakro contained L shaped theatres that could hold up to 500 spectators, and central courts ideal for bull-leaping. The Minoans had extensive trading contact with the Egyptians and the sporting influence from Egypt may have passed to the Minoans and then to Greece. A subsequent invasion of the aggressive Dorians from the North may have added the competitive spirit to the games we know of in Greece.

2

Ancient Olympic Games

Although records cannot verify games earlier than 776 B.C., the contests in Homer's Iliad indicate a much earlier competitive tradition. The ancient Greek games were held, every fourth summer, at Olympia, in honor of Zeus. They reached their height in the 5th–4th cent. B.C.; thereafter they became more and more professionalized until, in the Roman period, they provoked much censure. They were eventually discontinued by Emperor Theodosius I of Rome at the end of the 4th cent. A.D.

Among the Greeks, the games were nationalistic in spirit; states were said to have been prouder of Olympic victories than of battles won. Women, foreigners, slaves, and dishonored persons were forbidden to compete. Contestants were required to train faithfully for 10 months before the games, had to remain 30 days under the eyes of officials in Elis, who had charge of the games, and had to take an oath that they had fulfilled the training requirements before participating. At first, the Olympic games were confined to running, but over time new events were added: the long run (720 B.C.), when the loincloth was abandoned and athletes began competing naked; the pentathlon (708 B.C.); boxing (688 B.C.); chariot racing (680 B.C.); the pankration (648 B.C.), involving boxing and wrestling contests for boys (632 B.C.); and the foot race with armor (580 B.C.).

Greek women, forbidden not only to participate in but also to watch the Olympic games, held games of their own, called the Heraea. Those were also held every four years but had fewer events than the Olympics. Known to have been conducted as early as the 6th cent. B.C., the Heraea games were discontinued about the time the Romans conquered Greece. The winners of the Olympics (and of the Heraea) were crowned with chaplets of wild olive, and in their home city-states male champions were also awarded valuable gifts and privileges.

The ancient Olympics were rather different from the modern Games. There were fewer events, and only free men who spoke Greek could compete, instead of athletes from any country. Also, the games were always held at Olympia instead of moving around to different sites every time.

Like our Olympics, though, winning athletes were heroes who put their home towns on the map. One young Athenian nobleman defended his political reputation by mentioning how he entered seven chariots in the Olympic chariotrace. This high number of entries made both the aristocrat and Athens look very wealthy and powerful.

Like their modern counterparts, ancient athletes had a way of capturing the public's imagination. Several ancient authors such as Pindar, Pausanias, Strabo, and Dio Chrysostom record the noteworthy exploits of some of the best-known Olympic victors of ancient times.

The Olympic Games were supposed to start in the Peloponnese, in Greece, some 3 000 years ago. Sports competitions were organised at Olympia and were named after their location, hence their name of Olympic Games. Nobody knows exactly when they began, but the first written mention of the competitions is dated to 776 BC years before the birth of Christ. It can be said to be the time when human civilization was at its infancy. Olympics derived its name from the ancient Greek city of Olympia where the game show was founded as a part of a big festival. Olympia had a temple of

Zeus. And the festival was used to be held in the honor of Zeus. The earth goddess Gaea was originally worshiped at Olympia.

In the course of time, her importance reduced. And it was the sky god Zeus in whose honor priestly officials conducted quadrennial athletic contests. Sacred also were the games held at Delphi, in honor of Apollo, and at Corinth and Nemea. These four events were known as the periodos, and great athletes, such as Theagenes of Thasos, prided themselves on victories at all four sites. The athletic triumphs brought with it special prestige. Both in the form of statues of the victors and also material benefits. The festival witnessed the gathering of talents in different fields from different parts of the globe.

The great festival of Olympia earned so much of awe those days that even soldiers would lift no weapon during the festival. Its influence was so great that even the two warring states in Greece would announce a 'cease war' for the time being. All were eligible for taking part in the game show. Any independent Greek could take part in any event following a ten-month's training. And every state would vie for seeing their player clinching the title. Accordingly, Greeks would attach special attention to the physical culture of all boys since an early age.

Some of the events those days included penthalon,pancresia, wrestling, discuss throwing, javelin throwing, running, chariot racing. The winner of each event was awarded a crown made of green olive bough. This apart, the winners were greeted with honors and a hero's welcome back home. Of all the events pancresian was the most challenging one. It was a play-until-dead type of game. The winner had to be highly skilled in multiple disciplines like wrestling, boxing, kicking.

On the other hand the winner of the penthalon had to be an expert in high jump, race, discuss and javelin throwing, and, the stand-up wrestling. Unlike the three categories found in modern boxing, ancient Olympics had no such category. Thus the heaviest weighted one would eventually wear the boxing crown. But Olympic was not only confined among the players, musicians, artists, poets - all would come to take part in events marked for them.

Since the Greeks were devoted to secular sports as well as to sacred games, no polis, or city-state, was considered a proper community if it lacked a gymnasium where, as the word gymnos indicates, naked male athletes trained and competed. Except at militaristic Sparta, Greek girls rarely participated in sports of any kind. Women were excluded from the Olympic Games even as spectators (except for the priestess of Demeter). Pausanias, the 2nd-century-AD traveler, wrote of races for girls at Olympia, but these events in honor of Hera were of minor importance.

Unfortunately the curtain fell on ancient Olympics game during the regime of the Roman emperor Theodosius. He had a strong dislike to all games and sports. He was driven by a credo that there should be no place for a barbarian game show like Olympics in the Christian civilization.

Not only he ended the tradition of Olympic games, but ordered the destruction of the Olympic temple and the stadium. And it was under his instruction the statue of Zeus was carried away to Constantinople. Later the statue was destroyed by a fire. Later his successor Theodosius II asked the destruction of all Greek temples including that of Zeus. Still, what was left out was wiped by flood and earthquake. Thus the ancient game came to an end.

Although the ancient Olympic games were first recorded in 776 BC, they originated at least a century before that and possibly as early as the 13th century BC. One Greek legend said that the great Herakles (Hercules, in the Roman form) won a race at Olympia, a plain in the small state of Elis, and then decreed that the race should be re-enacted every four years. Another said that Zeus himself had originated the festival after defeating Cronus for the sovereignty of heaven.

The more likely story is that the Olympic festival was a local religious event until 884 BC, when Iphitus, the king of

Elis, decided to turn it into a broader, pan-Hellenic festival. To accomplish that, he entered into a temporary truce with other rulers, allowing athletes and others to travel peacefully to Olympia while the festival was going on. The Greeks based their chronology on four-year periods called Olympiads, and the Olympic festival marked the beginning of each Olympiad. Evidently, the festival was reorganized in 776 BC, which was considered the start of the first Olympiad.

The festival was basically a religious gathering to celebrate the gods worshipped in common by all Hellenes, primarily Zeus. There were three other major pan-Hellenic festivals, the Pythian, the Nemean, and the Isthmian, all of which included fairs, but the festival at Olympia became pre-eminent by 572 BC, when Elis and Sparta entered into an alliance under which Elis was in charge of the event itself while Sparta enforced the sacred truce.

A single foot race was the only athletic event until the fifteenth Olympiad. The race was the length of the stadium, approximately 200 yards. As time went on, the games associated with the festival expanded and became increasingly important. A race of two stadium lengths was added in 724 and a long-distance race of 24 stadium lengths (about 2.5 miles) was added in 720. Other types of sports followed quickly: Wrestling and the pentathlon in 708, boxing in 688, chariot racing in 680, and the pancratium, a combination of boxing and wrestling, in 748. At one time or another, there were 23 Olympic sports events, although they were never all held at the same festival.

A branch of wild olive was the only official prize for an Olympic winner, but there were also usually some unofficial prizes awarded by his city-state. For example, Athens allowed an Olympic champion to live free of charge in the Pyrtaneum, a special hall set aside for distinguished citizens. Other city-states exempted winners from taxes for an Olympiad, and in some cases citizens contributed to a cash award. Athletes had to arrive in Elis a month before the games to undergo spiritual, moral, and physical training under the supervision of the judges, who then decided which of them were genuinely qualified to compete. Each competitor had to swear an oath that he was a free-born Greek who had committed no sacrilege against the gods.

At first, the games took up only one day of the festival. That was extended to two days in 680, with the addition of chariot racing, and to five days in 632. However, only three of those days were actually devoted to competition. The first day was devoted to religious sacrifices, the registration of athletes, and the taking of the Olympic oath. Prizes were awarded and thanksgiving sacrifices were offered on the fifth day. Athletes usually competed nude. They originally wore shorts but, according to one ancient writer, Pausanias, a competitor deliberately lost his shorts so that he could run more freely during the race in 720 BC, and clothing was then abolished.

Women were not allowed to watch the games, but that had nothing to do with the nudity of the male athletes. Rather, it was because Olympia was dedicated to Zeus and was therefore a sacred area for men. The chariot races, which were held outside the sacred precinct, were open to women spectators. At its peak during the 4th century BC, the Olympic festival drew crowds not only from the Pelopponesian Peninsula but from colonies as far away as Libya and Egypt. Poets and other writers recited spontaneously, sculptors worked on statues while surrounded by spectators, vendors sold food from stalls, traders from throughout the peninsula sold horses.

Traveling to Olympia took on the nature of a pilgrimage, which attracted some of the greatest names of Greece's classic period. Plato attended the festival when he was seventy. Demosthenes, Diogenes the Cynic, Pythagoras, and Themistocles all visited Olympia at one time or another. The young Thucydides was in the audience when Herodotus, the "father of history," read from his works.

Even after the glory that was Greece vanished, the Olympics lived on, but in a debased form under the Romans, who replaced the traditional games with their own gladiatorial contests, in which slaves replaced free-born Greeks as the competitors. In 394 AD, Theodosius the Great decreed an end to the Olympic Games. But they had lasted more than a thousand years, perhaps as long as 1600 years, and certainly longer than any other secular institution in history.

The Games were held at Olympia every four years. This four-year period acquired the name Olympiad, and was used as a date system : time was counted in Olympiads, rather than years.

The Panhellenic Games

The Games organised at Olympia led to the development of the Panhellenic Games, which also included :

— The Games at Delphi (Pythian Games)

— The Games at Corinth (Isthmian Games)

— The Games at Nemea (Nemean Games)

These Games were special because they brought the Greek world together at a time when Greece was not a single state, but a series of city-states (politically and economically independent communities). From Greece and the colonies (in Italy, North Africa and Asia Minor), people travelled to take part in or attend these Games, inspired by the shared feeling of belonging to the same culture or religion. It should be noted that the four Panhellenic Games were never held during the same year. It is difficult to know exactly what gave rise to these Games. Mythology is mixed up with history, and events which happened at the time were often explained as the consequences of divine intervention. This was the case for the Panhellenic Games, for which there are numerous stories attempting to explain their origin.

The Sacred Truce

On the occasion of the four Panhellenic Games, a sacred truce was proclaimed. Messengers (spondorophoroi) went from city to city announcing the date of the competitions. They called for all wars to be halted before, during and after the Games in order to enable the athletes, as well as the spectators, to travel to and from the Games sites in total safety. A climate of peace was considered important during the period of competition.

The Panhellenic Games were of major religious significance. Each of the Games was celebrated in honour of a specific god :

— Zeus, the king of the gods, at Olympia and Nemea

— Apollo, the god of light and of reason, at Delphi

— Poseidon, the god of the sea and of horses, at Corinth

Site of the Olympia

Of the four Panhellenic Games, those at Olympia were the most important and were regarded as a special event throughout the Greek world. The site consisted of a sacred area, the Altis, marked by a boundary wall, and a secular (nonreligious) area. The sacred area contained the temples, including the one to Zeus, the altars on which sacrifices were made, and the Treasuries, small buildings erected by the city-states in which precious offerings were kept (e.g. vases and statues).

The secular area was outside the boundary wall. It contained the sporting structures of the gymnasium, palaestra, stadium and hippodrome, plus all the buildings used for the administration of the Games and to welcome important guests. Only the priests and the staff responsible for looking after the sanctuary lived at Olympia.

At the time of the competitions, the atmosphere was very different. In addition to the athletes and spectators, merchants of all kinds flocked to the site : the number of people present for the Olympic Games is estimated to have been over 40 000.

In addition to the Panhellenic Games, major sports competitions were held in Athens. These were known as the Panathenian Games. They were part of the Great Panathenaea, the biggest festival in Athens, which was held every four years in honour of the goddess Athena. Everywhere in Greece and the colonies, there were numerous local competitions, some better known than others. Each city made a point of organising them.

The Athlete

A number of objects made by the Ancient Greeks have survived until today. Archaeological excavations have uncovered sculptures, vases, coins and tools. These objects give us a good idea about how people lived at the time. We can use them to find out more about the athletes and the competitions they participated in.

When looking at a sculpture or a scene painted on a vase, it is easy to identify the athlete by his nakedness. Indeed, for both training and competitions, athletes were always nude. Their bodies, shaped by exercise, were used as models by sculptors and painters who drew inspiration for their works directly from the athletes and their movements whilst practising sport. The beauty of the naked body was considered to reflect internal beauty and to illustrate the harmonious balance between body and mind. Practising sport helped to develop and attain this harmony.

Gymnasium and Palaestra

There was a gymnasium and a palaestra in every Greek city. These places were where athletes trained and young boys were educated. It was an allround education, including exercise for the body as well as the mind. Physical education, music, arithmetic, grammar and reading were all part of the programme. Depending on the sports practised, the training took place in one or the other building.

Hygiene and Body Care

When they arrived at the gymnasium or palaestra, athletes stripped completely. Without the protection of a layer of clothing, they had to take special care of their skin. To prepare for training, an athlete would cover his body with olive oil and then dust it with fine sand. The oil and sand combination helped to regulate his body temperature as well as providing protection from the sun and from the stick that the trainer would use to beat him if he didn't perform the exercises correctly ! After the events, the athlete would take his strigil, a curved instrument, and scrape the sweat, oil and sand off his skin. He then finished cleaning himself with water and a sponge. During competitions, athletes cared for their skin in the same way. The equipment that the athlete needed was extremely simple :

— an aryballos, a kind of small bottle, often earthenware, containing oil
— a strigil
— a sponge

These were held together by a ring which the athlete attached to the wall of the gymnasium or palaestra.

Participation in the Games

There were three main criteria for participation in the Games: one had to be male, of Greek origin and a free man. Women, slaves and foreigners were excluded. To begin with, the athletes were not professionals. Though they were mostly from rich families, some of the athletes also came from more modest sections of the population. Over time, the situation changed, and most of the athletes became professionals. After Greece was conquered by Rome in 146 BC, Romans were allowed to join the Greek athletes. Later, participation was also extended to athletes of foreign origin, after the granting of Roman citizenship to all the inhabitants of the provinces during the 248th Olympiad.

For the Olympic Games, a city selected the best athletes from its gymnasium. The athletes chosen still had to train hard for several months. Once the sacred truce had been proclaimed and the date of the Games announced, the athletes and their trainers left for Olympia. The journey could be long and difficult. When they arrived in Elis, near Olympia, the athletes trained for one month at the city's gymnasium, the last stage of qualifying for the Games. Those who were finally selected went to Olympia and took an oath, as did the judges. They promised to take part in the competitions in an honourable way, abiding by the rules.

Cheating and Fines

Some athletes did not always respect their oath and tried to win by unauthorised means. This kind of cheating was punished and the dishonest athletes had to pay fines. With this money, statues of Zeus were erected, known as the Zanes. Each of these statues were placed along the passageway that led to the stadium, with the name of the cheat inscribed on its base. To get to the competition site, the athletes had to walk past all the statues. This reminded them of the example not to follow !

Famous Athletes

In the history of the modern Games, great champions are headline news. They are admired and respected : they are real heroes. The Games of Antiquity also had their champions. Thanks to their performances, the names of these famous athletes are still known today.

The fabulous wrestler Milo of Croton, several times Olympic champion in a career spanning 26 years. Milo was a true hero and enjoyed many other victories in competitions outside Olympia. Famous for his legendary power, he was also known for his great appetite ! The extraordinary Leonidas of Rhodes, fourtime Olympic running champion, was considered the equal of a god by his fellow countrymen. There was also the boxer Melankomas of Caria (Asia Minor), who was famous not only for his magnificent body, but also for his unusual fighting technique. Melankomas did not strike his opponents but instead wore them out by skilfully dodging their blows ! After they died, the great champions had special honours bestowed upon them. So that their victories at the Games were never forgotten, their tombs were decorated with a gravestone on which images of the wreaths won during their careers were carved.

Sports on the programme

In the ancient world, the Olympic Games were a reference point. The sports on the programme in Olympia were often taken up with slight variations at other Panhellenic sites or, with further minor variations, in local competitions. It is the Olympic programme that is presented here. The programme of the Games comprised only individual sports - team sports were not included. No water sports figured on the programme either.

Arrangements for the Games

The opening of the Games was marked by animal sacrifices on the altar of Zeus. The competitions, which eventually lasted for some five days, took place in the stadium and the hippodrome. The stadium was made of hard-packed earth and was rectangular in shape. There were no terraces and the spectators sat on the banks, except for the officials who were provided with a stand. Free men, slaves and young girls were able to watch the Games. Only married women were excluded from the crowd of spectators. The Games ended with banquets organised in honour of the winner and with sacrifices in honour of Zeus.

Features of the Sports

With the exception of the equestrian sports, which were staged in the hippodrome, all the competitions were held in the stadium.

There were different types of race :

— The stade or stadion, which consisted of one length of the stadium

— The diaulos, two lengths or double stadium

— The dolichos, a long-distance race (from 7 to 24 laps)

— The armed race (in Olympia it was a diaulos), where the athletes wore a helmet and greaves, and carried a shield

The competitors took their place at a starting line marked out by white limestone slabs. They ran in a straight line and not around the stadium as they do today.

Discus Throwing

The discus was made of stone or metal. A famous statue by the sculptor Myron represents an athlete about to throw a discus. This sculpture is called Discobolus (circa 40 BC). The original was destroyed, but there are many copies dating from Roman times. For example, one of them is on show at the Termes Museum in Rome.

Javelin Throwing

A leather strap was fixed to the shaft of the javelin to form a loop. When throwing, the athlete inserted his index and second fingers into the loop, which allowed him to increase the distance the javelin travelled.

Long Jump

The athlete used weights. With his feet together and without a run-up, the athlete jumped, throwing his arms forward. In the air, arms and legs were almost parallel. Before landing, the athlete swung his arms backwards, dropping the weights at the same time. This movement propelled his legs forward and extended the distance of the jump. The use of weights meant that the athletes' movements had to be co-ordinated. Flute music accompanied the event in order to aid the participants in this respect. The weights were made of stone or metal and their shape varied.

Combat Sports

There are several hypotheses concerning the place where wrestling, pugilism and pankration events took place. Some researchers think that these competitions took place in the Altis, in front of the altar of Zeus. Others believe they took place in the stadium. The drawing of lots decided which athletes would compete against each other. Unlike today, there were no weight categories.

Wrestling

The opponents fought standing up, with bare hands. There were different types of hold. The person who first touched the ground three times was the loser.

Pankration

A type of wrestling. All moves were allowed in pankration, except for biting, gouging out eyes and putting fingers in the opponent's nose.

Boxing

The fighters' hands were protected by long leather thongs. These ancestors of boxing gloves underwent numerous modifications over time. Pieces of metal were added on the knuckles, making the punches much more violent.

Penathlon

The pentathlon comprised five events : running, jumping, discus throwing, javelin throwing and wrestling. The athlete who took part in this competition was called a pentathlos. It was the most all-round sport, and the body of the pentathlos was considered to be the most perfect.

Equestrian Events

Chariot racing and horse riding took place in the hippodrome. Chariot races were spectacular and particularly popular with the public. There were quadriga races, where the chariots were pulled by four horses, and biga races, where the chariots were pulled by two horses. The drivers were called charioteers. Unlike the athletes, the charioteers were not naked but instead wore long tunics. In the horse races, the jockeys were naked. They rode bare-back (without a saddle) and did not wear spurs. Thanks to the equestrian events, women participated indirectly in the Games ! As owners, they could race their horses, driven or ridden by male charioteers or jockeys.

Music and Singing

Music and singing competitions were not on the programme of the Olympic Games. They were a speciality of the Games at Delphi !

Well before the appearance of sports competitions, musical competitions were organised in Delphi. These comprised singing accompanied by the cithara (a type of lyre), flute solos or singing with flute accompaniment. Music and singing remained a feature of the Pythian Games even after the integration of sports competitions. Poetry and drama competitions also figured on the programme.

Prizes

Crowns, Ribbons and Palm Fronds

At the modern Olympic Games, the first, second and third - placed athletes are rewarded, respectively, by gold, silver and bronze medals. At the Panhellenic Games, there was only one winner whose prize was a wreath or crown of leaves. At each of the venues, the crowns were made with different types of leaves : As well as a crown, the winner received a red woollen ribbon, the taenia. A famous statue by the sculptor Polycletus (dating from the second half of the 5th century BC) shows a victor tying the ribbon around his head. The statue is called Diadumenos and there is a bronze copy of it at the entrance to the Olympic Museum in Lausanne. Finally, the winner often held a palm frond, another symbol of victory.

The Ancient Greeks considered that it was the gods who decided to grant victory to an athlete. Victory was often represented in the form of a winged female character known as Nike, which means " victory " in Greek. As the servant or messenger of the Gods, Nike flew down to the chosen person, to bring them their divine reward in the form of a crown or ribbon.

Fame

The glory of the victorious athlete brought reflected glory to all the inhabitants of his home town. When he returned from the Games, he was given a hero's welcome and received numerous benefits for the rest of his life. To show that he had become famous, the victor had the right to have a statue of himself erected. He could also ask a poet to write verses telling of his feats. Because they were proud of him, his fellow citizens sometimes made coins with his effigy on them, so as not to forget him and to make him known throughout the Greek world.

Prizes in Local Competitions

The prizes awarded in local competitions had a greater material value. Amphorae filled with olive oil were often given to the winner. During this period, olive oil was extremely precious and worth a lot of money. Other treasures, such as bronze tripods (big vases with three feet), bronze shields or silver cups were also given as prizes.

A Progressive Decline

Throughout their history, the Olympic Games grew hugely in importance. Originating as simple running competitions, they became a major sports event. However, the quality of the competitions and the ethical values of the participants were not always of the highest standard. These phenomena would become obvious after the conquest of Greece by Rome, in 146 BC, when a period of " decline " started, which would eventually lead to the end of the Games. There are several reasons for the Games' disappearance :

— *The professionalism of the athletes :* The Games became a contest between professionals, whose principal motivation was to collect victories by participating a great number of competitions not only in the Panhellenic Games, but in local contests as well.

— *The presence of Romans amongst the Greek athletes :* The Romans were advocates of sport as a show. They sought above all to satisfy the spectators. The spirit of competition, of measuring oneself against others in a climate of excellence, was of no interest to them. The essential ideal of the Games was threatened.

— *The paganism of the Games :* Believing in several gods was a particularity of the religions in Antiquity. The Games

> were no exception, as they were dedicated to pagan divinities. The birth of Christianity, with its belief in a single God, and the conversion of emperors to this new religion meant that pagan Games could no longer be tolerated.

After the abolition of the Games, Olympia became prey to acts of vandalism. Fires and earthquakes also had their effect and over time destroyed the buildings. Little by little, the site disappeared under several metres of earth and vanished from memory. Thanks to the writings of ancient historians, the memory of the Games and their place in the Greek world was not totally forgotten. The Games were known to have existed, but the knowledge of their exact location had been lost. In the 18th century, research work started, and in the 19th century, archaeological digs finally revealed the ruins of Olympia. Today, the exploration of these ruins allows the visitor to appreciate the importance of Olympia and to imagine the past glory of the Panhellenic Games.

3

Modern Olympic Games: 1896-1964

The modern revival of the Olympic games is due in a large measure to the efforts of Pierre, baron de Coubertin, of France. They were held, appropriately enough, in Athens in 1896, but that meeting and the ones that followed at Paris (1900) and at St. Louis (1904) were hampered by poor organization and the absence of worldwide representation. The first successful meet was held at London in 1908; since then the games have been held in cities throughout the world. World War I prevented the Olympic meeting of 1916, and World War II the 1940 and 1944 meetings. The number of entrants, competing nations, and events have increased steadily.

To the traditional events of track and field athletics, which include the decathlon and heptathlon, have been added a host of games and sports—archery, badminton, baseball and softball, basketball, boxing, canoeing and kayaking, cycling, diving, equestrian contests, fencing, field hockey, gymnastics, judo and taekwondo, the modern pentathlon, rowing, sailing, shooting, soccer, swimming, table tennis, team (field) handball, tennis, trampoline, the triathlon, volleyball, water polo, weight lifting, and wrestling. Olympic events for women made their first appearance in 1912.

A separate series of winter Olympic meets, inaugurated (1924) at Chamonix, France, now includes ice hockey, curling, bobsledding, luge, skeleton, and skiing, snowboarding, and skating events. Since 1994 the winter games have been held in even-numbered years in which the summer games are not contested. Until late in the 20th cent. the modern Olympics were open only to amateurs, but the governing bodies of several sports now permit professionals to compete as well. As a visible focus of world energies, the Olympics have been prey to many factors that thwarted their ideals of world cooperation and athletic excellence. As in ancient Greece, nationalistic fervor has fostered intense rivalries that at times threatened the survival of the games. Although officially only individuals win Olympic medals, nations routinely assign political significance to the feats of their citizens and teams. Between 1952 and 1988 rivalry between the United States and the Soviet Union, rooted in mutual political antagonism, resulted in each boycotting games hosted by the other.

Politics has influenced the Olympic games in other ways, from the propaganda of the Nazis in Berlin to pressures leading to the exclusion of white-ruled Rhodesia from the Munich games. At Munich, nine Israeli athletes were kidnapped and murdered by Palestinian terrorists. The International Olympic Committee (IOC), which sets and enforces Olympic policy, has struggled with the licensing and commercialization of the games, the need to schedule events to accommodate American television networks, and the monitoring of athletes who seek illegal competitive advantages, often through the use of performance-enhancing drugs. The IOC itself has also been the subject of controversy. In 1998 a scandal erupted with revelations that bribery and favoritism had played a role in the awarding of the 2002 Winter Games to Salt Lake City, Utah, and in the selection of some earlier venues. As a result, the IOC instituted a number of reforms including, in 1999, initiating age and term limits for members and barring them from visiting cities bidding to be Olympic sites.

Today, the Olympic Games are the world's largest pageant of athletic skill and competitive spirit. They are also displays of nationalism, commerce and politics. These two opposing elements of the Olympics are not a modern invention. The conflict between the Olympic movement's high ideals and the commercialism or political acts which accompany the Games has been noted since ancient times.

The 19th-Century Olympic Movement

Baron Pierre de Coubertin, a Frenchman, is justly given credit for establishing the modern Olympics, but it was England that revived the idea, and it was in England that Coubertin was introduced to it.

As early as 1612, Robert Dover established an English version of the Olympic Games in the Cotswold Hills in Gloucestershire. Events included card games, chess, and dancing, as well as running, jumping, the hammer throw, pitching the bar, wrestling, and horse racing. During the 18th century, students at Cambridge University staged some kind of Olympic Games, but it's not known exactly when they were held or what sports were involved, if any.

The Olympic idea was definitely in the air in 19th-century England. The Baron de Berenger held an Olympic Festival at Chelsea Stadium in London in 1832. To commemorate Queen Victoria's coronation, he staged another festival in 1838, which included archery, gymnastics, cricket, fencing, rowing, sailing, and target shooting with both rifle and pistol.

By far the most important of such events was the annual Olympic festival at Much Wenlock, Shropshire, which began in 1850. William "Penny" Brooke, a life-long campaigner for physical education, organized the games, which included cricket, hurdling, jumping, quoits, running, and soccer.

The Much Wenlock Games were originally designed for youngsters—there was an even a race for children under seven—but they eventually grew to include older athletes. They also drew some attention from Europe and the German Gymnastics Society began sending a team to England to compete in various events.

In 1861, Brooke organized the Shropshire Olympian Association, which led to the founding of the National Olympian Association four years later. Brooke's goal was to create an international Olympics, primarily to promote physical education in participating countries.

Brooke never achieved that goal. But, in 1890, he was visited by Coubertin, who was eager to learn about the Much Wenlock games and the Olympian Society, and Brooke was very helpful to the young Frenchman who shared his interest in physical education and his dream of an international Olympic festival.

Born in 1863, Coubertin had grown up in the shadow of his country's devastating defeat in the Franco-Prussian War of 1870-71. He decided that France had lost the war due to physical and spiritual flabbiness caused primarily by poor educational methods.

A boxer, fencer, and rower as a young man, Coubertin determined to devote his life to education and, especially, to physical education. His ideas fit in exactly with England's "muscular Christianity" movement, which espoused moral and intellectual development based on physical fitness.

Coubertin visited England several times to see first-hand how sport was used in public schools, and he also traveled to the United States with the same goal. In 1889, he organized the Congress of Physical Education in Paris and the following year he made his visit to Much Wenlock to talk to "Penny" Brooke about the Olympian Society.

The idea of reviving the Olympics as a true international festival grew out of that meeting. Coubertin began openly espousing the idea in 1892, but attracted little notice. Despite repeated rebuffs, not only from his own countrymen but from the English and the Americans as well, Coubertin persisted. On June 23, 1894, he presided over a meeting of 79 delegates, representing 12 countries, who unanimously voted for the restoration of the Olympic games.

As a result, the International Olympic Committee (IOC) was organized, with the goal of staging the first modern Olympics in Paris in 1900. Pressed by Coubertin, the IOC soon decided to aim for 1896, with Athens as the site.

That idea, too, met with resistance, especially from the government of Greece. But when Georgios Averoff of Alexandria donated 920,000 gold drachmas to build an Olympic stadium in Athens, the resistance folded, and the King of Greece himself opened the first modern Olympic Games on April 5, 1896 (March 24 on the Greek calendar).

The 1896 Olympics: Athens, Greece

Fast Facts

Host City:	Athens, Greece
Opening date:	April 6, 1896
Closing date:	April 15, 1896
Nations:	14
Athletes:	245 (all male)
Events:	43 events in nine sports

There were 245 athletes registered for the inaugural 1896 Games at Athens, but 164 of them were Greek. They and 81 other athletes, representing 13 other countries, competed in the 43 events. The program included nine sports: cycling, fencing, gymnastics, shooting, swimming, tennis, track and field, weightlifting, and wrestling. (Rowing and sailing races had also been planned, but they were canceled because of bad weather.)

Most of the foreign athletes paid their own way, and there were no standards of eligibility. Some of the competitors, in fact, were tourists who just happened to be visiting Greece at the time and decided to enter on the spur of the moment. Germany and France had the largest representation, with 19 athletes each, followed by the United States with 14. There were no national teams as such, but the Boston Athletic Association brought a contingent of athletes, as did the German Gymnastics Society, the Union of French Athletic Associations, and the British Athletic Association.

Although the winners are listed, retroactively, as gold medalists, there were no gold medals in 1896 and only the first two finishers in each event received prizes: A silver medal and a crown of olive branches for first place, a bronze medal and crown of laurel for second.

The first champion of the modern Olympics was James Connolly of the United States, who won the triple jump. Paul Masson of France won three of the six cycling events and Hungary's Alfred Hajos won two of the four swimming races, while the U. S. dominated track and field, winning nine of twelve events.

The marathon was run for the first time in 1896. It retraced the legendary 25-mile route that had been run by Pheidippides in 490 BC to tell Athenians that the invading Persians had been beaten back at Marathon. (According to the legend, Pheidippides died of exhaustion after delivering the message. There was another legend, recorded by Herodotus, that Pheidippides had run the 150 miles from Athens to Sparta before the battle in order to enlist the aid of the Spartans.)

A previously unknown Greek shepherd, Spyridon Louis, became a national hero by winning the race. Along with his Olympic prizes, Louis won free shaves for the rest of his life from a patriotic barber and free meals, any time he asked, at an Athens restaurants.

Although the competition was not of the highest quality, the 1896 Olympics were considered a great success, in large part because of the enthusiasm of the Greek spectators. At the closing banquet, King George of Greece suggested that Athens should become the permanent home of the Olympic Games, but Coubertin and the IOC stuck to the original idea of holding the 1900 games in Paris.

Leading Medal Winners:

Athlete	Country	Sport	G-S-B	Total
Hermann Weingärtner,	GER	Gymnastics	3-2-1	6
Karl Schuman,	GER	Gymnastics /Wrestling	4-0-0	4
Alfred Flatow,	GER	Gymnastics	3-1-0	4
Bob Garrett,	USA	Track	2-1-1	4
Viggo Jensen,	DEN	Shooting /Weightlifting	1-2-1	4
Paul Masson,	FRA	Cycling	3-0-0	3
Teddy Flack,	AUS	Track/Tennis	2-0-1	3
Jules Zutter,	SWI	Gymnastics	1-2-0	3
James Connolly,	USA	Track	1-1-1	3
Leon Flameng,	FRA	Cycling	1-1-1	3
Adolf Schmal,	AUT	Cycling	1-0-2	3
Efstathios Choraphas,	GRE	Swimming	0-1-2	3
Holger Nielsen,	DEN	Shooting	0-1-2	3

Medals by Nation:

No.	Nation	G	S	B
1.	United States of America (USA)	11	7	2
2.	Greece (GRE)	10	18	17
3.	Germany (GER)	6	5	2
4.	France (FRA)	5	4	2
5.	Great Britain (GBR)	2	3	2
6.	Hungary (HUN)	2	1	2
7.	Austria (AUT)	2	1	2
8.	Australia (AUS)	2	0	0
9.	Denmark (DEN)	1	2	3
10.	Switzerland (SUI)	1	2	0
11.	Mixed team	1	0	0

The 1900 Olympics: Paris, France

Fast Facts

Host City: Paris, France

Opening date: May 14, 1900

Closing date: October 28, 1900

Nations: 24

Athletes: 1,225 (1,206 male, 19 female)

Events: 87 events in 20 sports

Coubertin was resented by many chauvinistic French sports officials because of his international outlook and because of what was seen as his desire to import English ideas about education into the country. As a result, the 1900 Games almost didn't happen and, when they did happen, they were very poorly organized. Progress began only after Coubertin resigned from the Union of French Athletic Associations (USFSA) in 1899. The USFSA then decided to hold the Olympics in conjunction with the Universal Paris Exhibition of 1900. That led to some absurdities, such as the fencing competition being held as a sort of sideshow in the exhibition's cutlery area.

Because there were other sporting events held in connection with the exposition, there was a great deal of confusion about which were Olympic contests and which weren't. Some athletes didn't even know they were taking part in the Olympics, while others thought they were in the Olympics when they really weren't. As an example of the confusion, Margaret Abbott of the United States won a nine-hole golf tournament, which she entered as a lark. She is now on record as the first woman ever to win a gold medal but she died in 1955 without knowing it. Another problem was that the French staged some events on Sunday, when a number of American athletes refused to compete because they believed in honoring the Lord's Day, including both entrants in 1500-meter run and the country's Prix des Nations equestrian team.

Myer Prinstein, the world record holder in the long jump, entered into a gentleman's agreement with other U. S. athletes not to compete on Sunday even though he was Jewish and it was not his Sabbath. However, Alvin Kraenzlein of the U. S. entered the long jump finals on Sunday, July 14, and won the gold medal. That led to a fist fight between the two athletes on Monday, when Prinstein discovered the deception.

Kraenzlein emerged as the game's big winner, taking four gold medals. In addition to his high jump victory, he won the 60-meter dash, the 110-meter hurdles, and the 200-meter hurdles. Ray Ewry of the U. S. won three now-obsolete events, the standing high jump, standing broad jump, and standing triple jump. Irving Baxter won an unusual double, in the high jump and pole vault, and Walter Tewksbury won gold medals in the 200-meter dash and the 400-meter hurdles. All told, the United States won 17 of the 23 track and field events.

Despite all the confusion, 1,225 athletes competed in 1900, representing 24 countries, according to the official IOC numbers, which have been revised several times. Swimming, wrestling, and weightlifting were dropped from the program and gymnastics was reduced to a single event, the all-around competition. Cricket, croquet, equestrian events, golf, rowing, rugby, soccer, tennis, and water polo were added, though several of those sports disappeared from the Olympics almost immediately. Women competed for the first time, in croquet and tennis as well as golf. Charlotte Cooper of Great Britain became the first female Olympic champion, winning the women's singles tennis title.

Leading Medal Winners:

Men				
Athlete	Country	Sport	G-S-B	Total
Irving Baxter,	USA	Track	2-3-0	5
John W. Tewksbury,	USA	Track	2-2-1	5
Alvin Kraenzlein,	USA	Track	4-0-0	4

Konrad Stäheli,	SWI	Shooting	3-0-1	4
Achille Paroche,	FRA	Shooting	1-2-1	4
Stan Rowley,	AUS	Track	1-0-3	4
Ole Östmo,	NOR	Shooting	0-2-2	4
Ray Ewry,	USA	Track	3-0-0	3
Charles Bennett,	AUS	Track	2-1-0	3
Emil Kellenberger,	SWI	Shooting	2-1-0	3
Laurie Doherty,	GBR	Tennis	2-0-1	3
Reggie Doherty,	GBR	Tennis	2-0-1	3
E. Michelet,	FRA	Yachting	1-0-2	3
F. Michelet,	FRA	Yachting	1-0-2	3
Anders Nielsen,	DEN	Shooting	0-3-0	3
Zoltán Halmay,	HUN	Swimming	0-2-1	3
Léon Moreaux,	FRA	Shooting	0-2-1	3

Women

Athlete	Country	Sport	G-S-B	Total
Charlotte Cooper,	GBR	Tennis	2-0-0	2
Marion Jones,	USA	Tennis	0-0-2	2

Medals by Nation

No.	Nation	G	S	B
1.	France (FRA)	25	36	31
2.	United States of America (USA)	20	14	15
3.	Great Britain (GBR)	16	6	9
4.	Switzerland (SUI)	6	1	1
5.	Belgium (BEL)	5	5	5
6.	Mixed teams	4	3	3
7.	Germany (GER)	3	2	2
8.	Italy (ITA)	2	1	0
9.	Australia (AUS)	2	0	3
10.	Denmark (DEN)	1	3	2

11.	Hungary (HUN)	1	3	2
12.	Cuba (CUB)	1	1	0
13.	Austria (AUT)	0	3	3
14.	Norway (NOR)	0	2	3
15.	India (IND)	0	2	0
16.	Netherlands (NED)	0	1	3
17.	Bohemia (BOH)	0	1	1
18.	Sweden (SWE)	0	0	1

The 1904 Olympics: St. Louis, Missouri

Fast Facts

Host City:	St. Louis, Missouri
Opening date:	July 1, 1904
Closing date:	Nov. 23, 1904
Nations:	13
Athletes:	689 (681 male, 8 female)
Events:	94 events in 17 sports

The confusion of the Paris Games seriously damaged the Olympic movement, and the 1904 games almost killed it. Chicago was originally selected as the host, but St. Louis officials feared that the Olympics would cut into attendance at the World Fair.

They threatened to hold athletic competitions in conjunction with the fair if the Olympic Games weren't moved to St. Louis. The IOC finally decided to let President Theodore Roosevelt arbitrate the question, and he chose St. Louis. The IOC went along with that.

European tension caused by the Russo-Japanese War and the difficulty of getting to St. Louis kept many of the world's top athletes away. There were only 687 competitors, most of them from the United States, though Canada sent a good-sized contingent. Only 12 countries were represented.

In a number of sports, the U. S. national championship was combined with the Olympic championship, because there were no competitors from other nations. The United States won 80 of the 100 gold medals and 238 of the 300 total medals.

Boxing was added to the program and wrestling was restored, but all the competitors in both sports were from the United States. Swimming returned, along with weightlifting, and a full gymnastics program was held. Rowing events were held for the first time.

Ray Ewry again won all three standing jumps. Three other U. S. track and field athletes, Archibald Hahn, Jim Lightbody, and Harry Hillman, won three gold medals apiece. The top foreign athlete was Emil Rausch of Germany, who won three swimming events. Zoltan Halmay of Hungary and Charles Daniels of the United States each won two swimming gold medals.

The St. Louis Games did make one major contribution to the Olympic tradition: gold, silver, and bronze medals were awarded to the top three finishers for the first time.

Leading Medal Winners:

Men

Athlete	Country	Sport	G-S-B	Total
Irving Baxter,	USA	Track	2-3-0	5
Anton Heida,	USA	Gymnastics	5-1-0	6
George Eyser,	USA	Gymnastics	3-2-1	6
Burton Downing,	USA	Cycling	2-3-1	6
Marcus Hurley,	USA	Cycling	4-0-1	5
Charles Daniels,	USA	Swimming	3-1-1	5
Albertson Van Zo Post,	USA	Fencing	2-1-2	5

William Merz,	USA	Gymnastics	0-1-4	5
Jim Lightbody,	USA	Track	3-1-0	4
Francis Gailey,	USA	Swimming	0-3-1	4
Teddy Billington,	USA	Cycling	0-1-3	4
Frank Kungler,	USA	Weightlifting /Wrestling /Tug of War	0-1-3	4
Ray Ewry,	USA	Track	3-0-0	3
Ramón Fonst,	CUB	Fencing	3-0-0	3
Archie Hahn,	USA	Track	3-0-0	3
Harry Hillman,	USA	Track	3-0-0	3
Julius Lenhart,	AUT	Gymnastics	2-1-0	3
George "Phil" Bryant,	USA	Archery	2-0-1	3
Emil Rausch,	GER	Swimming	2-0-1	3
Robert Williams,	USA	Archery	1-2-0	3
Ralph Rose,	USA	Track	1-1-1	3
William Thompson,	USA	Archery	1-0-2	3
Charles Tatham,	USA	Fencing	0-2-1	3
William Hogenson,	USA	Track	0-1-2	3
Emil Voigt,	USA	Gymnastics	0-1-2	3

Women

Athlete,	Country	Sport	G-S-B	Tot
Lida Howell,	USA	Archery	2-0-0	2
Emma Cooke,	USA	Archery	0-2-0	2
Jessie Pollack,	USA	Archery	0-0-2	2

Medals by Nation

No.	Nation	G	S	B
1.	United States of America (USA)	78	83	77

2.	Germany (GER)	4	4	5
3.	Cuba (CUB)	4	2	3
4.	Canada (CAN)	4	1	0
5.	Hungary (HUN)	2	1	1
6.	Mixed team	1	1	0
7.	Great Britain (GBR)	1	1	0
8.	Greece (GRE)	1	0	1
9.	Switzerland (SUI)	1	0	1
10.	Austria (AUT)	0	0	1

The 1906 "Intercalated" Olympics: Athens, Greece

Fast Facts

Host City: Athens, Greece

Nations: 20

Athletes: 877 (870 male, 7 female)

With his beloved Olympic movement in disarray, Baron de Coubertin felt the best way to restore it to health would be to return to Athens as soon as possible. Rome had been selected as the site for 1908 games, but Coubertin entered into a tentative agreement with the Greek government that Athens would host interim or "intercalated" games in 1906 and 1910, with the possibility that such games would be held every four years thereafter.

The IOC as a whole wasn't particularly pleased with the idea, so Coubertin withheld formal sanctioning of the 1906 games. Despite that fact, however, and despite the fact that the program was cut back substantially from those of 1900 and 1904, more than 900 athletes from 20 countries competed in Athens.

Among them was Virner Jarvinen, the first Finnish competitor. He won the Greek-style discus event and finished in the standard discus. He was welcomed home as a national hero, which inspired many young Finnish athletes to strive for future Olympic glory.

The United States won 11 of 21 track and field events, led by Paul Pilgrim, who won the 400- and 800-meter runs; Martin Sheridan, the winner in the shot put and the standard discus; and Ray Ewry, who won the standing long and high jumps.

Archie Hahn, who had won medals in the 60-, 100-, and 200-meter dashes in 1904, repeated in the 100, but the other events weren't on the program in Athens. Swimming events were cut way back, from ten in 1904 to only four, and gold medals went to four different countries, Austria, Great Britain, Hungary, and the United States.

The lack of archery competition was more than made up for by a wide variety of target shooting events. In fact, there were so many of them that five different athletes won four or more medals in shooting.

The "intercalated" games were discontinued after 1906, and the IOC doesn't consider the 1906 games official. Nevertheless, Coubertin was grateful to Athens for celebrating the 10th anniversary of the Olympics with a well-organized and well-run program that helped restore belief in the movement.

Leading Medal Winners:

Men				
Athlete	Country	Sport	G-S-B	Total
Louis Richardet,	SWI	Shooting	4-2-0	6
Martin Sheridan,	USA	Track	2-3-0	5
Konrad Stäheli,	SWI	Shooting	2-2-1	5
Léon Moreaux,	FRA	Shooting	2-1-2	5
Jean Reich,	SWI	Shooting	1-1-3	5

Gudbrand Skatteboe,	NOR	Shooting	3-1-0	4
Gustav Casmir,	GER	Fencing	2-2-0	4
Eric Lemming,	SWE	Track/ Tug of War	1-0-3	4
Francesco Verri,	ITA	Cycling	3-0-0	3
Enrico Bruna,	ITA	Rowing	3-0-0	3
Georgio Cesana,	ITA	Rowing	3-0-0	3
Max Decugis,	FRA	Tennis	3-0-0	3
Emilio Fontanella,	ITA	Rowing	3-0-0	3
Georges Dillon-Cavanaugh,	FRA	Fencing	2-1-0	3
Henry Taylor,	GBR	Swimming	1-1-1	3
Fernand Vast,	FRA	Cycling	1-0-2	3
Raoul de Boigne,	FRA	Shooting	0-1-2	3
John Jarvis,	GBR	Swimming	0-1-2	3

Women

Athlete	Country	Sport	G-S-B	Total
Sophia Marinou,	GRE	Tennis	0-2-0	2

Medals by Nation

Rk.	Nation	G	S	B	Total
1.	France	5	9	16	40
2.	Greece	8	13	12	33
3.	United States	12	6	6	24
4.	Great Britain	8	11	5	24
5.	Italy	7	6	3	16
6.	Sweden	2	5	7	14

7.	Germany	4	5	4	13
8.	Switzerland	5	4	2	11
9.	Hungary	2	5	3	10
10.	Austria	3	3	2	8
11.	Belgium	2	2	3	7
12.	Norway	4	1	0	5
13.	Denmark	2	2	1	5
14.	Finland	2	0	1	3
15.	Australia	0	1	2	3
16.	Holland	0	0	3	3
17.	Canada	1	1	0	2
18.	Czechoslovakia	0	0	2	2
19.	South Africa	0	0	1	1

The 1908 Olympics: London, England

Fast Facts

Host City: London, England

Opening date: April 27, 1908

Closing date: Oct. 31, 1908

Nations: 22

Athletes: 2,035 athletes (36 women, 1,999 men)

Events: 109 events in 22 sports

Rome had originally been selected to host the 1908 Olympics, but the Italian organizers withdrew after a 1906 eruption of Mount Vesuvius created havoc in the country. The IOC asked the British Olympic Association to take over.

In many respects, it was the ideal solution. England had much more collective experience in organizing large sports events than any other country, with the Henley Royal Regatta, the All-England (Wimbledon) tennis tournament, and the 30-year-old Amateur Athletic Association's national track and field championships. The English organizers did bring considerably more order to the Olympics, primarily by limiting the number of athletes that could represent any one country in a given event. But the 1908 Games were the first to be marred by international politics and controversy over judging.

Finnish athletes were told that they would have to march under the Russian flag, not the flag of Finland, and they chose not to carry any flag at all. Similarly, Irish athletes who wanted to represent their country were ordered to compete on behalf of Great Britain, and many of them withdrew as a result.

Acrimony between the United States and the host country began at the opening ceremony, when the American flag bearer, Ralph Rose, refused to dip the flag to the royal box, as other countries did. He explained his action with the terse statement, "This flag dips to no earthly king."

Several decisions by British judges went against American athletes during the games, and U. S. spokesmen felt they stemmed from bias, caused in part by the flag incident. Other countries also complained about some official decisions. The Swedish Greco-Roman wrestling team withdrew because of several adverse rulings, and both Canada and France complained bitterly about what they felt were unfair decisions in cycling.

The biggest controversy arose from the final of the 400-meter run, in which there were only four runners, one Briton and three Americans. J. C. Carpenter, who apparently won the race, was disqualified for allegedly interfering with the British runner, Wyndham Halswelle. Judges ordered a rerun of the final, but the three Americans refused to take part and Halswelle won by running around the track all by himself.

One reason for the disqualification was that Great Britain and the United States had different rules governing obstruction in running races. As a result of the controversy, the IOC decided, after the 1908 Games, that judges would be drawn from an international pool, rather than being furnished by the host country, and that standardized rules would be drawn up for all sports. That led directly to the founding in 1912 of the International Amateur Athletic Federation to codify rules for track and field competition.

The marathon also ended in controversy when Dorando Pietri of Italy collapsed after entering the stadium ahead of the pack. He was revived by doctors and some of the officials helped him to his feet and then assisted him to the finish line. John Hayes of the United States was the second finisher. Pietri had been declared the winner, but the Americans lodged a protest that was finally upheld. However, the action by the British officials, and the unusually long time it took them to uphold the protest, didn't go over very well with the United States.

On the brighter side, the overall organization of the 1908 Olympics was nearly impeccable. The system of using qualifying standards and preliminary competition leading up to the medals events has been followed by the organizers of every Olympics since then.

Quite by accident, the standard marathon distance was established in 1908. The original course was 25 miles long, which was more or less the standard distance at the time. But the starting line was moved from its original location to Windsor Castle, in order to give the royal family a better view, and the resulting distance of 26 miles, 385 yards has been the standard ever since.

The British also set a standard for future international swimming competition by building a 100-meter pool, clearly marked into lanes. And they planted the seed of the future Winter Olympics by adding figure skating to the program.

Despite the disputed 400-meter result, the United States did well in track and field, winning 13 of the 24 events. Ray Ewry won the standing broad jump and standing high jump to increase his gold medal total to 10, which is still the all-time record. Mel Sheppard was the only other double gold medalist and track and field, winning the 800- and 1,500-meter runs. The biggest winner overall was Henry Taylor of Great Britain, who won three gold medals in swimming.

Leading Medal Winners:

Men

Athlete	Country	Sport	G-S-B	Total
Mel Sheppard,	USA	Track	3-0-0	3
Henry Taylor,	GBR	Swimming	3-0-0	3
Benjamin Jones,	GBR	Cycling	2-1-0	3
Martin Sheridan,	USA	Track	2-0-1	3
Oscar Swahn,	SWE	Shooting	2-0-1	3
Josiah Ritchie,	GBR	Tennis	1-1-1	3
Ted Ranken,	GBR	Shooting	0-3-0	3

Women

Athlete	Country	Sport	G-S-B	Total
Madge Syers,	GBR	Figure Skating	1-0-1	2

Medals by Nation

No. Nation	G	S	B
1. Great Britain (GBR)	56	51	35
2. United States of America (USA)	23	12	12
3. Sweden (SWE)	8	6	11
4. France (FRA)	5	5	9
5. Germany (GER)	3	5	6
6. Hungary (HUN)	3	4	2
7. Canada (CAN)	3	3	10
8. Norway (NOR)	2	3	3

9. Italy (ITA)	2	2	0
10. Belgium (BEL)	1	5	2
11. Australasia (ANZ)	1	2	2
12. Russia (RUS)	1	2	0
13. Finland (FIN)	1	1	3
14. South Africa (RSA)	1	1	0
15. Greece (GRE)	0	3	0
16. Denmark (DEN)	0	2	3
17. Bohemia (BOH)	0	0	2
18. Netherlands (NED)	0	0	2
19. Austria (AUT)	0	0	1

The 1912 Olympics: Stockholm, Sweden

Fast Facts

Host City: Stockholm, Sweden

Opening date: May 5, 1912

Closing date: July 27, 1912

Nations: 28

Athletes: 2,547 athletes (57 women, 2,490 men)

Events: 102 events in 14 sports

Ironically, with World War I only two years away, the 1912 Olympics were the most successful up to that time and they were distinguished by a high level of international amity. The Swedish organizers benefited from their observation of British organizational methods and from a full four years of preparation.

There were no important arguments or protests. In fact, for the first time it seemed that an Olympic community was genuinely taking shape. Many of the athletes had met in 1908, and they fraternized happily together. It was commonplace, after a medal event, for winners and losers to embrace in congratulation and commiseration. Officials from international sports organizations and national teams were also generally well-acquainted with one another, especially since many of them had been involved in regular meetings planning and preparing for the games.

At Stockholm, gymnastics became a major sport, with an astounding 1,275 athletes from 13 countries either competing or giving demonstrations. Swimming, too, was bigger than ever before, with 313 competitors from 18 countries. Both Australia and Japan served notice that they were beginning to produce world-class swimmers.

The 1912 Olympics introduced two technical innovations. For the first time, a public address system kept spectators informed about what was happening and electrical timing was used for running events. This was also notable as the first Olympics to draw extensive, front-page newspaper coverage in the United States.

The only real problems were that boxing was dropped from the program because it was illegal in Sweden, and freestyle wrestling was also dropped because the sport was unknown to the Swedes. The IOC took over the responsibility of determining which sports would be on the Olympic program after 1912. The modern pentathlon, a new event created specifically for the Olympics at the urging of Coubertin, was added in 1912. Equestrian competition was another new sport, and there were two women's events for the first time.

Hannes Kohlemainen of Finland was the top track and field athlete, winning gold medals in the 5,000-meter, 10,000-meter and cross-country runs. Finns also won four other track gold medals. Hannes and his brother, Willie Kohlemainen, had spent considerable time in the United States, studying American training methods, and had then helped train other Finnish athletes. Because of their success, several other European countries hired coaches from the United States to help them prepare for future Olympics.

The top U. S. runner was Ralph Craig, who won both sprints, but the great Jim Thorpe was the major story. Thorpe won both the pentathlon and decathlon with ease. "Sir, you are the most wonderful athlete in the world," he was told by the king of Sweden, and Czar Nicholas of Russia sent him the silver model of a Viking ship to reward his performance.

But in January of 1913, Thorpe was ordered to return his medals because it was discovered that he had played semi-pro baseball for $60 a month. The medals were finally returned to his family in 1983, 30 years after Thorpe's death.

Leading Medal Winners:

Men

Athlete	Country	Sport	G-S-B	Total
Louis Richardet,	SWI	Shooting	4-2-0	6
Wilhelm Carlberg,	SWE	Shooting	3-2-0	5
Hannes Kolehmainen,	FIN	Track	3-1-0	4
Eric Carlberg,	SWE	Shooting	2-2-0	4
Johan von Holst,	SWE	Shooting	2-1-1	4
Carl Osburn,	USA	Shooting	1-2-1	4
Alfred Lane,	USA	Shooting	3-0-0	3
Åke Lundeberg,	SWE	Shooting	2-1-0	3
Frederick Hird,	USA	Shooting	2-0-1	3
Jean Cariou,	FRA	Equestrian	1-1-1	3
Charles Dixon,	GBR	Tennis	1-1-1	3
Harold Hardwick,	AUS	Swimming	1-0-2	3
Jack Hatfield,	GBR	Swimming	0-2-1	3
Charles Stewart,	GBR	Shooting	0-0-3	3

Women

Athlete	Country	Sport	G-S-B	Total
Edith Hannam,	GBR	Tennis	2-0-0	2

Jennie Fletcher,	GBR	Swimming	1-0-1	2
Sigrid Fick,	SWE	Tennis	0-1-1	2

Medals by Nation

No.	Nation	G	S	B
1.	United States of America (USA)	25	18	20
2.	Sweden (SWE)	23	24	17
3.	Great Britain (GBR)	10	15	16
4.	Finland (FIN)	9	8	9
5.	France (FRA)	7	4	3
6.	Germany (GER)	5	13	7
7.	South Africa (RSA)	4	2	0
8.	Norway (NOR)	3	2	4
9.	Hungary (HUN)	3	2	3
10.	Canada (CAN)	3	2	2
11.	Italy (ITA)	3	1	2
12.	Australasia (ANZ)	2	2	3
13.	Belgium (BEL)	2	1	3
14.	Denmark (DEN)	1	6	5
15.	Greece (GRE)	1	0	1
16.	Russia (RUS)	0	2	3
17.	Austria (AUT)	0	2	2
18.	Netherlands (NED)	0	0	3

The 1920 Olympics: Antwerp, Belgium

Fast Facts

Host City: Antwerp, Belgium

Opening date: April 20, 1920

Closing date: Sept. 12, 1920

Nations: 29

Athletes: 2,669 athletes (78 women, 2,591 men)

Events: 154 events in 22 sports

Coubertin and other members of the IOC had the quixotic idea that awarding the 1916 Olympics to Berlin might help avert war by mobilizing the opinions of those in Germany who favored peace. Even after war broke in 1914, plans went ahead for the Berlin Olympics. Almost everyone thought that it would be very short, well over before 1916, possibly even before 1915 arrived.

But the war went on. Coubertin was pressured by some members of the IOC to move the 1916 Olympics to the United States or to a Scandinavian country, since they weren't yet involved in the conflict, but he refused. He wasn't willing to take the games away from Germany unless Germany offered to withdraw. Finally, in 1915, after it had become apparent that Germany couldn't possibly host the games, the IOC reluctantly announced that the 1916 Olympics had been canceled.

Belgium, which had fought heroically after being victimized by Germany's surprise attack in 1914, was awarded the 1920 Olympics as a tribute. But taking on the games wasn't easy for the organizers in a country that already faced an enormous rebuilding task.

Visiting athletes slept on cots in schoolrooms, but for the most part they accepted the accommodations and many of them even praised the food. The American athletes weren't so happy, though. Their anger was directed, not at the Belgians, but at their own team officials.

Most members of the U. S. national team sailed to Europe on an overcrowded Army transport ship with poor sleeping facilities and even worse food. When they saw the abandoned schoolhouse in which they were to stay during the Olympics, they were ready to revolt.

Triple jumper Dan Ahearn simply found another place to stay and was thrown off the team. That was the last straw. About 200 American athletes signed a petition demanding better accommodations and Ahearn's reinstatement, and they threatened not to compete if their demands weren't met. After a long meeting between athletes and officials, Ahearn was reinstated, but the accommodations remained the same.

The United States didn't do quite as well as usual in track and field, but that undoubtedly had more to do with improved competition than with their sleeping conditions. The Finns won eight gold medals, including two by Paavo Nurmi, the great "flying Finn," in the 10,000-meter track run and 10,000-meter cross country. Finland was also strong in the weight competitions, sweeping the javelin medals and finishing first and second in both the shot-put and discus.

The major surprise of the games was Albert G. Hill, a 36-year-old British railway guard who had spent four years in the army during the war. Several years earlier, Hill had won his only major championship, the 4-mile run in the British national championships. At Antwerp, he won both the 800- and the 1500-meter runs.

The only triple gold medalist of the games was Etheida Bleibtrey of the U. S., who won both individual swimming events and swam on the champion 400-meter relay team. Tiny, 14-year-old Aileen Riggin of the U. S. became the first gold medalist in women's springboard diving. Duke Kahanamoku won two gold medals in men's swimming and his fellow Hawaiian, Warren Kealoha, claimed another.

In rowing, the single sculls event featured a great final between Jack Beresford of Great Britain and John B. Kelly of the U.S. Kelly, who later became better known as the father of actress-princess Grace Kelly, edged Beresford for the gold medal. Half an hour later, he also won the doubles sculls final with his cousin, Paul V. Costello.

Belgium and Antwerp were hailed for an outstanding job of staging the games, despite all of the difficulties. Even though Germany, Austria, Bulgaria, and Hungary were banned because they had been the aggressors in World War I, the Antwerp games set new records with participation by 29 countries and 2,669 athletes.

Leading Medal Winners:

Men				
Athlete	Country	Sport	G-S-B	Total
Willis Lee,	USA	Shooting	5-1-1	7
Lloyd Spooner,	USA	Shooting	4-1-2	7
Hubert van Innis,	BEL	Archery	4-2-0	6
Carl Osburn,	USA	Shooting	4-1-1	6
Nedo Nadi,	ITA	Fencing	5-0-0	5
Otto Olsen,	NOR	Shooting	3-2-0	5
Larry Nuesslein,	USA	Shooting	2-1-2	5
Julien Brulé,	FRA	Archery	1-3-1	5
Dennis Fenton,	USA	Shooting	3-0-1	4
Aldo Nadi,	ITA	Fencing	3-1-0	4
Paavo Nurmi,	FIN	Track	3-1-0	4
Harold Natvig,	NOR	Shooting	2-1-1	4
Östen Östensen,	NOR	Shooting	0-2-2	4
Erik Backman,	SWE	Track	0-1-3	4
Fritz Kuchen,	SWI	Shooting	0-0-4	4
Norman Ross,	USA	Swimming	3-0-0	3
Albert Hill,	GBR	Track	2-1-0	3
Morris Kirksey,	USA	Track/Rugby	2-1-0	3
Charley Paddock,	USA	Track	2-1-0	3
Bevil Rudd,	S. Afr.	Track	1-0-2	3
Ettore Caffaratti,	ITA	Equestrian	0-1-2	3

Women

Athlete	Country	Sport	G-S-B	Total
Ethelda Bleibtrey,	USA	Swimming	3-0-0	3
Suzanne Lenglen,	FRA	Tennis	2-0-1	3
Kitty McKane,	GBR	Tennis	1-1-1	3
Frances Schroth,	USA	Swimming	1-0-2	3
Irene Guest,	USA	Swimming	1-1-0	2
Margaret Woodbridge,	USA	Swimming	1-1-0	2
Dorothy Holman,	GBR	Tennis	0-2-0	2

Medals by Nation

No.	Nation	G	S	B
1.	United States of America (USA)	41	27	27
2.	Sweden (SWE)	19	20	25
3.	Great Britain (GBR)	15	15	13
4.	Finland (FIN)	15	10	9
5.	Belgium (BEL)	14	11	11
6.	Norway (NOR)	13	9	9
7.	Italy (ITA)	13	5	5
8.	France (FRA)	9	19	13
9.	Netherlands (NED)	4	2	5
10.	Denmark (DEN)	3	9	1
11.	South Africa (RSA)	3	4	3
12.	Canada (CAN)	3	3	3
13.	Switzerland (SUI)	2	2	7
14.	Estonia (EST)	1	2	0
15.	Brazil (BRA)	1	1	1
16.	Australia (AUS)	0	2	1
17.	Spain (ESP)	0	2	0
18.	Japan (JPN)	0	2	0

19.	Luxembourg (LUX)	0	1	0
20.	Greece (GRE)	0	1	0
21.	Czechoslovakia (TCH)	0	0	2
22.	New Zealand (NZL)	0	0	1

The 1924 Olympics: Paris, France

Fast Facts

Host City: Paris, France

Opening date: May 4, 1924

Closing date: July 27, 1924

Nations: 44

Athletes: 3,092 athletes (136 women, 2,956 men)

Events: 126 events in 17 sports

When Paris became the first city to host the Olympics for a second time, it was a major triumph for Baron Pierre de Coubertin. He had announced his retirement as president of the IOC, and the 1924 games gave him a chance to go out in glory by showing his native country that his idea had succeeded and also, incidentally, by showing the rest of the world that France could successfully host the Olympics, despite the debacle of 1900.

Despite the country's financial problems and a major flood in the spring before the Olympics, the 1924 games were very successful. In fact, 1924 is often considered the beginning of a truly modern Olympic era. International sports became big during the 1920s, mainly because of Wimbledon and the French Open in tennis, the British and French Opens in golf, and major cycling events in Europe. As a result, the international press followed the 1924 Olympics in much greater detail before. An estimated 1,000 journalists were on hand for part or all of the Olympics.

More than 3,000 athletes from 45 countries took part. And, in 1924, virtually every participating country had its own Olympic committee that conducted trials to select a national team, so most of the world's first-class athletes in every sport were in Paris. Women's swimming was greatly expanded and women's fencing was added to the program, paving the way for much greater future participation by female athletes.

The French were happy because their athletes outdid the Italians in cycling and fencing. Roger Ducret became a national hero by winning three golds and two silvers in fencing.

In track and field, the U. S. returned to something like its former dominance, winning 10 gold medals, including a tie for the pole vault gold between Lee Barnes and Glenn Graham. The Finns again won eight gold medals and dominated distance running, Paavo Nurmi won the 1500- and 5000-meter runs and the 10,000-meter cross-country, while teammate Ville Ritola won the 10,000-meter run and 3,000-meter steeplechase.

The surprise winner of the games was Harold Abrahams of Great Britain in the 100-meter dash. His story was later fictionalized in the movie, "Chariots of Fire." Johnny Weismuller, who later became Hollywood's best-known Tarzan, not only won three gold medals in swimming, he was a member of the American bronze medal water polo team. In all, the United States won all but three swimming and diving events, and they swept all medals in six of them.

Two American gold medalists in boxing later became world professional champions: Fidel LaBarba, who won the flyweight championship in 1925, and Jackie Fields, who captured the welterweight title in 1929.

In 1924, France also hosted a "Winter Sports Festival" at Chamonix that was sanctioned by the International Olympic Committee, over Coubertin's opposition. The festival retroactively became the first Winter Olympics.

Leading Medal Winners:

Men				
Athlete	Country	Sport	G-S-B	Total
Ville Ritola,	FIN	Track	4-2-0	6
Paavo Nurmi,	FIN	Track	5-0-0	5
Roger Ducret,	FRA	Fencing	3-2-0	5
Johnny Weissmuller,	USA	Swimming /Water Polo	3-0-1	4
Ole Lilloe-Olsen,	NOR	Shooting	2-1-0	3
Vincent Richards,	USA	Tennis	2-1-0	3
Albert Séquin,	FRA	Gymnastics	1-2-0	3
Boy Charlton,	AUS	Swimming	1-1-1	3
August Güttinger,	SWI	Gymnastics	1-0-2	3
Robert Prazák,	CZE	Gymnastics	0-3-0	3
Arne Borg,	SWE	Swimming	0-2-1	3
Jean Gutweniger,	SWI	Gymnastics	0-2-1	3
Henri Hoevenaers,	BEL	Cycling	0-2-1	3

Women				
Athlete	Country	Sport	G-S-B	Total
Gertrude Ederle,	USA	Swimming	1-0-2	3
Ethel Lackie,	USA	Swimming	2-0-0	2
Hazel Wightman,	USA	Tennis	2-0-0	2
Helen Wills,	USA	Tennis	2-0-0	2
Betty Becker,	USA	Diving	1-1-0	2
Mariechen Wehselau,	USA	Swimming	1-1-0	2
Kitty McKane,	GBR	Tennis	0-1-1	2
Aileen Riggin,	USA	Swimming /Diving	0-1-1	2

Medals by Nation

No.	Nation	G	S	B
1.	United States of America (USA)	45	27	27
2.	Finland (FIN)	14	13	10
3.	France (FRA)	13	15	10
4.	Great Britain (GBR)	9	13	12
5.	Italy (ITA)	8	3	5
6.	Switzerland (SUI)	7	8	10
7.	Norway (NOR)	5	2	3
8.	Sweden (SWE)	4	13	12
9.	Netherlands (NED)	4	1	5
10.	Belgium (BEL)	3	7	3
11.	Australia (AUS)	3	1	2
12.	Denmark (DEN)	2	5	2
13.	Hungary (HUN)	2	3	4
14.	Yugoslavia (YUG)	2	0	0
15.	Czechoslovakia (TCH)	1	4	5
16.	Argentina (ARG)	1	3	2
17.	Estonia (EST)	1	1	4
18.	South Africa (RSA)	1	1	1
19.	Uruguay (URU)	1	0	0
20.	Austria (AUT)	0	3	1
21.	Canada (CAN)	0	3	1
22.	Poland (POL)	0	1	1
23.	Portugal (POR)	0	0	1
24.	Romania (ROM)	0	0	1
25.	New Zealand (NZL)	0	0	1
26.	Japan (JPN)	0	0	1
27.	Haiti (HAI)	0	0	1

The 1928 Olympics: Amsterdam, Holland

Fast Facts

Host City: Amsterdam, Holland

Opening date: May 17, 1928

Closing date: Aug. 12, 1928

Nations: 46

Athletes: 3,014 athletes (290 women, 2,724 men)

Events: 109 events in 14 sports

Although Coubertin and the Vatican were outspoken in their opposition, women's track and field events were added to the Olympic program in 1928. As a result, the number of women competing more than doubled, from 136 to 290, even though the number of total athletes declined slightly. Germany and its World War I allies were re-admitted, and the tradition of the Olympic torch being carried from Athens to the site of the games was initiated.

The list of medal winners became truly international at Amsterdam, as athletes from 28 nations won gold medals, a record that stood until 1968. Argentina won two gold medals in boxing and one in swimming, Uruguay won the soccer championship, India won the field hockey title, Japanese athletes clamed golds in the triple jump and the men's 200-meter breast stroke, an Egyptian won a gold medal in wrestling, South Africa took two in track and field, and a long jumper from Haiti won the silver medal in his event.

The growing international importance of Olympic sports was illustrated by the results in equestrian and rowing competition. Sweden had previously dominated equestrian events, but in 1928 Holland and Germany both won two gold medals, while Czechoslovakia and Spain had one champion each. Swedish equestrians were limited to just two bronze medals.

The five rowing events produced gold medals for five different countries: Australia, Great Britain, Italy, Switzerland, and the U.S. The United States had its poorest showing ever in track events. Both men's relay teams won gold medals, but Ray Barbuti was the only individual track gold medalist, in the 400-meter dash. Percy Williams of Canada won the 100- and 200-meter events and the Finns again dominated in the distances, with four different runners taking gold medals.

However, U. S. athletes did win five of the nine field events and Betty Robinson became the first gold medalist in the women's 100-meter. American divers were supreme, winning all four gold medals, and Johnny Weissmuller again won the 100-meter freestyle and anchored the U. S. freestyle relay team to a world record time.

With the success of the Amsterdam Games, it became obvious even to long-time skeptics that the modern Olympics had not only become permanently established, but were affecting the growth and development of competitive sports world-wide.

Leading Medal Winners:

Men				
Athlete	Country	Sport	G-S-B	Total
Georges Miez,	SWI	Gymnastics	3-1-0	4
Hermann Hänggi,	SWI	Gymnastics	2-1-1	4
Lucien Gaudin,	FRA	Fencing	2-1-0	3
Eugen Mack,	SWI	Gymnastics	2-0-1	3
Paavo Nurmi,	FIN	Track	1-2-0	3
Ladislav Vácha,	CZE	Gymnastics	1-2-0	3
Leon Stukelj,	YUG	Gymnastics	1-0-2	3
Emanuel Löffler,	CZE	Gymnastics	0-2-1	3

Women

Athlete	Country	Sport	G-S-B	Total
Joyce Cooper,	GBR	Swimming	0-1-2	3
Martha Norelius,	USA	Swimming	2-0-0	2
Albina Osipowich,	USA	Swimming	2-0-0	2
Maria Braun,	NED	Swimming	1-1-0	2
Eleanor Garatti,	USA	Swimming	1-1-0	2
Betty Robinson,	USA	Track	1-1-0	2
Fanny Rosenfeld,	CAN	Track	1-1-0	2
Ethel Smith,	CAN	Track	1-0-1	2
Ellen King,	GBR	Swimming	0-2-0	2
Georgia Coleman,	USA	Diving	0-1-1	2

Medals by Nation

No.	Nation	G	S	B
1.	United States of America (USA)	22	18	16
2.	Germany (GER)	10	7	14
3.	Finland (FIN)	8	8	9
4.	Sweden (SWE)	7	6	12
5.	Italy (ITA)	7	5	7
6.	Switzerland (SUI)	7	4	4
7.	France (FRA)	6	10	5
8.	Netherlands (NED)	6	9	4
9.	Hungary (HUN)	4	5	0
10.	Canada (CAN)	4	4	7
11.	Great Britain (GBR)	3	10	7
12.	Argentina (ARG)	3	3	1
13.	Denmark (DEN)	3	1	2

14.	Czechoslovakia (TCH)	2	5	2
15.	Japan (JPN)	2	2	1
16.	Estonia (EST)	2	1	2
17.	Egypt (EGY)	2	1	1
18.	Austria (AUT)	2	0	1
19.	Australia (AUS)	1	2	1
20.	Norway (NOR)	1	2	1
21.	Poland (POL)	1	1	3
22.	Yugoslavia (YUG)	1	1	3
23.	South Africa (RSA)	1	0	2
24.	Spain (ESP)	1	0	0
25.	Uruguay (URU)	1	0	0
26.	New Zealand (NZL)	1	0	0
27.	India (IND)	1	0	0
28	Ireland (IRL)	1	0	0
29.	Belgium (BEL)	0	1	2
30.	Chile (CHI)	0	1	0
31.	Haiti (HAI)	0	1	0
32.	Portugal (POR)	0	0	1
33.	Philippines (PHI)	0	0	1

The 1932 Olympics: Los Angeles, California

Fast Facts

Host City: Los Angeles, CA

Opening date: July 30, 1932

Closing date: Aug. 14, 1932

Nations: 37

Athletes: 1,408 athletes (127 women, 1,281 men)

Events: 116 events in 14 sports

The difficulty and cost of traveling to California, combined with the international economic depression, severely reduced participation in the 1932 Olympics. The number of countries represented dropped from 46 to 37, and only 1,408 athletes participated, compared to 3,014 at Amsterdam.

Yet the 1932 games were successful financially and competitively. More than 1,250,000 spectators attended the various events and the Los Angeles Organizing Committee ended with a surplus of more than $1 million. Led by William May Garland, the LAOC took a bold step to increase participation, offering food, housing, and local transportation to every athlete for only $2 a day. To make the offer economic feasible, organizers constructed the first Olympic Village.

Another tradition that began in Los Angeles was the use of the victory stand, with the national anthem of the gold medal winner's country played during ht medal ceremony. While quantity was way down, the overall quality of the athletes didn't seem to suffer. Sixteen world records and 33 Olympic records were set in 1932. The United States returned to form in the track events, with Eddie Tolan leading an American sweep in both sprints and the 400-meter relay team setting a world record of 40.0, beating the second-place Germans by nearly a second.

American women did exceptionally well in both swimming and track. Helene Madison won gold medals in both individual freestyle races and as a member of the 400-meter freestyle relay team. Mildred "Babe" Didrikson also won three medals, two of them gold. She scored a very unusual double in the 80-meter hurdles and the javelin throw. Didrikson actually tied with teammate Jean Shiley with a world record in the high jump, but she was disqualified for a technical violation in the jump-off and had to settle for a silver medal.

Men's swimming was dominated by the Japanese, who won four of the five races. The only U. S. champion was Clarence "Buster" Crabbe, who later became known as Hollywood's Buck Rogers.

Leading Medal Winners:

Men

Athlete	Country	Sport	G-S-B	Total
István Pelle,	HUN	Gymnastics	2-2-0	4
Giulio Gaudini,	ITA	Fencing	0-3-1	4
Heikki Savolainen,	FIN	Gymnastics	0-1-3	4
Romeo Neri,	ITA	Gymnastics	3-0-0	3
Alex Wilson,	CAN	Track	0-1-2	3
Philip Edwards,	CAN	Track	0-0-3	3

Women

Athlete	Country	Sport	G-S-B	Total
Helene Madison,	USA	Swimming	3-0-0	3
Babe Didrikson,	USA	Track	2-1-0	3
Georgia Coleman,	USA	Diving	1-1-0	2
Eleanor Garatti,	USA	Swimming	1-0-1	2
Willy den Ouden,	NED	Swimming	0-2-0	2
Valerie Davies,	GBR	Swimming	0-0-2	2

Medals by Nation

No.	Nation	G	S	B
1.	United States of America (USA)	41	32	30
2.	Italy (ITA)	12	12	12
3.	France (FRA)	10	5	4
4.	Sweden (SWE)	9	5	9

5.	Japan (JPN)	7	7	4
6.	Hungary (HUN)	6	4	5
7.	Finland (FIN)	5	8	12
8.	Great Britain (GBR)	4	7	5
9.	Germany (GER)	3	12	5
10.	Australia (AUS)	3	1	1
11.	Argentina (ARG)	3	1	0
12.	Canada (CAN)	2	5	8
13.	Netherlands (NED)	2	5	0
14.	Poland (POL)	2	1	4
15.	South Africa (RSA)	2	0	3
16.	Ireland (IRL)	2	0	0
17.	Czechoslovakia (TCH)	1	2	1
18.	Austria (AUT)	1	1	3
19.	India (IND)	1	0	0
20.	Denmark (DEN)	0	3	3
21.	Mexico (MEX)	0	2	0
22.	Switzerland (SUI)	0	1	0
23.	New Zealand (NZL)	0	1	0
24.	Latvia (LAT)	0	1	0
25.	Philippines (PHI)	0	0	3
26.	Spain (ESP)	0	0	1
27.	Uruguay (URU)	0	0	1

The 1936 Olympics: Berlin, Germany

Fast Facts

Host City: Berlin, Germany

Opening date: Aug. 1, 1936

Closing date: Aug. 16, 1936

Nations: 49

Athletes: 4,066 athletes (328 women, 3,738 men)

Events: 129 events in 19 sports

Berlin was awarded the 1936 Olympics in 1931, two years before the Nazi party came to power. Adolf Hitler immediately seized on the games as an opportunity to showcase the efficiency and might of his regime.

There were doubts in many quarters about the wisdom of attending the Berlin Olympics. An alternative, to be called the "People's Olympics," was actually scheduled for Barcelona, but that plan was destroyed by the outbreak of the Spanish Civil War. In the United States, a move to boycott the Olympics was led by Judge Jeremiah T. Murphy, president of the Amateur Athletic Union (AAU). Murphy and his supporters were concerned chiefly about Nazi anti-Semitism, since Jewish sports clubs throughout Germany had been shut down.

However, in 1935 the AAU voted by a narrow margin to sanction participation and Murphy resigned. He was replaced by Avery Brundage, who went to Germany on an inspection tour and reported that everything looked just fine. Despite the preliminary doubts and the growing international tensions that were to culminate in World War II, the 1936 Olympics attracted more countries (49) and more athletes (4,066) than any previous Olympics.

On the positive side, the Berlin Games were noted mainly for technological achievements. Events were televised on a closed-circuit system throughout the Olympic village and to public halls and theaters throughout the country. Zeppelins carried newsreel film to other European cities, while results were transmitted to news media by telex as soon as events were completed.

But many athletes and members of the press were alarmed by the nationalistic and militaristic atmosphere in

Berlin. The ever-present swastika and icon-like portraits of Hitler and the martial music that blared endlessly through loudspeakers were deeply disturbing to many. Nor did it help that many journalists, suspected of anti-Nazi sentiments, discovered that their rooms had been searched by the secret police. In Nazi Germany's pro-Aryan setting, it was ironic that the greatest athletic hero was Jesse Owens, the black American sprinter. Owens won the 100- and 200-meter dashes and the long jump and also anchored the U. S. 400-meter relay team to a gold medal.

Hitler's "snub" of Owens is a well-known story, but it's not accurate. The German leader, who was prominently on display in his regal box, personally congratulated the first three gold medal winners in track and field—two Germans and a Finn. With darkness looming and rain threatening, he left the stadium after all the German competitors had been eliminated from the high jump. The winner was another black American, Cornelius Johnson, who led a U. S. sweep of the event. If Hitler is to be blamed for snubbing someone, Johnson was the victim.

That evening, Hitler was told by Count Baillet-Latour, the president of the IOC, that he should congratulate either all of the winners or none of them. He opted to congratulate none. When Owens won the first of his four gold medals the following day, therefore, he was not congratulated by the Fuehrer. (It is, of course, quite possible that Hitler made his decision knowing that Owens was very likely to win at least one event and possibly more.)

Black athletes were certainly denigrated, though, by the semi-official newspaper, *Der Angriff* (The Attack), which referred to them as America's "black auxiliaries" and did not include them in its daily scoring chart. The publisher of the paper was Hitler's minister of propaganda, Joseph Goebbels.

Besides Owens, the top individual athletes in 1936 were two German gymnasts, Konrad Frey and Alfred Schwarzmann; Dutch swimmer Hendrika "Rie" Mastenbroek; French cyclists Robert Charpentier and Guy Lapebie; and U. S. sprinter Helen Stephens.

Frey was the top medalist with three golds, one silver, and two bronze, while Schwarzmann collected three gold and two bronze medals. Mastenbroek won three golds and a silver. Charpentier won three gold medals, Lapebie two golds and a silver. Stephens won the women's 100-meter dash and also anchored the 400-meter relay team to victory.

In part because of a greatly expanded men's gymnastics program, Germany led all countries with 89 medals, including 33 gold, to 56 total and 24 gold for the United States.

To no one's surprise, one of the American gold medals came in basketball, which was added to the Olympic program in 1936. The games were played outdoors, often in rain, but that couldn't prevent the U. S. team from rolling through its opposition. The biggest threat to American victory actually came just after the games started, when the International Basketball Federation decided to ban any players 6-foot-3 or taller. The ban, which would have applied to only three players, all Americans, was quickly rescinded.

The Japanese dominated men's swimming, winning four of the six events, while Holland won four of the five women's events. Jack Medica and Adolph Kiefer were the only American gold medalists in swimming, although Medica added two silvers to finish among the top total medalists.

Four different U. S. athletes won the diving events. Marjorie Gestring, the women's springboard champion, was only 13 years and 9 months. She is still the youngest individual gold medalist in Olympic history.

Leading Medal Winners:

Men				
Athlete	Country	Sport	G-S-B	Total
Konrad Frey,	GER	Gymnastics	3-1-2	6
Alfred Schwarzmann,	GER	Gymnastics	3-0-2	5
Eugen Mack,	SWI	Gymnastics	0-4-1	5

Jesse Owens,	USA	Track	4-0-0	4
Robert Charpentier,	FRA	Cycling	3-0-0	3
Guy Lapébie,	FRA	Cycling	2-1-0	3
Jack Medica,	USA	Swimming	1-2-0	3
Matthias Volz,	GER	Gymnastics	1-0-2	3

Women

Athlete	Country	Sport	G-S-B	Total
Rie Mastenbroek,	NED	Swimming	3-1-0	4
Helen Stephens,	USA	Track	2-0-0	2
Dorothy Poynton Hill,	USA	Diving	1-0-1	2
Gisela Arendt,	GER	Swimming	0-1-1	2

Medals by Nation

No.	Nation	G	S	B
1.	Germany (GER)	33	26	30
2.	United States of America (USA)	24	20	12
3.	Hungary (HUN)	10	1	5
4.	Italy (ITA)	8	9	5
5.	Finland (FIN)	7	6	6
6.	France (FRA)	7	6	6
7.	Sweden (SWE)	6	5	9
8.	Japan (JPN)	6	4	8
9	Netherlands (NED)	6	4	7
10.	Great Britain (GBR)	4	7	3
11.	Austria (AUT)	4	6	3
12.	Czechoslovakia (TCH)	3	5	0
13.	Argentina (ARG)	2	2	3
14.	Estonia (EST)	2	2	3

15.	Egypt (EGY)	2	1	2
16.	Switzerland (SUI)	1	9	5
17.	Canada (CAN)	1	3	5
18.	Norway (NOR)	1	3	2
19.	Turkey (TUR)	1	0	1
20.	New Zealand (NZL)	1	0	0
21.	India (IND)	1	0	0
22.	Poland (POL)	0	3	3
23.	Denmark (DEN)	0	2	3
24.	Latvia (LAT)	0	1	1
25.	Romania (ROM)	0	1	0
26.	South Africa (RSA)	0	1	0
27.	Yugoslavia (YUG)	0	1	0
28.	Mexico (MEX)	0	0	3
29.	Belgium (BEL)	0	0	2
30.	Australia (AUS)	0	0	1
31.	Portugal (POR)	0	0	1
32.	Philippines (PHI)	0	0	1

The 1948 Olympics: London, England

Fast Facts

Host City: London, England

Opening date: July 29, 1948

Closing date: Aug. 14, 1948

Nations: 59

Athletes: 4,099 athletes (385 women, 3,714 men)

Events: 136 events in 17 sports

The IOC in 1936 selected Tokyo to host the 1940 Games. It was a bold idea to stage the Olympics in Asia and in a country which was still rather mysterious to the West. But Japan and China went to war in 1938 and the Japanese government ordered the organizing committee to stop preparation after sixteen sites had already been pretty well prepared to host Olympic events.

The IOC then called on Helsinki to take over. War again intervened, as the Soviet Union invaded Finland in 1939. By September, most of Europe was engulfed in war and it became obvious, even to the stubborn IOC, that the Olympics would have to be canceled. In June of 1939, the IOC awarded the 1944 Olympics to London. Again, World War II forced cancellation. A year after the war ended, London was once again selected, this time to host the 1948 Olympics.

As in Antwerp after World War II, a lot of improvisation was necessary to prepare London for the 1948 Olympics. Again, school buildings were used to house athletes. A temporary track was built at Wembley Stadium, and many government buildings were converted to temporary uses, especially for the media.

There truly were media in 1948. Many events were broadcast on television, though only within the British Isles, while radio coverage was carried around the world via short-wave transmission. London set new records with 59 countries and 4,099 athletes competing. The number of male competitors was down slightiy, from 3,738 to 3,714, but the number of women increased from 328 to 385.

And it was a woman, Fanny Blankers-Koen of the Netherlands, who emerged as the star of the 1948 games. A 30-year-old mother of two children, Blankers-Koen won individual gold medals in the 100- and 200-meter dashes and the 80-meter hurdles, and won a fourth gold running the anchor leg on Holland's 400-meter relay team.

At the other end of the track-and-field age spectrum was 17-year-old Bob Mathias. Just two months after graduating from high school in Tulare, California, Mathias was competing in only his third decathlon. He was third after the first day of competition, but he pulled into the lead with a tremendous discus throw on the second day and held on to win with a plodding but gutsy 5:11 in the concluding 1500-meter run.

The surprising winner in the men's 100-meter dash was Harrison "Bones" Dillard of the United States. The world record holder in the 120-yard hurdles, Dillard failed to qualify in that event and barely made the team by finishing third in the 100-meter trials. He and teammate Barney Ewell were both clocked in 10.3 seconds, tying the world record, but judges awarded Dillard the gold medal after studying the photo-finish results. (This was the first time, incidentally, that the photo-finish camera was used at the Olympics.)

Dillard won a second gold as a member of the 400-meter relay team. Mel Patton, the winner of the 200-meter dash, also won gold in the relay. The only other double gold medalist in track and field was Mal Whitfield, who won the 800-meter run and ran the anchor leg on the 4 by 400-meter relay team. Whitfield also took a bronze in the 400-meter run.

Although there was no really dominant swimmer, the United States won all six men's events. Jimmy McLane, Wally Ris, and Bill Smith each won an individual gold medal and a second gold in the freestyle relay. Ann Curtis was the only individual gold medalist among American women, in the 400-meter freestyle, and she too added a second in the relay, swimming the anchor leg in an incredible 1:04.4. That was nearly two seconds better than the winning time in the 100-meter freestyle, in which Curtis had finished second.

For the fifth straight time, Americans took gold medals in all four diving events, with Vicki Draves becoming the first woman to win both the springboard and the platform.

Leading Medal Winners:

Men				
Athlete	Country	Sport	G-S-B	Total
Veikko Huhtanen,	FIN	Gymnastics	3-1-1	5
Paavo Aaltonen,	FIN	Gymnastics	3-0-1	4
Jimmy McLane,	USA	Swimming	2-1-0	3
Humberto Mariles,	MEX	Equestrian	2-0-1	3
Mal Whitfield,	USA	Track	2-0-1	3
Barney Ewell,	USA	Track	1-2-0	3
Michael Reusch,	SWI	Gymnastics	1-2-0	3
Josef Stalder,	SWI	Gymnastics	1-1-1	3
Ferenc Pataki,	HUN	Gymnastics	1-0-2	3
Walter Lehmann,	SWI	Gymnastics	0-3-0	3
Edoardo Mangiarotti,	ITA	Fencing	0-2-1	3
János Mogyorósi,	HUN	Gymnastics	0-1-2	3

Women				
Athlete	Country	Sport	G-S-B	Total
Fanny Blankers-Koen,	NED	Track	4-0-0	4
Ann Curtis,	USA	Swimming	2-1-0	3
Micheline Ostermeyer,	FRA	Track	2-0-1	3
Karen-Margrete Harup,	DEN	Swimming	1-2-0	3
Shirley Strickland,	AUS	Track	0-1-2	3

Medals by Nation

No.	Nation	G	S	B
1.	United States of America (USA)	38	27	19
2.	Sweden (SWE)	16	11	17
3.	France (FRA)	10	6	13

4.	Hungary (HUN)	10	5	12
5.	Italy (ITA)	8	11	8
6.	Finland (FIN)	8	7	5
7.	Turkey (TUR)	6	4	2
8.	Czechoslovakia (TCH)	6	2	3
9.	Switzerland (SUI)	5	10	5
10.	Denmark (DEN)	5	7	8
11.	Netherlands (NED)	5	2	9
12.	Great Britain (GBR)	3	14	6
13.	Argentina (ARG)	3	3	1
14.	Australia (AUS)	2	6	5
15.	Belgium (BEL)	2	2	3
16.	Egypt (EGY)	2	2	1
17.	Mexico (MEX)	2	1	2
18.	South Africa (RSA)	2	1	1
19.	Norway (NOR)	1	3	3
20.	Jamaica (JAM)	1	2	0
21.	Austria (AUT)	1	0	3
22.	India (IND)	1	0	0
23.	Peru (PER)	1	0	0
24.	Yugoslavia (YUG)	0	2	0
25.	Canada (CAN)	0	1	2
26.	Uruguay (URU)	0	1	1
27.	Portugal (POR)	0	1	1
28.	Spain (ESP)	0	1	0
29.	Sri Lanka (SRI)	0	1	0
30.	Trinidad and Tobago (TRI)	0	1	0
31.	Cuba (CUB)	0	1	0
32.	Korea (KOR)	0	0	2

33.	Panama (PAN)	0	0	2
34.	Poland (POL)	0	0	1
35.	Puerto Rico (PUR)	0	0	1
36.	Islamic Republic of Iran (IRI)	0	0	1
37.	Brazil (BRA)	0	0	1

The 1952 Olympics: Helsinki, Finland

Fast Facts

Host City:	Helsinki, Finland
Opening date:	July 19, 1952
Closing date:	Aug. 3, 1952
Nations:	69
Athletes:	4,925 athletes (518 women, 4,407 men)
Events:	149 events in 17 sports

The "Olympic cold war" began in 1952, when the Soviet Union entered competition for the first time. Originally, the USSR had planned to base its athletes in Leningrad and to fly them into Helsinki as needed. As it turned out, a separate Olympic village was set up in Helsinki for the Communist bloc countries - Bulgaria, Czechoslovakia, Hungary, Poland, Rumania, the Soviet Union, and Yugoslavia.

For the hosting Finns, the high point of the games came at the opening ceremony, when the great Paavo Nurmi entered the stadium bearing the Olympic torch. Still a national hero though he had retired from competition nearly 20 years earlier, the 55-year-old Nurmi was greeted with a mighty burst of applause, accompanied by tears from many spectators.

He passed the torch on to Hannes Kohlemainen, the winner of three gold medals in 1912, who jogged up the stadium steps to light the official Olympic flame. With the addition of several Communist countries and the re-admission of Japan and Germany (actually represented only by West Germany), the number of countries represented in 1952 increased from 59 to 69 and the number of athletes leaped by nearly 25 percent, from 4,099 to 4,925.

More than 100 Olympic records were broken at Helsinki, and there were many outstanding performances, by any standard. Emil Zatopek of Czechoslovakia scored a remarkable triple in the 5,000- and 10,000-meter runs and the marathon—the first time he had ever run that event.

As in 1948, the men's 100-meter final featured an upset winner in a photo finish. Four runners crossed the finish line within 14 inches of each other. Lindy Remigino, the second-place runner at the U. S. Olympic trials, congratulated Herb McKenley of Jamaica, who had broken the tape. But the judges concluded, after a long study of the photograph, that Remigino's right shoulder had crossed the line before McKenley's chest hit the tape, and Remigino was awarded the gold medal while McKenley received the silver.

An even more remarkable upset occurred in the 1500-meter run. Roger Bannister, who was to become the first man to break the 4-minute barrier two years later, was one of the favorites in the race, along with Robert McMillen of the United States and Werner Lueg of Germany. But a virtual unknown, Josef Barthel of Luxembourg, beat them all, running 3.3 seconds faster than he had ever run before. His victory was so unexpected that the medal ceremony had to be delayed while officials searched for the music to Luxembourg's national anthem.

The United States won 14 of the 23 men's events in track and field. Harrison Dillard, the surprise winner of the 100-meter in 1948, won his "real" event, the 110-meter hurdles, and claimed his fourth career gold medal with the U. S. 400-meter relay team. Mal Whitfield was the 800-meter champion for the second time, and Bob Mathias won his second Olympic decathlon championship by more than 900 points, shattering the world record.

In women's track, Marjorie Jackson of Australia won the 100- and 200-meter dashes and her teammate, Shirley Strickland, won the 80-meter hurdles. Gold medals for women's field events were well distributed: Two to the Soviet Union and one each to Czechoslovakia, New Zealand, and South Africa. Hungary dominated women's swimming, winning four of the five events, while the United States won four of the six men's swimming events. As usual, United States divers captured all four gold medals and Pat McCormick became the second woman to win both the platform and the springboard events.

Two future heavyweight champions, Floyd Patterson and Ingemar Johansson, were Olympic competitors in 1952. Patterson won the middleweight title, but Johansson not only lost in the heavyweight final, he was denied the silver medal by judges for failing to put up a fight.

Those two later combined to make boxing history. Johansson in 1959 upset Patterson with a third-round knockout to win the heavyweight championship. In a rematch a year later, Patterson scored a fifth-round knockout to become the first fighter ever to regain the title.

Leading Medal Winners:

Men				
Athlete	Country	Sport	G-S-B	Total
Viktor Chukárin,	USSR	Gymnastics	4-2-0	6
Edoardo Mangiarotti,	ITA	Fencing	2-2-0	4
Grant Shaginyan,	USSR	Gymnastics	2-2-0	4
Josef Stalder,	SWI	Gymnastics	0-2-2	4
Emil Zátopek,	CZE	Track	3-0-0	3
Ford Konno,	USA	Swimming	2-1-0	3
Herb McKenley,	JAM	Track	1-2-0	3

Hans Eugster,	SWI	Gymnastics	1-1-1	3

Women

Athlete	Country	Sport	G-S-B	Total
Maria Gorokhovskaya,	USSR	Gymnastics	2-5-0	7
Margit Korondi,	HUN	Gymnastics	1-1-4	6
Nina Bocharova,	USSR	Gymnastics	2-2-0	4
Ágnes Keleti,	HUN	Gymnastics	1-1-2	4
Yekaterina Kalinchuk,	USSR	Gymnastics	2-1-0	3
Éva Novák,	HUN	Swimming	1-2-0	3
Galina Minaicheva,	USSR	Gymnastics	1-1-1	3
Aleksandra Chudina,	USSR	Track	0-2-1	3

Medals by Nation

No.	Nation	G	S	B
1.	United States of America (USA)	40	19	17
2.	USSR (URS)	22	30	19
3.	Hungary (HUN)	16	10	16
4.	Sweden (SWE)	12	13	10
5.	Italy (ITA)	8	9	4
6.	Czechoslovakia (TCH)	7	3	3
7.	France (FRA)	6	6	6
8.	Finland (FIN)	6	3	13
9.	Australia (AUS)	6	2	3
10.	Norway (NOR)	3	2	0
11.	Switzerland (SUI)	2	6	6
12.	South Africa (RSA)	2	4	4
13.	Jamaica (JAM)	2	3	0
14.	Belgium (BEL)	2	2	0

15.	Denmark (DEN)	2	1	3
16.	Turkey (TUR)	2	0	1
17.	Japan (JPN)	1	6	2
18.	Great Britain (GBR)	1	2	8
19.	Argentina (ARG)	1	2	2
20.	Poland (POL)	1	2	1
21.	Canada (CAN)	1	2	0
22.	Yugoslavia (YUG)	1	2	0
23.	Romania (ROM)	1	1	2
24.	New Zealand (NZL) 1 0 2			
25.	Brazil (BRA)	1	0	2
26.	India (IND)	1	0	1
27.	Luxembourg (LUX)	1	0	0
28.	Germany (GER)	0	7	17
29.	Netherlands (NED)	0	5	0
30.	Islamic Republic of Iran (IRI)	0	3	4
31.	Chile (CHI)	0	2	0
32.	Austria (AUT)	0	1	1
33.	Lebanon (LIB)	0	1	1
34.	Mexico (MEX)	0	1	0
35.	Spain (ESP)	0	1	0
36.	Ireland (IRL)	0	1	0
37.	Trinidad and Tobago (TRI)	0	0	2
38.	Korea (KOR)	0	0	2
39.	Uruguay (URU)	0	0	2
40.	Venezuela (VEN)	0	0	1
41.	Portugal (POR)	0	0	1
42.	Bulgaria (BUL)	0	0	1
43.	Egypt (EGY)	0	0	1

The 1956 Olympics: Melbourne, Australia

Fast Facts

Host City:	Melbourne, Australia
Opening date:	Nov. 22, 1956
Closing date:	Dec. 8, 1956
Nations:	67
Athletes:	3,184 athletes (371 women, 2,813 men)
Events:	145 events in 17 sports

Many members of the IOC had doubts about Melbourne from the beginning. Its location in the Southern Hemisphere, where the seasons are reversed, was a big strike against it, since it would require that the Olympics be held in the Northern Hemisphere's off-season, so to speak, when many athletes were accustomed to resting from the rigors of one year and gathering themselves for the rigors of the next.

But Melbourne was selected, in 1949, to host the 1956 Olympics by a one-vote margin. The first sign of trouble was the revelation that Australian equine quarantine would prevent the country from hosting the equestrian events. Stockholm was selected as the alternate site, so equestrian competition began on June 10, five and a half months before the rest of the Olympic games were to open, half the world away.

Then bickering over financing broke out among Australian politicians. Faced with a housing shortage, the premier of Victoria, in which Melbourne is located, refused to allocate money for the Olympic village, and the country's prime minister barred the used of federal funds.

IOC President Avery Brundage, suggested that Rome, which was to host the 1960 games, was so far ahead of Melbourne in preparations that it might be ready as a replacement site in 1956.

As late as April of 1955, Brundage was still doubtful about Melbourne, and an inspection trip didn't satisfy him. Construction was well underway by then, thanks to a $4.5 million federal loan to Victoria, but it was behind schedule. He still held out the possibility that Rome might have to step in. By the beginning of 1956, though, it was obvious that Melbourne would be ready for the Olympics. The question then arose: Would the rest of the world be ready?

Great Britain and France took over the Suez Canal after Israel attacked Egypt. In protest, Egypt, Iraq, and Lebanon announced they wouldn't participate in the Olympics. The Soviet Union invaded a rebellious Hungary, leading to the withdrawal of the Netherlands, Spain, and Switzerland. Less than two weeks before the Nov. 22 opening ceremony, the People's Republic of China also pulled out because the Republic of China (Taiwan) had been allowed to compete.

Although the number of countries participating was almost the same—67, compared to 69 in 1952—the number of athletes dropped sharply, from 4,925 to 3,342. (Another 158 athletes, from 29 countries, took part in the Stockholm equestrian competition.)

Once the games were underway, though, they certainly went well. The Aussies were excellent hosts, both friendly and efficient. They were also well represented in competition. Betty Cuthbert, an 18-year-old from Sydney, won the 100- and 200-meter dashes and ran a great final leg in the 4 x 100-meter relay to overcome Great Britain's lead and claim her third gold medal. The veteran Shirley Strickland repeated in the 80-meter hurdles and also ran on the relay team, running her career total to seven, three golds, a silver, and three bronze medals.

But it was in swimming that the Australians really shone. They won all of the freestyle races, men's and women's, and collected a total of eight gold, four silver and two bronze medals. Murray Rose became the first male swimmer to win two freestyle events since Johnny Weissmuller in 1924, while Dawn Fraser won gold medals in the 100-meter freestyle and as the leadoff swimmer on the 4 x 100-meter relay team.

Controversial judging prevented the United States from winning all four diving events, which had become almost customary. Pat McCormick again took gold medals in both the springboard and the platform, and Bob Clotworthy won the men's springboard. However, Gary Tobian was given unusually low scores by the Russian and Hungarian judges, and he finished second by just .03 to Mexico Joaquim Capilla in the platform event.

United States men dominated track and field. They not only won 15 of 24 events, they swept four of them and finished first and second in five others. Bobby Morrow led the way with gold medals in the 100- and 200-meter dashes and the 4 x 100-meter relay. Tom Courtney barely overtook Great Britain's Derek Johnson in the 800-meter run, then collapsed from the exertion and needed medical attention.

Vladimir Kuts of the Soviet Union ran away from his competition in the 5,000- and 10,000-meter runs, while Ireland's Ron Delaney ran a briiliant 53.8 over the last 400 meters to win the 1,500-meter run, in which favorite John Landy of Australia finished third.

There was a major upset, marred briefly by controversy, in the 3,000-meter steeplechase. Little-known Chris Brasher of Great Britain finished well ahead of the field, but judges announced that he was disqualified for interfering with Norway's Ernst Larsen, and they anointed Sandor Rozsnyoi of Hungary as the winner. Brasher's appeal, remarkably, was supported by Larsen, Rozsnyoi, and fourth-place finisher Heinz Laufer of Germany. The decision was reversed and Brasher became the first Briton to win a gold medal in track and field since 1932.

Only two world records were set in track and field. Mildred McDaniel, the only American woman to win gold in the sport, set a high jump record of 5 feet, 9 1/4 inches, and Egil Danielsen of Norway overcame a troublesome wind with a remarkable javelin throw of 281 feet, 2 1/2 inches.

Throughout the Olympics, Hungarian athletes were cheered by fans from Australia and other countries. Many of them gathered in the boxing arena when thirty-year-old Laszlo Papp of Hungary won his third gold medal by beating Jose Torres for the light-middleweight championship.

A few days later, the crowd was with the Hungarian water polo team in its match against the Soviet Union. The game became rough and, when a Hungarian was forced to leave the pool with blood streaming from a cut over his eye, a riot almost broke out. But police restored order and the game was called early, with Hungary leading 4-0. The Hungarians went on to win the gold medal.

Despite the international tensions of 1956—or perhaps because of them—the Australian organizers came up with a new idea for the closing ceremony. Instead of marching as teams, behind their national flags, the athletes mingled with one another as they paraded into and around the arena for a final appearance before the spectators. That began an Olympic tradition that has been followed ever since.

Leading Medal Winners:

Men				
Athlete	Country	Sport	G-S-B	Total
Viktor Chukarin,	USSR	Gymnastics	3-1-1	5
Takashi Ono,	JPN	Gymnastics	1-3-1	5
Valentin Muratov,	USSR	Gymnastics	3-1-0	4
Yuriy Titov,	USSR	Gymnastics	1-1-2	4
Masao Takemoto,	JPN	Gymnastics	0-1-3	4
Bobby Morrow,	USA	Track	3-0-0	3
Murray Rose,	AUS	Swimming	3-0-0	3
Edoardo Mangiarotti,	ITA	Fencing	2-0-1	3
Thane Baker,	USA	Track	1-1-1	3
Masami Kubota,	JPN	Gymnastics	0-2-1	3

George Breen,	USA	Swimming	0-1-2	3

Women

Athlete	Country	Sport	G-S-B	Total
Agnes Keleti,	HUN	Gymnastics	4-2-0	6
Larissa Latynina,	USSR	Gymnastics	4-1-1	6
Tamara Manina,	USSR	Gymnastics	1-2-1	4
Sofiya Muratova,	USSR	Gymnastics	1-0-3	4
Betty Cuthbert,	AUS	Track	3-0-0	3
Lorraine Crapp,	AUS	Swimming	2-1-0	3
Dawn Fraser,	AUS	Swimming	2-1-0	3
Olga Tass,	HUN	Gymnastics	1-1-1	3

Medals by Nation

No.	Nation	G	S	B
1.	USSR (URS)	37	29	32
2.	United States of America (USA)	32	25	17
3.	Australia (AUS)	13	8	14
4.	Hungary (HUN)	9	10	7
5.	Italy (ITA)	8	8	9
6.	Sweden (SWE)	8	5	6
7.	United Team of Germany (EUA)	6	13	7
8.	Great Britain (GBR)	6	7	11
9.	Romania (ROM)	5	3	5
10.	Japan (JPN)	4	10	5
11.	France (FRA)	4	4	6
12.	Turkey (TUR)	3	2	2
13.	Finland (FIN)	3	1	11
14.	Islamic Republic of Iran (IRI)	2	2	1
15.	Canada (CAN)	2	1	3

16.	New Zealand (NZL)	2	0	0
17.	Poland (POL)	1	4	4
18.	Czechoslovakia (TCH)	1	4	1
19.	Bulgaria (BUL)	1	3	1
20.	Denmark (DEN)	1	2	1
21.	Ireland (IRL)	1	1	3
22.	Norway (NOR)	1	0	2
23.	Mexico (MEX)	1	0	1
24.	India (IND)	1	0	0
25.	Brazil (BRA)	1	0	0
26.	Yugoslavia (YUG)	0	3	0
27.	Chile (CHI)	0	2	2
28.	Belgium (BEL)	0	2	0
29.	Argentina (ARG)	0	1	1
30.	Korea (KOR)	0	1	1
31.	Pakistan (PAK)	0	1	0
32.	Iceland (ISL)	0	1	0
33.	South Africa (RSA)	0	0	1
34.	Austria (AUT)	0	0	2
35.	Bahamas (BAH)	0	0	1
36.	Greece (GRE)	0	0	1
37.	Switzerland (SUI)	0	0	1
38.	Uruguay (URU)	0	0	1

The 1960 Olympics: Rome, Italy

Fast Facts

Host City: Rome, Italy

Opening date: Aug. 25, 1960

Closing date: Sept. 11, 1960

Nations:	83
Athletes:	5,348 athletes (610 women, 4,738 men)
Events:	150 events in 17 sports

In Rome, where the ancient Olympics had ended more than 1600 years earlier, the 1960 Olympic venues were a curious blend of ancient and modern architecture. Near the brand-new Olympic stadium, sports palace and velodrome, wrestling was contested in the Basilica of Maxentius, which had hosted matches 2,000 years before; gymnastics took place in the Baths of Caracalla, and the marathon was run along the Appian Way, finishing at the Arch of Constantine.

Italian preparations for the games set a new standard for Olympic sites, in that the entire infrastructure was upgraded. Superhighways and tunnels were built to ease the traffic burden, and an entire new water supply system was constructed. The Villagio Olympico, which housed a record 5,348 athletes from 84 nations, was a true village, with parks, play areas, and shops. After the athletes left, it became low-cost housing for government workers.

The Rome Olympics were the first to be thoroughly covered on broadcast television. Eurovision brought live telecasts of many events to Europe, and CBS paid $394,000 for U. S. rights. Since there was no way of relaying broadcasts across the Atlantic, the network flew tapes to New York City daily.

For the United States, the track and field star was the graceful Wilma Rudolph, who won both sprints and ran the anchor leg on the 4 x 100-meter relay team to win a third gold medal. She helped make up for disappointments in the men's sprints. Armin Hary of Germany won the 100-meter and Livio Berrutti of Italy was the surprise winner of the 200-meter sprint, in world record time. The American sprint relay team had a good shot at a gold medal, but was disqualified for an illegal pass.

However, Otis Davis of the U. S. set a world record in the 400-meter and two Americans won their second straight gold medals in the hurdles, Lee Calhoun in the 110-meter and Glenn Davis in the 400-meter. Both Davises, Otis and Glenn, were on the gold medal 4 x 400-meter relay team. Other world records were set by Australia's Herb Elliott, in the 1500-meter run; barefoot runner Abibè Bikila, in the marathon; and by the German 4 x 100-meter relay team, led by Hary.

American men were more successful in the field events than on the track. Don Bragg won the pole vault, Ralph Boston the long jump. Bill Nieder beat favored teammate Parry O'Brien in the shotput and Al Oerter won the second of his historic four gold medals in the discus. The marathon featured an intensely close competition between two good friends and UCLA teammates, Rafer Johnson of the United States and C. K. Yang, representing the Republic of China. Yang had better scores than Johnson in seven of the ten events, but Johnson's great superiority in weight throws gave him a 58-point victory, the narrowest margin in Olympic history.

The Soviet Union dominated women's track and field, aside from the sprints. Led by sisters Tamara and Irina Press, they won six of the other seven events. Irina took the 80-meter hurdles, Tamara the shot put. The 800-meter run, restored to the program for the first time since 1924, was won by Soviet Lyudmila Shevtsova in world record time.

Men's swimming was pretty much a contest between Australia and the United States. The Aussies won four of the six individual races, but U. S. depth led to victories and world records in both relays. There was some controversy over the 100-meter freestyle, where Lance Larson of the U. S. appeared to win by a touch, but Australia's John Devitt was awarded the gold medal by the judges after much discussion.

In women's swimming, Dawn Fraser of Australia won the second of her three gold medals in the 100-meter freestyle, but American teen-agers ruled five of the other six events. Sixteen-year-old Chris Von Saltza led the way with three gold medals. She won the 400-meter freestyle and anchored both relay teams which, like their male counterparts, won gold medals in world record times. Another teen-ager, 17-year-old Ingrid Kramer of Germany, won both diving events, breaking an American stranglehold. She was the first woman from outside the U. S. to win a gold medal in diving since 1920. However, Bob Webster won the platform event and Gary Tobian the springboard event to give American men a gold-medal sweep.

Italian fans cheered wildly at the boxing arena, where six of their countrymen reached the finals and three won gold medals. Among them was Nino Benvenuti, who went on to become world middleweight champion. The United States also had three gold medalists, led by 18-year-old Cassius Marcellus Clay in the light-heavyweight division. He later became better known as Muhammad Ali.

The term "Dream Team" hadn't been coined yet, but it could have been applied to the 1960 U. S. basketball squad, probably the greatest team put together until professionals were allowed to play in 1992. The roster included Walt Bellamy, Terry Dischinger, Jerry Lucas, Oscar Robertson, and Jerry West. All went on to stardom in the NBA, four of them won the league's rookie of the year award, and three of them - Lucas, Robertson, and West - are in the basketball hall of fame. Unfortunately, a tragedy marred the 1960 cycling competition. Danish cyclist Knud Jensen collapsed and died during the road race, and it was discovered that drug use was a contributing factor. That was a precursor of what was to become a major problem, not only in the Olympics, but in all of sports.

Leading Medal Winners:

Men

Athlete	Country	Sport	G-S-B	Total
Boris Shakhlin,	USSR	Gymnastics	4-2-1	7
Takashi Ono,	JPN	Gymnastics	3-1-2	6

Murray Rose,	AUS	Swimming	1-1-1	3
John Konraads,	AUS	Swimming	1-0-2	3
Yuri Titov,	USSR	Gymnastics	0-2-1	3

Women

Athlete	Country	Sport	G-S-B	Total
Larissa Latynina,	USSR	Gymnastics	3-2-1	6
Chris von Saltza,	USA	Swimming	3-1-0	4
Polina Astakhova,	USSR	Gymnastics	2-1-1	4
Sofia Muratova,	USSR	Gymnastics	1-2-1	4
Wilma Rudolph,	USA	Track	3-0-0	3
Dawn Fraser,	AUS	Swimming	1-2-0	3
Tamara Lyukhina,	USSR	Gymnastics	1-0-2	3

Medals by Nation

No.	Nation	G	S	B
1.	USSR (URS)	43	29	31
2.	United States of America (USA)	34	21	16
3.	Italy (ITA)	13	10	13
4.	United Team of Germany (EUA)	12	19	11
5.	Australia (AUS)	8	8	6
6.	Turkey (TUR)	7	2	0
7.	Hungary (HUN)	6	8	7
8.	Japan (JPN)	4	7	7
9.	Poland (POL)	4	6	11
10.	Czechoslovakia (TCH)	3	2	3
11.	Romania (ROM)	3	1	6
12.	Great Britain (GBR)	2	6	12
13.	Denmark (DEN)	2	3	1
14.	New Zealand (NZL)	2	0	1

15.	Bulgaria (BUL)	1	3	3
16.	Sweden (SWE)	1	2	3
17.	Finland (FIN)	1	1	3
18.	Austria (AUT)	1	1	0
19.	Yugoslavia (YUG)	1	1	0
20.	Pakistan (PAK)	1	0	1
21.	Ethiopia (ETH)	1	0	0
22.	Greece (GRE)	1	0	0
23.	Norway (NOR)	1	0	0
24.	Switzerland (SUI)	0	3	3
25.	France (FRA)	0	2	3
26.	Belgium (BEL)	0	2	2
27.	Islamic Republic of Iran (IRI)	0	1	3
28.	Netherlands (NED)	0	1	2
29.	South Africa (RSA)	0	1	2
30.	Egypt (EGY)	0	1	1
31.	Argentina (ARG)	0	1	1
32.	Ghana (GHA)	0	1	0
33.	India (IND)	0	1	0
34.	Canada (CAN)	0	1	0
35.	Chinese Taipei (TPE)	0	1	0
36.	Singapore (SIN)	0	1	0
37.	Portugal (POR)	0	1	0
38.	Morocco (MAR)	0	1	0
39.	Mixed team	0	0	2
40.	Brazil (BRA)	0	0	2
41.	Iraq (IRQ)	0	0	1
42.	Mexico (MEX)	0	0	1
43.	Spain (ESP)	0	0	1
44.	Venezuela (VEN)	0	0	1

The 1964 Olympics: Tokyo, Japan

Fast Facts

Host City:	Tokyo, Japan
Opening date:	Oct. 10, 1964
Closing date:	Oct. 24, 1964
Nations:	93
Athletes:	5,140 athletes (683 women, 4,457 men)
Events:	163 events in 19 sports

The 1940 Olympics had been scheduled for Japan, but they were cancelled because of the Sino-Japanese War and then World War II. Twenty-four years later, the games finally came to Tokyo. Japan spent an estimated $3 billion getting ready, including construction of a new transportation system and renovation of public buildings as well as the construction necessary for the Olympics.

The opening ceremony was a major pageant. An orchestra of 560 musicians and a choir of 350 singers performed the Olympic Anthem. The final torchbearer was Yoshinori Sakai, who had been born in Hiroshima on Aug. 6, 1945, the day the atomic bomb destroyed that city. Emperor Hirohito proclaimed the games open.

Two new sports, judo and volleyball, were added to the program. Three countries were absent: South Africa was disqualified because of its apartheid policies. Indonesia was also banned for refusing to allow athletes from Israel and Taiwan to take part in the 1962 Asian Games, and North Korea withdrew in support of Indonesia.

Three athletes won gold medals in an event for the third time: Vyacheslav Ivanov of the Soviet Union in single sculls, Dawn Fraser of Australia in 100-meter freestyle swimming, and Al Oerter of the United States in the discus. Abebe Bekila of Ethiopia became the first runner to repeat as the marathon champion and Hungarian water polo player Dezso Gyarmati won a medal for the fifth consecutive Olympics. Ukrainian gymnast Larysa Latynina won four medals, two gold and two silver, bringing her career total to 18, including a record-tying nine golds.

The individual hero was American Don Schollander, who became the first swimmer to win four gold medals at a single Olympics. Billy Mills, a native American from South Dakota, provided the biggest upset of the Games. While favorite Ron Clark of Australia and Mohamed Camundi of Tunis were battling through the last lap of the 10,000-meter run, the virtually unknown Mills passed them both to win by three yards. Mills improved his personal best in the event by an incredible 47 seconds.

Leading Medal Winners:

Men

Athlete	Country	Sport	G-S-B	Total
Don Schollander,	USA	Swimming	4-0-0	4
Yukio Endo,	JPN	Gymnastics	3-1-0	4
Shuji Tsurumi,	JPN	Gymnastics	1-3-0	4
Boris Shakhlin,	USSR	Gymnastics	1-2-1	4
Viktor Lisitsky,	USSR	Gymnastics	0-4-0	4
Hans-Joachim Klein,	GER	Swimming	0-3-1	4
Steve Clark,	USA	Swimming	3-0-0	3
Franco Menichelli,	ITA	Gymnastics	1-1-1	3
Frank Wiegard,	GER	Swimming	0-3-0	3

Women

Athlete	Country	Sport	G-S-B	Total
Larissa Latynina,	USSR	Gymnastics	2-2-2	6
Vera Cáslavská,	CZE	Gymnastics	3-1-0	4
Polina Astakhova,	USSR	Gymnastics	2-1-1	4

Sharon Stouder,	USA	Swimming	3-1-0	4
Kathy Ellis,	USA	Swimming	2-0-2	4
Irena Kirszenstein,	POL	Track	1-2-0	3
Ada Kok,	NED	Swimming	1-2-0	3
Edith Maguire,	USA	Track	1-2-0	3
Mary Rand,	GBR	Track	1-1-1	3

Medals by Nation

No.	Nation	G	S	B
1.	United States of America (USA)	36	26	28
2.	USSR (URS)	30	31	35
3.	Japan (JPN)	16	5	8
4.	United Team of Germany (EUA)	10	22	18
5.	Italy (ITA)	10	10	7
6.	Hungary (HUN)	10	7	5
7.	Poland (POL)	7	6	10
8.	Australia (AUS)	6	2	10
9.	Czechoslovakia (TCH)	5	6	3
10.	Great Britain (GBR)	4	12	2
11.	Bulgaria (BUL)	3	5	2
12.	Finland (FIN)	3	0	2
13.	New Zealand (NZL)	3	0	2
14.	Romania (ROM)	2	4	6
15.	Netherlands (NED)	2	4	4
16.	Turkey (TUR)	2	3	1
17.	Sweden (SWE)	2	2	
18.	Denmark (DEN)	2	1	3
19.	Yugoslavia (YUG)	2	1	
20.	Belgium (BEL)	2	0	1
21.	France (FRA)	1	8	6
22.	Canada (CAN)	1	2	1

23.	Switzerland (SUI)	1	2	1
24.	Ethiopia (ETH)	1	0	0
25.	Bahamas (BAH)	1	0	0
26.	India (IND)	1	0	0
27.	Korea (KOR)	0	2	1
28.	Trinidad and Tobago (TRI)	0	1	2
29.	Tunisia (TUN)	0	1	1
30.	Pakistan (PAK)	0	1	0
31.	Philippines (PHI)	0	1	0
32.	Argentina (ARG)	0	1	0
33.	Cuba (CUB)	0	1	0
34.	Islamic Republic of Iran (IRI)	0	0	2
35.	Ireland (IRL)	0	0	1
36.	Ghana (GHA)	0	0	1
37.	Brazil (BRA)	0	0	1
38.	Nigeria (NGR)	0	0	1
39.	Mexico (MEX)	0	0	1
40.	Kenya (KEN)	0	0	1
41.	Uruguay (URU)	0	0	1

4

Modern Olympic Games: 1968-2004

The 1968 Olympics: Mexico City, Mexico

Fast Facts

Host City: Mexico City, Mexico

Opening date: Oct. 12, 1968

Closing date: Oct. 27, 1968

Nations: 112

Athletes: 5,530 athletes (780 women, 4,750 men)

Events: 172 events in 20 sports

The over polite fiction is that the Olympics are somehow above politics. Of course, they never have been, but in 1968 politics became a much more noticeable aspect of the Olympic scene than ever before. The choice of Mexico City had been controversial anyway. The high altitude, more than 7500 feet above sea level, meaning a 30-percent reduction in available oxygen, was the problem that most critics fastened on. But there was also the fact that the Olympics had never before been awarded to an underdeveloped country, and there were doubts as to whether Mexico could possibly be ready in time.

The International Olympic Committee added its own untimely controversy by deciding to readmit segregated South Africa to competition, on the grounds that the country planned to enter an integrated team. About 40 countries announced that they would boycott the games if South Africa were admitted. In the United States, sociologist Harry Edwards was already trying to persuade black athletes to boycott the Olympics, and his movement, the Olympic Project for Human Rights, gained even more momentum.

The IOC eventually decided to continue its ban of South Africa, and the boycotts didn't take place. Nevertheless, the Black Power movement was to manifest itself in Mexico City. About two months before the Olympics, Warsaw Pact troops moved into Czechoslovakia to put down an anti-Soviet uprising. Czech gymnast Vera Caslavska, who had signed a resolution advocating democratic change, had to go into hiding in a small town where she couldn't train. She, too, was make a reappearance at the Olympics.

Ten days before the opening ceremonies, students demonstrated in Mexico City as part of a movement that had begun several months earlier. Troops fired into the crowd, killing about 250 unarmed demonstrators.

Despite all the doubts and turmoil, the Olympics went on as planned. The high altitude did take its toll on distance runners, but it also contributed to some remarkable records in shorter events. Bob Beamon's long jump of 29 feet 2 1/2 inches, the first jump ever to exceed 28 feet, was the most dramatic example, but there were others. Lee Evans' time of 43.86 in the 400-meter run stood for nearly 20 years; the United States 4x100-meter relay team set a record of 2:56.16 that lasted 24 years; and two triple jumpers exceeded the former world record without even winning medals, because three other competitors broke the record by even greater margins.

There were many other highlights. Al Oerter won his fourth gold medal in the discus. Dick Fosbury started a revolution in the high jump by winning the event with his unorthodox "Fosbury Flop," clearing the bar head first and backwards. Wyomia Tyus became the first runner of either sex to repeat as the 100-meter champion, and Debbie Myer became the first swimmer to win three individual gold medals at a single Olympics.

The biggest winner, though, was Vera Caslavska. After three weeks in hiding, she was given permission to compete in Mexico City. She responded by winning six medals, four gold and two silver. A day after the gymnastics competition ended, Caslavska was married to Josef Odlozil, a runner on the Czech track team.

Tommie Smith turned in perhaps the most courageous victory of the Olympics. He suffered a severe groin pull in the semi-finals of the 200-meter and thought he would probably be unable to run in the final. But he made it to the starting line, his thighs heavily wrapped in tape. Somehow, he fought through the pain and not only won the gold medal but set a new record of 19.83 seconds.

Smith's teammate at San Jose State, John Carlos, finished third. They were both members of the Olympic Project for Human Rights and they had agreed to stage some kind of protest if they won medals. When Smith and Carlos mounted the dais for the victory ceremony, they wore black socks and no shoes. Each wore one black glove, Smith on his right hand, Carlos on his left hand. When the National Anthem began, they lowered their heads, refusing to look at the flag, and each raised his gloved fist in the Black Power salute.

The IOC ordered the U. S. Olympic Committee to ban Smith and Carlos from further competition and to throw them out of the Olympic Village. To its credit, the USOC initially refused. Then the IOC threatened to ban the entire U. S. track and field team from competition, forcing the USOC to give in. Incidentally, this was the same IOC that had declined to comment when Mexican troops shot down students, calling it "an internal affair."

Leading Medal Winners:

Men				
Athlete	Country	Sport	G-S-B	Total
Mikhail Voronin,	USSR	Gymnastics	2-4-1	7

Akinori Nakayama,	JPN	Gymnastics	4-1-1	6
Charles Hickcox,	USA	Swimming	3-1-0	4
Sawao Kato,	JPN	Gymnastics	3-0-1	4
Mark Spitz,	USA	Swimming	2-1-1	4
Mike Wenden,	AUS	Swimming	2-1-1	4
Roland Matthes,	E. Ger	Swimming	2-1-0	3
Ken Walsh,	USA	Swimming	2-1-0	3
Pierre Trentin,	FRA	Cycling	2-0-1	3
Vladimir Kosinski,	USSR	Swimming	0-2-1	3
Leonid Ilyichev,	USSR	Swimming	0-1-2	3

Women

Athlete	Country	Sport	G-S-B	Total
Vera Cáslavská,	CZE	Gymnastics	4-2-0	6
Sue Pedersen,	USA	Swimming	2-2-0	4
Natalya Kuchinskaya,	USSR	Gymnastics	2-0-2	4
Jan Henne,	USA	Swimming	2-1-1	4
Zinaida Voronina,	USSR	Gymnastics	1-1-2	4
Debbie Meyer,	USA	Swimming	3-0-0	3
Kaye Hall,	USA	Swimming	2-0-1	3
Larissa Petrik,	USSR	Gymnastics	2-0-1	3
Ellie Daniel,	USA	Swimming	1-1-1	3
Linda Gustavson,	USA	Swimming	1-1-1	3
Elaine Tanner,	CAN	Swimming	0-2-1	3

Medals by Nation

No.	Nation	G	S	B
1.	United States of America (USA)	45	28	34
2.	USSR (URS)	29	32	30
3.	Japan (JPN)	11	7	7

4.	Hungary (HUN)	10	10	12
5.	German Democratic Republic (GDR)	9	9	7
6.	France (FRA)	7	3	5
7.	Czechoslovakia (TCH)	7	2	4
8.	Federal Republic of Germany (FRG)	5	11	10
9.	Australia (AUS)	5	7	5
10.	Great Britain (GBR)	5	5	3
11.	Poland (POL)	5	2	11
12.	Romania (ROM)	4	6	5
13.	Italy (ITA)	3	4	9
14.	Kenya (KEN)	3	4	2
15.	Mexico (MEX)	3	3	3
16.	Yugoslavia (YUG)	3	3	2
17.	Netherlands (NED)	3	3	1
18.	Bulgaria (BUL)	2	4	3
19.	Islamic Republic of Iran (IRI)	2	1	2
20.	Sweden (SWE)	2	1	1
21.	Turkey (TUR)	2	0	0
22.	Denmark (DEN)	1	4	3
23.	Canada (CAN)	1	3	1
24.	Finland (FIN)	1	2	1
25.	Ethiopia (ETH)	1	1	0
26.	Norway (NOR)	1	1	0
27.	New Zealand (NZL)	1	0	2
28.	Tunisia (TUN)	1	0	1
29.	Venezuela (VEN)	1	0	0
30.	Pakistan (PAK)	1	0	0
31.	Cuba (CUB)	0	4	0
32.	Austria (AUT)	0	2	2
33.	Switzerland (SUI)	0	1	4
34.	Mongolia (MGL)	0	1	3
35.	Brazil (BRA)	0	1	2

36.	Belgium (BEL)	0	1	1
37.	Korea (KOR)	0	1	1
38.	Uganda (UGA)	0	1	1
39.	Jamaica (JAM)	0	1	0
40.	Cameroon (CMR)	0	1	0
41.	Argentina (ARG)	0	0	2
42.	Chinese Taipei (TPE)	0	0	1
43.	Greece (GRE)	0	0	1
44.	India (IND)	0	0	1

The 1972 Olympics: Munich, Germany

Fast Facts

Host City: Munich, Germany

Opening date: Aug. 26, 1972

Closing date: Sept. 11, 1972

Nations: 121

Athletes: 7,123 athletes (1,058 women, 6,065 men)

Events: 195 events in 23 sports

The 1972 Olympics were supposed to celebrate peace. But, on Sept. 5, the 11th day of the games, Palestinian terrorists destroyed the illusion of peace by raiding the Olympic Village, killing two Israelis and taking nine others hostage. The tragedy culminated in a battle at a military airport, where the other hostages were killed, along with five of the terrorists and a German policemen. The Olympics were put on hold while a memorial service was held in the main stadium. After a 34-hour hiatus, they resumed.

Bracketing the bloodshed, the Munich games delivered more than the usual Olympic share of athletic excitement and disappointment. U. S. swimmer Mark Spitz won a record-setting seven gold medals, giving him nine for his career. Tiny Soviet gymnast Olga Korbut was the television star of the games, winning the nickname "the Munchkin of Munich" as she won two gold medals and a silver.

Liselott Linsenhoff of West Germany became the first woman to win an individual gold medal in an equestrian event when she captured the dressage championship. Finland's Lasse Viren fell while running fifth halfway through the 10,000-meter final. But he picked himself up, quickly moved into second place, and not only won the gold but set a world record by running an incredible 56.4-second final lap. Viren went on to win three more gold medals in subsequent Olympics.

In basketball, the United States' 62-game winning streak came to a controversial end in the gold medal game against the Soviet Union. With three seconds left on the clock, the U. S. led, 50-49. Two seconds after the Soviet team inbounded the ball, the head referee suddenly called an official timeout for a consultation at the scorers' table. The Soviet coach insisted that he had called a timeout while Doug Collins was making the free throw that gave the U. S. its lead.

The timeout was awarded with one second left, and the U. S. team celebrated when time ran out after the Soviets inbounded the ball without getting a shot off.

But the secretary-general of the international federation, R. William Jones of Great Britain, ordered that three seconds be put back on the clock and the Soviet team was given another chance. This time, Aleksandr "Sasha" Belov caught the long inbounds pass and scored after pushing through two U. S. defenders, giving the USSR a victory. A protest was rejected on a 3-2 vote by a jury of appeal and the U. S. team voted not to accept its silver medals. They are still stored in a Swiss bank vault.

There was further disappointment for the United States in track, as Valery Borzov of the Soviet Union won gold medals in both the 100- and 200-meter dashes. The top two

U. S. sprinters failed to reach the 100-meter final because they missed their quarter-final heats due to a coach's error in reading the schedule. However, Borzov won the 200-meter so convincingly that it's doubtful an American runner could have beaten him in the shorter sprint, anyway.

For the record, the Munich Olympics were the biggest ever, up to that time. A record 121 nations and 7,123 athletes competed in a 195 events, also a record. Two former Olympic sports were restored to the program, archery after 52 years and team handball after 36 years. Slalom (whitewater) canoeing was also added.

Leading Medal Winners:

Men

Athlete	Country	Sport	G-S-B	Total
Mark Spitz,	USA	Swimming	7-0-0	7
Sawao Kato,	JPN	Gymnastics	3-2-0	5
Jerry Heidenreich,	USA	Swimming	2-1-1	4
Roland Matthes,	E. Ger	Swimming	2-1-1	4
Akinori Nakayama,	JPN	Gymnastics	2-1-1	4
Shigeru Kasamatsu,	JPN	Gymnastics	1-1-2	4
Eizo Kenmotsu,	JPN	Gymnastics	1-1-2	4
Valery Borsov,	USSR	Track	2-1-0	3
Mitsuo Tsukahara,	JPN	Gymnastics	2-0-1	3
Steve Genter,	USA	Swimming	1-2-0	3
Viktor Klimenko,	USSR	Gymnastics	1-2-0	3
Mike Stamm,	USA	Swimming	1-2-0	3
Vladimir Bure,	USSR	Swimming	0-1-2	3

Women

Athlete	Country	Sport	G-S-B	Total
Shane Gould,	AUS	Swimming	3-1-1	5

Karin Janz,	E. Ger	Gymnastics	2-2-1	5
Olga Korbut,	USSR	Gymnastics	3-1-0	4
Lyudmila Tourischeva,	USSR	Gymnastics	2-1-1	4
Tamara Lazakovitch,	USSR	Gymnastics	1-1-2	4

Medals by Nation

No.	Nation	G	S	B
1.	USSR (URS)	50	27	22
2.	United States of America (USA)	33	31	30
3.	German Democratic Republic (GDR)	20	23	23
4.	Federal Republic of Germany (FRG)	13	11	16
5.	Japan (JPN)	13	8	8
6.	Australia (AUS)	8	7	2
7.	Poland (POL)	7	5	9
8.	Hungary (HUN)	6	13	16
9.	Bulgaria (BUL)	6	10	5
10.	Italy (ITA)	5	3	10
11.	Sweden (SWE)	4	6	6
12.	Great Britain (GBR)	4	5	9
13.	Romania (ROM)	3	6	7
14.	Finland (FIN)	3	1	4
15.	Cuba (CUB)	3	1	4
16.	Netherlands (NED)	3	1	1
17.	France (FRA)	2	4	7
18.	Czechoslovakia (TCH)	2	4	2
19.	Kenya (KEN)	2	3	4
20.	Yugoslavia (YUG)	2	1	2
21.	Norway (NOR)	2	1	1
22.	People's Republic of Korea (PRK)	1	1	3
23.	New Zealand (NZL)	1	1	2
24.	Uganda (UGA)	1	1	0

25.	Denmark (DEN)	1	0	0
26.	Switzerland (SUI)	0	3	0
27.	Canada (CAN)	0	2	3
28.	Islamic Republic of Iran (IRI)	0	2	1
29.	Greece (GRE)	0	2	0
30.	Belgium (BEL)	0	2	0
31.	Austria (AUT)	0	1	2
32.	Colombia (COL)	0	1	2
33.	Argentina (ARG)	0	1	0
34.	Korea (KOR)	0	1	0
35.	Lebanon (LIB)	0	1	0
36.	Mexico (MEX)	0	1	0
37.	Mongolia (MGL)	0	1	0
38.	Pakistan (PAK)	0	1	0
39.	Tunisia (TUN)	0	1	0
40.	Turkey (TUR)	0	1	0
41.	Brazil (BRA)	0	0	2
42.	Ethiopia (ETH)	0	0	2
43.	Ghana (GHA)	0	0	1
44.	Jamaica (JAM)	0	0	1
45.	Niger (NIG)	0	0	1
46.	Nigeria (NGR)	0	0	1
47.	India (IND)	0	0	1
48.	Spain (ESP)	0	0	1

The 1976 Olympics: Montreal, Canada

Fast Facts

Host City: Montreal, Canada

Opening date: July 17, 1976

Closing date: Aug. 1, 1976

Nations:	92
Athletes:	6,028 athletes (1,247 women, 4,781 men)
Events:	198 events in 21 sports

The Montreal Games ran into serious problems before they even began. The original budget of $310 million (American) grew to nearly $1 billion because of bad management, poor planning, and just plain corruption, plunging the city of Montreal, the province of Quebec, and the nation of Canada into heavy debt to pay the tab.

Meanwhile, Tanzania exhorted African nations to boycott the Olympics if New Zealand was allowed to compete. The rationale was that New Zealand's national rugby team had toured South Africa, which was still following its apartheid policy. Even though rugby isn't an Olympic sport, 23 nations took part in the boycott.

A few weeks before the games were to begin, Canadian Prime Minister Pierre Trudeau announced that athletes from Taiwan wouldn't be allowed to compete under the name of the Republic of China. Trudeau held firm against protests from the International Olympic Committee, and Taiwanese athletes stayed home. Once the opening ceremony began,though, everything went smoothly. It was a very quiet Olympics for the United States, which won only 84 medals, finishing third behind the Soviet Union and East Germany. The men's swimming team was dominant, winning 12 of 13 events and capturing both gold and silver in 11 of the individual events. John Naber was the top performer, winning four gold medals.

As in 1972, the media star was a young female gymnast, 14-year-old Nadia Comaneci of Romania, who supplanted Olga Korbut. Comaneci was actually a much better gymnast than Korbut. She became a focus of attention when her performance on the uneven bars during the team competition won her the first perfect score of 10.0 in Olympic history. She went on to win six more perfect scores, along with five individual medals, including three golds.

The biggest track and field star was Alberto Juantorena of Cuba, the first runner to score a double in the 400- and 800-meter runs. Two athletes won gold in their events for the third straight time: Klaus Dibiasi of Italy in platform diving and Viktor Saneyev of the Soviet Union in the triple jump.

East Germany's strong showing, led by its women's swimming team, was the surprise of the 1976 Olympics. In 1972, East German women didn't win a single gold medal in swimming. In 1976, they won 11 of the 13 events. Many suspected that this sudden emergence owed at least as much to steroids as to skill and training. Sadly, they were to be proven right more than 20 years later, after Germany was reunified and former East German coaches and doctors went on trial for giving steroids to young athletes, usually without their knowledge. No new sports were added to the 1976 Olympic program, but women competed in basketball, rowing, and team handball for the first time.

Leading Medal Winners:

		Men		
Athlete	Country	Sport	G-S-B	Total
Nikolai Andrianov,	USSR	Gymnastics	4-2-1	7
John Naber,	USA	Swimming	4-1-0	5
Mitsuo Tsukahara,	JPN	Gymnastics	2-1-2	5
Jim Montgomery,	USA	Swimming	3-0-1	4
John Hencken,	USA	Swimming	2-1-0	3
Sawao Kato,	JPN	Gymnastics	2-1-0	3
Eizo Kenmotsu,	JPN	Gymnastics	1-2-0	3
Rüdiger Helm,	E. Ger	Canoeing	1-0-2	3

		Women		
Athlete	Country	Sport	G-S-B	Total
Kornelia Ender,	E. Ger	Swimming	4-1-0	5

Nadia Comaneci,	ROM	Gymnastics	3-1-1	5
Shirley Babashoff,	USA	Swimming	1-4-0	5
Nelli Kim,	USSR	Gymnastics	3-1-0	4
Andrea Pollack,	E. Ger	Swimming	2-2-0	4
Lyudmila Tourischeva,	USSR	Gymnastics	1-2-1	4
Ulrike Richter,	E. Ger	Swimming	3-0-0	3
Annagret Richter,	W. Ger	Track	1-2-0	3
Renate Stecher,	E. Ger	Track	1-1-1	3
Teodora Ungureanu,	ROM	Gymnastics	0-2-1	3

Medals by Nation

No.	Nation	G	S	B
1.	USSR (URS)	49	41	35
2.	German Democratic RepublicGDR	40	25	25
3.	United States of America (USA)	34	35	25
4.	Federal Republic of Germany (FRG)	10	12	17
5.	Japan (JPN)	9	6	10
6.	Poland (POL)	7	6	13
7.	Bulgaria (BUL)	6	9	7
8.	Cuba (CUB)	6	4	3
9.	Romania (ROM)	4	9	14
10.	Hungary (HUN)	4	5	13
11.	Finland (FIN)	4	2	0
12.	Sweden (SWE)	4	1	0
13.	Great Britain (GBR)	3	5	5
14.	Italy (ITA)	2	7	4
15.	France (FRA)	2	3	4
16.	Yugoslavia (YUG)	2	3	3
17.	Czechoslovakia (TCH)	2	2	4

18.	New Zealand (NZL)	2	1	1
19.	Korea (KOR)	1	1	4
20.	Switzerland (SUI)	1	1	2
21.	Norway (NOR)	1	1	0
22.	Jamaica (JAM)	1	1	0
23.	People's Republic of Korea (PRK)	1	1	0
24.	Denmark (DEN)	1	0	2
25.	Mexico (MEX)	1	0	1
26.	Trinidad and Tobago (TRI)	1	0	0
27.	Canada (CAN)	0	5	6
28.	Belgium (BEL)	0	3	3
29.	Netherlands (NED)	0	2	3
30.	Portugal (POR)	0	2	0
31.	Spain (ESP)	0	2	0
32.	Australia (AUS)	0	1	4
33.	Islamic Republic of Iran (IRI)	0	1	1
34.	Mongolia (MGL)	0	1	0
35.	Venezuela (VEN)	0	1	0
36.	Brazil (BRA)	0	0	2
37.	Thailand (THA)	0	0	1
38.	Puerto Rico (PUR)	0	0	1
39.	Pakistan (PAK)	0	0	1
40.	Austria (AUT)	0	0	1
41.	Bermuda (BER)	0	0	1

The 1980 Olympics: Moscow, Russia

Fast Facts

Host City: Moscow, Russia

Opening date: July 19, 1980

Closing date: Aug. 3, 1980

Nations: 80

Athletes: 5,217 athletes (1,124 women, 4,093 men)

203 events in 21 sports

In 1980, the Olympics were held in a Communist bloc country for the first time. They also faced the first genuinely major boycott in Olympic history. After the Soviet Union invaded Afghanistan in December of 1979, President Jimmy Carter threatened to boycott the Games if the invasion continued. The Soviets didn't back down. Led by the United States, 65 nations refused to send teams to Moscow.

The governments of Great Britain and Italy supported the boycott but allowed their athletes to compete if they wanted to. Two of those who did were British middle distance runners Steve Ovett and Sebastian Coe. Though they were countrymen, they hadn't raced against one another since 1978. Coe had set new world records in the 800-meter, 1500-meter, and 1-mile runs in 1979, but Ovett broke Coe's 1-mile record and tied his 1500-meter mark less than a month before the Olympics.

The 800-meter final was anti-climactic, as Ovett won easily but in a very slow time, nearly three seconds slower than Coe's world record, though he finished well ahead of Coe. The 1500-meter was an exciting, three-man race. Jurgen Straub of East Germany held the lead with 200 meters to go, but Coe and Ovett then turned on their finishing sprints. Straub held off Ovett, but Coe passed him to win by 4 meters, thanks to a remarkable 52.2 seconds in the final lap.

Despite the fact that only 80 nations competed, the lowest number since 1956, the Moscow Olympics produced 74 Olympic records and 36 world records, more than had been set in Montreal four years earlier. Cuba's Teófilo Stevenson breezed through the super-heavyweight division with ease, becoming the first boxer to win three gold medals in the same weight class.

The swimming field was seriously depleted by the absence of U. S. competitors, but Vladimir Salnikov of the Soviet Union not only won gold in the 1500-meter freestyle, he became the first to break the 15-minute mark in the event. Salnikov also won two other gold medals.

Another Soviet, gymnast Aleksandr Dityatin, became the first athlete to win eight medals at a single Olympics.

Leading Medal Winners:

Men				
Athlete	Country	Sport	G-S-B	Total
Aleksandr Dityatin,	USSR	Gymnastics	3-4-1	8
Nikolai Andrianov,	USSR	Gymnastics	2-2-1	5
Roland Brückner,	E. Ger	Gymnastics	1-1-2	4
Vladimir Parfenovich,	USSR	Canoeing	3-0-0	3
Vladimir Salnikov,	USSR	Swimming	3-0-0	3
Sergei Kopliakov,	USSR	Swimming	2-1-0	3
Aleksandr Tkachyov,	USSR	Gymnastics	2-1-0	3
Andrei Krylov,	USSR	Swimming	1-2-0	3
Arsen Miskarov,	USSR	Swimming	0-2-1	3

Women				
Athlete	Country	Sport	G-S-B	Total
Ines Diers,	E. Ger	Swimming	2-2-1	5
Caren Metschuck,	E. Ger	Swimming	3-1-0	4
Nadia Comaneci,	ROM	Gymnastics	2-2-0	4
Natalya Shaposhnikova,	USSR	Gymnastics	2-0-2	4
Maxi Gnauck,	E. Ger	Gymnastics	1-1-2	4
Barbara Krause,	E. Ger	Swimming	3-0-0	3
Rica Reinisch,	E. Ger	Swimming	3-0-0	3
Yelena Davydova,	USSR	Gymnastics	2-1-0	3

Steffi Kraker,	E. Ger	Gymnastics	0-1-2	3
Melita Ruhn,	ROM	Gymnastics	0-1-2	3

Medals by Nation

No.	Nation	G	S	B
1.	USSR (URS)	80	69	46
2.	German Democratic Republic (GDR)	47	37	42
3.	Bulgaria (BUL)	8	16	17
4.	Cuba (CUB)	8	7	5
5.	Italy (ITA)	8	3	4
6.	Hungary (HUN)	7	10	15
7.	Romania (ROM)	6	6	13
8.	France (FRA)	6	5	3
9.	Great Britain (GBR)	5	7	9
10.	Poland (POL)	3	14	15
11.	Sweden (SWE)	3	3	6
12.	Finland (FIN)	3	1	4
13.	Czechoslovakia (TCH)	2	3	9
14.	Yugoslavia (YUG)	2	3	4
15.	Australia (AUS)	2	2	5
16.	Denmark (DEN)	2	1	2
17.	Ethiopia (ETH)	2	0	2
18.	Brazil (BRA)	2	0	2
19.	Switzerland (SUI)	2	0	0
20.	Spain (ESP)	1	3	2
21.	Austria (AUT)	1	2	1
22.	Greece (GRE)	1	0	2
23.	India (IND)	1	0	0
24.	Belgium (BEL)	1	0	0

25.	Zimbabwe ZIM	1	0	0
26.	People's Republic of Korea (PRK)	0	3	2
27.	Mongolia (MGL)	0	2	2
28.	Tanzania (TAN)	0	2	0
29.	Mexico (MEX)	0	1	3
30.	Netherlands (NED)	0	1	2
31.	Ireland (IRL)	0	1	1
32.	Uganda (UGA)	0	1	0
33.	Venezuela (VEN)	0	1	0
34.	Jamaica (JAM)	0	0	3
35.	Lebanon (LIB)	0	0	1
36.	Guyana (GUY)	0	0	1

The 1984 Olympics: Los Angeles, California

Fast Facts

Host City: Los Angeles, California

Opening date: July 28, 1984

Closing date: Aug. 12, 1984

Nations: 140

Athletes: 6,797 athletes (1 567 women, 5,230 men)

Events: 221 events in 23 sports

In 1932, Los Angeles created the Olympic Village. In 1984, the city's organizing committee, led by Peter Ueberroth, created an entirely new model for the games. The 1984 Olympics were the first since 1896 to be organized without major government financing. Ueberroth led a much-criticized drive for private money that even included sponsorship of the Olympic torch run, at $3,000 a kilometer.

The drive was so successful that the Games actually turned a profit of well over $200 million. The Soviet Union boycotted the Olympics, in retribution for the U. S.-led boycott of its 1980 Games, and was joined by 13 other nations. Nevertheless, a record 140 nations competed at Los Angeles, compared to only 80 at Moscow, and the number of athletes reached nearly 7,000, very close to the previous record.

The women's program continued to expand with the addition of the marathon in track and the road race in cycling, along with two sports for women only, rhythmic gymnastics and synchronized swimming.

Although the Soviet-led boycott had much less impact on the total numbers than the boycott of 1980, or even the African boycott of 1976, it had a major impact on competition. The 14 Soviet bloc countries that stayed away had won more than half the gold medals in 1976.

The sports most affected were gymnastics, weightlifting, freestyle wrestling, and women's track. The U. S. team was the chief beneficiary, increasing its medal total to 174, nearly double its total of 94 medals in 1976.

The presence of the boycotting countries wouldn't have had any effect on Carl Lewis's record-tying performance, though. Before the Olympics, Lewis had vowed to match Jesse Owens' 1936 feat of winning gold medals in both sprints, the long jump, and the 4x100-meter relay. He did it with relative ease. Lewis won the 100-meter dash by 8 feet, the largest margin in Olympic history. His 200-meter victory margin was an ample 4 feet, his gold medal long jump was nearly a foot better than anyone else's, and he anchored the relay team to a world record 37.83 seconds, nearly 8/10 of a second better than second-place Jamaica.

Women's gymnastics produced its first U. S. heroine, 16-year-old Mary Lou Retton, who scored two perfect 10s while winning the all-around championship. She also won a silver and two bronze medals. Sebastian Coe of Great Britain became the first man to repeat as 1500-meter medalist and Pertti

Karpinnen of Finland won the single sculls event for the third straight time.

Leading Medal Winners:

Men				
Athlete	Country	Sport	G-S-B	Total
Li Ning,	CHN	Gymnastics	3-2-1	6
Koji Gushiken,	JPN	Gymnastics	2-1-2	5
Carl Lewis,	USA	Track	4-0-0	4
Mike Heath,	USA	Swimming	3-1-0	4
Michael Gross,	W. Ger	Swimming	2-2-0	4
Mitch Gaylord,	USA	Gymnastics	1-1-2	4
Rick Carey,	USA	Swimming	3-0-0	3
Ian Ferguson,	NZE	Canoeing	3-0-0	3
Rowdy Gaines,	USA	Swimming	3-0-0	3
Peter Vidmar,	USA	Gymnastics	2-1-0	3
Victor Davis,	CAN	Swimming	1-2-0	3
Pablo Morales,	USA	Swimming	1-2-0	3
Lou Yun,	CHN	Gymnastics	1-2-0	3
Shinji Morisue,	JPN	Gymnastics	1-1-1	3
Lars-Erik Moberg,	SWE	Canoeing	0-3-0	3
Mark Stockwell,	AUS	Swimming	0-2-1	3

Women				
Athlete	Country	Sport	G-S-B	Total
Ecaterina Szabó,	ROM	Gymnastics	4-1-0	5
Mary Lou Retton,	USA	Gymnastics	1-2-2	5
Nancy Hogshead,	USA	Swimming	3-1-0	4
Valerie Brisco-Hooks,	USA	Track	3-0-0	3
Tracy Caulkins,	USA	Swimming	3-0-0	3

Mary T. Meagher,	USA	Swimming	3-0-0	3
Agneta Andersson,	SWE	Canoeing	2-1-0	3
Chandra Cheeseborough,	USA	Track	2-1-0	3
Simona Pauca,	ROM	Gymnastics	2-0-1	3
Julie McNamara,	USA	Gymnastics	1-2-0	3
Anne Ottenbrite,	CAN	Swimming	1-1-1	3
Karin Seick,	W. Ger	Swimming	0-1-2	3
Annemarie Verstappen,	NED	Swimming	0-1-2	3

Medals by Nation

No.	Nation	G	S	B
1.	United States of America (USA)	83	61	30
2.	Romania (ROM)	20	16	17
3.	Federal Republic of Germany (FRG)	17	19	23
4.	People's Republic of China (CHN)	15	8	9
5.	Italy (ITA)	14	6	12
6.	Canada (CAN)	10	18	16
7.	Japan (JPN)	10	8	14
8.	New Zealand (NZL)	8	1	2
9.	Yugoslavia (YUG)	7	4	7
10.	Korea (KOR)	6	6	7
11.	Great Britain (GBR)	5	11	21
12.	France (FRA)	5	7	16
13.	Netherlands (NED)	5	2	6
14.	Australia (AUS)	4	8	12
15.	Finland (FIN)	4	2	6
16.	Sweden (SWE)	2	11	6
17.	Mexico (MEX)	2	3	1
18.	Morocco (MAR)	2	0	0

19.	Brazil (BRA)	1	5	2
20.	Spain (ESP)	1	2	2
21.	Belgium (BEL)	1	1	2
22.	Austria (AUT)	1	1	1
23.	Kenya (KEN)	1	0	2
24.	Portugal (POR)	1	0	2
25.	Pakistan (PAK)	1	0	0
26.	Switzerland (SUI)	0	4	4
27.	Denmark (DEN)	0	3	3
28.	Norway (NOR)	0	1	2
29.	Jamaica (JAM)	0	1	2
30.	Nigeria (NGR)	0	1	1
31.	Greece (GRE)	0	1	1
32.	Puerto Rico (PUR)	0	1	1
33.	Syrian Arab Republic (SYR)	0	1	0
34.	Thailand (THA)	0	1	0
35.	Colombia (COL)	0	1	0
36.	Egypt (EGY)	0	1	0
37.	Peru (PER)	0	1	0
38.	Ireland (IRL)	0	1	0
39.	Ivory Coast (CIV)	0	1	0
40.	Turkey (TUR)	0	0	3
41.	Venezuela (VEN)	0	0	3
42.	Algeria (ALG)	0	0	2
43.	Cameroon (CMR)	0	0	1
44.	Chinese Taipei (TPE)	0	0	1
45.	Dominican Republic (DOM)	0	0	1
46.	Iceland (ISL)	0	0	1
47.	Zambia (ZAM)	0	0	1

The 1988 Olympics: Seoul, South Korea

Fast Facts

Host City: Seoul, South Korea

Opening date: Sept. 17, 1988

Closing date: Oct. 2, 1988

Nations: 149

Athletes: 8,465 athletes (2,186 women, 6,279 men)

Events: 237 events in 24 sports

The 1988 Olympics faced a small boycott, led by North Korea and joined by Cuba, Ethiopia, and Nicaragua. Nevertheless, a record 159 nations and 8,465 athletes competed in Seoul.

Table tennis was added to the Olympic program and tennis was restored after a 62-year absence. Another new event was the women's match sprint in cycling, which led to a record that will never be broken. East German Christa Luding-Rothenburger, who won the silver medal in the match sprint, had won gold and silver speed skating medals at the Winter Olympics in February. She's the only athlete to medal at both Olympics in the same year. Since the Summer and Winter games are now held in different years, no one will ever do it again.

The top winners in Seoul were both swimmers. Kristin Otto of East Germany won six gold medals and Matt Biondi of the U. S. won a total of seven medals, including two gold. In track, sisters-in-law Florence Griffith "Flo-Jo" Joyner and Jackie Joyner-Kersee won a total of six medals. Flo-Jo won four of them, including three golds, and Joyner-Kersee won gold medals in the long jump and the heptathlon.

The biggest story to emerge from the 1988 Olympics was the disqualification of Canadian sprinter Ben Johnson after he had apparently set a world record of 9.79 seconds in the 100-meter dash. Johnson tested positive for steroids, so his world record and gold medal were both disallowed. The medal went to second-place finisher Carl Lewis, who thus became the first athlete to win that event twice. Lewis also won the long jump in more straightforward fashion, and he was the first to win two golds in that event, as well.

U. S. Diver Greg Louganis turned in the Games' most courageous performance in the springboard competition. During his ninth dive of the preliminaries, Louganis hit his head on the board, suffering a gash that required four temporary stitches.

He returned 35 minutes later, just in time to perform his last dive and advance into the finals. He went on to win gold in the springboard and, a week later, in platform diving, becoming the first male diver to win both events at two Olympics.

Leading Medal Winners:

Men				
Athlete	Country	Sport	G-S-B	Total
Matt Biondi,	USA	Swimming	5-1-1	7
Vladimir Artemov,	USSR	Gymnastics	4-1-0	5
Dmitri Bilozerchev,	USSR	Gymnastics	3-0-1	4
Valeri Lyukin,	USSR	Gymnastics	2-2-0	4
Chris Jacobs,	USA	Swimming	2-1-0	3
Carl Lewis,	USA	Track	2-1-0	3
Holger Behrendt,	E. Ger	Gymnastics	1-1-1	3
Uwe Dassler,	E. Ger	Swimming	1-1-1	3
Paul McDonald,	NZE	Canoeing	1-1-1	3
Igor Polianski,	USSR	Swimming	1-0-2	3
Gennadi Prigoda,	USSR	Swimming	0-1-2	3
Sven Tippelt,	E. Ger	Gymnastics	0-1-2	3

Women

Athlete	Country	Sport	G-S-B	Total
Kristin Otto,	E. Ger	Swimming	6-0-0	6
Daniela Silivas,	ROM	Gymnastics	3-2-1	6
Florence Griffith Joyner,	USA	Track	3-1-0	4
Svetlana Boguinskaya,	USSR	Gymnastics	2-1-1	4
Elena Shushunova,	USSR	Gymnastics	2-1-1	4
Janet Evans,	USA	Swimming	3-0-0	3
Silke Hörner,	E. Ger	Swimming	2-0-1	3
Daniela Hunger,	E. Ger	Swimming	2-0-1	3
Katrin Meissner,	E. Ger	Swimming	2-0-1	3
Birgit Schmidt,	E. Ger	Canoeing	2-1-0	3
Birte Weigang,	E. Ger	Swimming	1-2-0	3
Vania Guecheva,	BUL	Canoeing	1-1-1	3
Gabriela Potorac,	ROM	Gymnastics	0-2-1	3
Heike Drechsler,	E. Ger	Track	0-1-2	3

Medals by Nation

No.	Nation	G	S	B
1.	USSR (URS)	55	31	46
2.	German Democratic Republic (GDR)	37	35	30
3.	United States of America (USA)	36	31	27
4.	Korea (KOR)	12	10	11
5.	Federal Republic of Germany (FRG)	11	14	15
6.	Hungary (HUN)	11	6	6
7.	Bulgaria (BUL)	10	12	13
8.	Romania (ROM)	7	11	6
9.	France (FRA)	6	4	6
10.	Italy (ITA)	6	4	4

11.	People's Republic of China (CHN)	5	11	12
12.	Great Britain (GBR)	5	10	9
13.	Kenya (KEN)	5	2	2
14.	Japan (JPN)	4	3	7
15.	Australia (AUS)	3	6	5
16.	Yugoslavia (YUG)	3	4	5
17.	Czechoslovakia (TCH)	3	3	2
18.	New Zealand (NZL)	3	2	8
19.	Canada (CAN)	3	2	5
20.	Poland (POL)	2	5	9
21.	Norway (NOR)	2	3	0
22.	Netherlands (NED)	2	2	5
23.	Denmark (DEN)	2	1	1
24.	Brazil (BRA)	1	2	3
25.	Finland (FIN)	1	1	2
26.	Spain (ESP)	1	1	2
27.	Turkey (TUR)	1	1	0
28.	Morocco (MAR)	1	0	2
29.	Suriname (SUR)	1	0	0
30.	Austria (AUT)	1	0	0
31.	Portugal (POR)	1	0	0
32.	Sweden (SWE)	0	4	7
33.	Switzerland (SUI)	0	2	2
34.	Jamaica (JAM)	0	2	0
35.	Argentina (ARG)	0	1	1
36.	Chile (CHI)	0	1	0
37.	Costa Rica (CRC)	0	1	0
38.	Indonesia (INA)	0	1	0
39.	Islamic Republic of Iran (IRI)	0	1	0

40.	Peru (PER)	0	1	0
41.	Netherlands Antilles AHO	0	1	0
42.	Senegal (SEN)	0	1	0
43.	Virgin Islands (ISV)	0	1	0
44.	Mexico (MEX)	0	0	2
45.	Belgium (BEL)	0	0	2
46.	Colombia (COL)	0	0	1
47.	Greece (GRE)	0	0	1
48.	Djibouti (DJI)	0	0	1
49.	Mongolia (MGL)	0	0	1
50.	Pakistan (PAK)	0	0	1
51.	Philippines (PHI)	0	0	1
52.	Thailand (THA)	0	0	1

The 1992 Olympics: Barcelona, Spain

Fast Facts

Host City: Barcelona, Spain

Opening date: July 25, 1992

Closing date: Aug. 9, 1992

Nations: 169

Athletes: 9,367 athletes (2,708 women, 6,659 men)

Events: 257 events in 28 sports

Spain's pitch for the 1992 Olympics emphasized the 500th anniversary of Christopher Columbus's discovery of America under the auspices of the Spanish monarchy. Columbus and the explorers who followed him obviously changed the world. But the world had also changed dramatically since the 1988 Olympics. South Africa had finally abandoned apartheid and was welcomed back to the Olympics for the first time since

1960. Every nation with a National Olympic Committee was represented at Barcelona. And there were more of them than ever before because of the breakup of the Soviet Union into 15 different countries. Lithuania had an independent team for the first time since 1928, and Estonia and Latvia returned to the Olympics after being absent since 1936. Other former Soviet republics competed as the "Unified Team." There was one less country in the world, though, because of the fall of the Berlin Wall and the reunification of Germany.

Badminton, baseball, and women's judo were added to the program in 1992. And basketball was opened to professionals for the first time, allowing the U. S. "Dream Team" to stock up on NBA players, led by Larry Bird, Magic Johnson, and Michael Jordan.

The biggest individual star was Belarus gymnast Vitaly Scherbo, who won six gold medals. Derartu Tulu of Ethiopia won the women's 10,000-meter run to become the first black African woman gold medalist ever. Andreas Keller of Germany extended a family tradition as a member of Germany's gold medal field hockey team. His father had played for the 1972 gold medal team, his grandfather for the 1936 silver medal team. The most exciting contest of the games was the women's 100-meter dash. Gail Devers of the United States won in 10.82 seconds, just 1/100 second ahead of Juliet Cuthbert of Jamaica and only 6/100 faster than Merlene Ottey, also of Jamaica, who finished fifth. The major surprise was Voula Patoulidou's victory in the women's 100-meter hurdles. Patoulidou, who had never before won a major championship, was the first Greek woman ever to win a medal and the first Greek athlete to win a track and field gold medal since 1912.

Leading Medal Winners:

Men

Athlete	Country	Sport	G-S-B	Total
Vitaly Scherbo,	UT	Gymnastics	6-0-0	6
Grigory Misiutin,	UT	Gymnastics	1-4-0	5

Aleksandr Popov,	UT	Gymnastics	2-2-0	4
Yevgeny Sadovyi,	UT	Swimming	3-0-0	3
Matt Biondi,	USA	Swimming	2-1-0	3
Jon Olsen,	USA	Swimming	2-0-1	3
Mel Stewart,	USA	Swimming	2-0-1	3
Vladimir Pychnenko,	UT	Swimming	1-2-0	3
Li Xiaosahuang,	CHN	Gymnastics	1-1-1	3
Li Jing,	CHN	Gymnastics	0-3-0	3
Anders Holmertz,	SWE	Swimming	0-2-1	3
Andreas Wecker,	GER	Gymnastics	0-1-2	3

Women

Athlete	Country	Sport	G-S-B	Total
Shannon Miller,	USA	Gymnastics	0-2-3	5
Tatiana Gutsu,	UT	Gymnastics	2-1-1	4
Lavinia Milosovici,	ROM	Gymnastics	2-1-1	4
Summer Sanders,	USA	Swimming	2-1-1	4
Franziska van Almsick,	GER	Swimming	0-2-2	4
Krisztina Egerszegi,	HUN	Swimming	3-0-0	3
Nicole Haislett,	USA	Swimming	3-0-0	3
Crissy Ahmann-Leighton	USA	Swimming	2-1-0	3
Jenny Thompson,	USA	Swimming	2-1-0	3
Gwen Torrence,	USA	Track	2-1-0	3
Tatyana Lysenko,	UT	Gymnastics	2-0-1	3
Lin Li,	CHN	Swimming	1-2-0	3
Dagmar Hase,	GER	Swimming	1-2-0	3
Zhuang Yong,	CHN	Swimming	1-2-0	3
Rita Koban,	HUN	Kayaking	1-1-1	3
Anita Hall,	USA	Swimming	1-1-1	3
Daniela Hunger,	GER	Swimming	0-1-2	3

Medals by Nation

No.	Nation	G	S	B
1.	Unified Team (EUN)	45	38	29
2.	United States of America (USA)	37	34	37
3.	Germany (GER)	33	21	28
4.	People's Republic of China (CHN)	16	22	16
5.	Cuba (CUB)	14	6	11
6.	Spain (ESP)	13	7	2
7.	Korea (KOR)	12	5	12
8.	Hungary (HUN)	11	12	7
9.	France (FRA)	8	5	16
10.	Australia (AUS)	7	9	11
11.	Canada (CAN)	7	4	7
12.	Italy (ITA)	6	5	8
13.	Great Britain (GBR)	5	3	12
14.	Romania (ROM)	4	6	8
15.	Czechoslovakia (TCH)	4	2	1
16.	People's Republic of Korea (PRK)	4	0	5
17.	Japan (JPN)	3	8	11
18.	Bulgaria (BUL)	3	7	6
19.	Poland (POL)	3	6	10
20.	Netherlands (NED)	2	6	7
21.	Kenya (KEN)	2	4	2
22.	Norway (NOR)	2	4	1
23.	Turkey (TUR)	2	2	2
24.	Indonesia (INA)	2	2	1
25.	Brazil (BRA)	2	1	0
26.	Greece (GRE)	2	0	0
27.	Sweden (SWE)	1	7	4

28.	New Zealand (NZL)	1	4	5
29.	Finland (FIN)	1	2	2
30.	Denmark (DEN)	1	1	4
31.	Morocco (MAR)	1	1	1
32.	Ireland (IRL)	1	1	0
33.	Ethiopia (ETH)	1	0	2
34.	Estonia (EST)	1	0	1
35.	Algeria (ALG)	1	0	1
36.	Lithuania (LTU)	1	0	1
37.	Switzerland (SUI)	1	0	0
38.	Nigeria (NGR)	0	3	1
39.	Jamaica (JAM)	0	3	1
40.	Latvia (LAT)	0	2	1
41.	Austria (AUT)	0	2	0
42.	Namibia NAM	0	2	0
43.	South Africa (RSA)	0	2	0
44.	Belgium (BEL)	0	1	2
45.	Croatia (CRO)	0	1	2
46.	Independant Participant (IOP)	0	1	2
47.	Islamic Republic of Iran (IRI)	0	1	2
48.	Israel (ISR)	0	1	1
49.	Chinese Taipei (TPE)	0	1	0
50.	Mexico (MEX)	0	1	0
51.	Peru (PER)	0	1	0
52.	Slovenia (SLO)	0	0	2
53.	Mongolia (MGL)	0	0	2
54.	Malaysia (MAS)	0	0	1
55.	Puerto Rico (PUR)	0	0	1
56.	Qatar (QAT)	0	0	1

57.	Philippines (PHI)	0	0	1
58.	Pakistan (PAK)	0	0	1
59.	Suriname (SUR)	0	0	1
60.	Thailand (THA)	0	0	1
61.	Colombia (COL)	0	0	1
62.	Bahamas (BAH)	0	0	1
63.	Argentina (ARG)	0	0	1
64.	Ghana (GHA)	0	0	1

The 1996 Olympics: Atlanta, Georgia

Fast Facts

Host City: Atlanta, Georgia

Opening date: July 19, 1996

Closing date: Aug. 4, 1996

Nations: 197

Athletes: 10,320 athletes (3,523 women, 6,797 men)

Events: 271 events in 26 sports

The Atlanta Olympics of 1996 were widely regarded as an athletic success but an artistic failure. A host of problems with logistics and organization plagued the games. The much-touted computerized scoring and results system kept crashing and the transportation system was inadequate. Atlanta never got around to building an Olympic village; instead, athletes were housed in dorms at Georgia Tech University.

On July 27, eight days after the opening ceremony, a bomb exploded in Centennial Olympic Park, killing one person and injuring more than 100 others. Although the park seemed to be part of the Olympic setting, it wasn't, and therefore it was not covered by Olympic security.

Atlanta set new records across the board: 197 nations send 10,320 athletes, 79 nations won medals, and 53 won gold medals. Beach volleyball, lightweight rowing, mountain biking, soccer, and women's softball were added to the program, bringing the number of events to a record 271.

Four was the lucky number for U. S. track star Carl Lewis. By taking the gold medal in the high jump, he became one of only three athletes to win the same event four times, and he also became the fourth athlete to win nine gold medals during his career.

But Lewis was overshadowed by teammate Michael Johnson, who set a world record of 19.32 seconds in the 200-meter dash and became the first male runner to double in the 200 and 400-meter events. Marie-Jose Perec of France scored the same double on the women's side.

Three athletes won their third gold medals in a single event: Krisztina Egerszegi of Hungary in the 200-meter backstroke, Aleksandr Karelin of Russia in Greco-Roman wrestling, and Naim Suleymanoglu of Turkey in weightlifting. They were surpassed by Birgit Schmidt of Germany, who won a fifth gold medal in kayaking. She had won her first in 1980.

Leading Medal Winners:

Men				
Athlete	Country	Sport	G-S-B	Total
Alexei Nemov,	RUS	Gymnastics	2-1-3	6
Gary Hall Jr.,	USA	Swimming	2-2-0	4
Aleksandr Popov,	RUS	Swimming	2-2-0	4
Josh Davis,	USA	Swimming	3-0-0	3
Denis Pankratov,	RUS	Swimming	2-1-0	3
Daniel Kowalski,	AUS	Swimming	0-1-2	3
Vitaly Scherbo,	BEL	Gymnastics	0-0-3	3

Women				
Athlete	Country	Sport	G-S-B	Total
Amy Van Dyken,	USA	Swimming	4-0-0	4
Michelle Smith,	IRE	Swimming	3-0-1	4
Angel Martino,	USA	Swimming	2-0-2	4
Simona Amanar,	ROM	Gymnastics	1-1-2	4
Dagmar Hase,	GER	Swimming	0-3-1	4
Gina Gogean,	ROM	Gymnastics	0-1-3	4
Jenny Thompson,	USA	Swimming	3-0-0	3
Lilia Podkopayeva,	UKR	Gymnastics	2-1-0	3
Amanda Beard,	USA	Swimming	1-2-0	3
Le Jingyi,	CHN	Swimming	1-2-0	3
Wendy Hedgepeth,	USA	Swimming	1-2-0	3
Susan O'Neill,	AUS	Swimming	1-1-1	3
Merlene Ottey,	JAM	Track	0-2-1	3
Franziska van Almsick,	GER	Swimming	0-2-1	3
Sandra Volker,	GER	Swimming	0-1-2	3

Medals by Nation

No.	Nation	G	S	B
1.	United States of America (USA)	44	32	25
2.	Russian Federation (RUS)	26	21	16
3.	Germany (GER)	20	18	27
4.	People's Republic of China (CHN)	16	22	12
5.	France (FRA)	15	7	15
6.	Italy (ITA)	13	10	12
7.	Australia (AUS)	9	9	23
8.	Cuba (CUB)	9	8	8
9.	Ukraine (UKR)	9	2	12

10.	Korea (KOR)	7	15	5
11.	Poland (POL)	7	5	5
12.	Hungary (HUN)	7	4	10
13.	Spain (ESP)	5	6	6
14.	Romania (ROM)	4	7	9
15.	Netherlands (NED)	4	5	10
16.	Greece (GRE)	4	4	0
17.	Czech Republic (CZE)	4	3	4
18.	Switzerland (SUI)	4	3	0
19.	Denmark (DEN)	4	1	1
20.	Turkey (TUR)	4	1	1
21.	Canada (CAN)	3	11	8
22.	Bulgaria (BUL)	3	7	5
23.	Japan (JPN)	3	6	5
24.	Kazakhstan (KAZ)	3	4	4
25.	Brazil (BRA)	3	3	9
26.	New Zealand (NZL)	3	2	1
27.	South Africa (RSA)	3	1	1
28.	Ireland (IRL)	3	0	1
29.	Sweden (SWE)	2	4	2
30.	Norway (NOR)	2	2	3
31.	Belgium (BEL)	2	2	2
32.	Nigeria (NGR)	2	1	3
33.	People's Republic of Korea (PRK)	2	1	2
34.	Ethiopia (ETH)	2	0	1
35.	Algeria (ALG)	2	0	1
36.	Great Britain (GBR)	1	8	6
37.	Belarus (BLR)	1	6	8
38.	Kenya (KEN)	1	4	3

39.	Jamaica (JAM)	1	3	2
40.	Finland (FIN)	1	2	1
41.	Indonesia (INA)	1	1	2
42.	Yugoslavia (YUG)	1	1	2
43.	Slovakia (SVK)	1	1	1
44.	Islamic Republic of Iran (IRI)	1	1	1
45.	Armenia (ARM)	1	1	0
46.	Croatia (CRO)	1	1	0
47.	Portugal (POR)	1	0	1
48.	Thailand (THA)	1	0	1
49.	Syrian Arab Republic (SYR)	1	0	0
50.	Costa Rica (CRC)	1	0	0
51.	Burundi (BDI)	1	0	0
52.	Hong-Kong (HKG)	1	0	0
53.	Ecuador (ECU)	1	0	0
54.	Argentina (ARG)	0	2	1
55.	Slovenia (SLO)	0	2	0
56.	Namibia (NAM)	0	2	0
57.	Austria (AUT)	0	1	2
58.	Moldova MDA	0	1	1
59.	Malaysia (MAS)	0	1	1
60.	Uzbekistan (UZB)	0	1	1
61.	Zambia (ZAM)	0	1	0
62.	Latvia (LAT)	0	1	0
63.	Philippines (PHI)	0	1	0
64.	Tonga (TGA)	0	1	0
65.	Azerbaijan (AZE)	0	1	0
66.	Bahamas (BAH)	0	1	0
67.	Chinese Taipei (TPE)	0	1	0

68.	Georgia (GEO)	0	0	2
69.	Trinidad and Tobago (TRI)	0	0	2
70.	Morocco (MAR)	0	0	2
71.	Mozambique (MOZ)	0	0	1
72.	Mongolia (MGL)	0	0	1
73.	Lithuania (LTU)	0	0	1
74.	Mexico (MEX)	0	0	1
75.	Tunisia (TUN)	0	0	1
76.	Puerto Rico (PUR)	0	0	1
77.	Israel (ISR)	0	0	1
78.	India (IND)	0	0	1
79.	Uganda (UGA)	0	0	1

The 2000 Olympics: Sydney, Australia

Fast Facts

Host City: Sydney, Australia

Opening date: Sept. 15, 2000

Closing date: Oct. 1, 2000

Nations: 199

Athletes: 10,651 athletes (4,069 women, 6,582 men)

Events: 300 events in 30 sports

When Juan Antonio Samaranch said that the 2000 Olympics were the best ever, it could have been taken as hyperbole. But the IOC president was simply echoing what had been said by thousands of spectators who had come to Sydney, Australia, from around the world, including many journalists who had covered several previous Olympics.

In terms of numbers, the Sydney Games surpassed all that had come before. Records were set for events (300), sports

(28), countries participating (199), athletes (10,651), and the number of countries winning medals (80). The quality of the 2000 Olympics went far beyond numbers, though. Bud Greenspan, producer of the official documentary on the games, said that the torch relay and the opening ceremony both earned perfect 10s and that the rest of the organization lived up to that standard. And Greenspan had attended every Olympics since 1952.

More than 50,000 unpaid volunteers worked to make the Games successful, and foreign visitors saluted them, almost unanimously, for their friendliness as well as their efficiency. Boston Globe columnist Dan Shaughnessy wrote, "Sydney's greatest tourist attraction is its population."

The only real black spot was that more than 30 athletes failed drug tests. Even that was seen by many as a positive indication that testing was catching up to methods of hiding drug use. But on to the athletes, who produced some remarkable accomplishments. British rower Steve Redgrave became the first athlete to win gold medals at five consecutive Olympics.

Birgit Fischer of Germany won two gold medals in canoeing, giving her a total of nine medals overall, six gold, and becoming the first woman to win medals 20 years apart.

Cuban heavyweight boxer Felix Savon, Czech javelin thrower Jan Zelezny, and Greek weightlifter Pyrros Dimas all won their third consecutive gold medals. But Turkey's Naim Suleymanoglu, trying for his fourth consecutive gold in weightlifting, was eliminated from medal contention in the 62-kilogram class.

The Australian three-day event team also won a third straight gold medal, the first time that had ever been accomplished in equestrian competition.

There were two major upsets. Domenico Fioravanti of Italy, ranked 14th in the world, won the 100-meter breaststroke. And Greco-Roman wrestler Rulon Gardner of the

U. S. went from obscurity to world fame by beating Russia's Alexander Kareline for the super heavyweight gold medal. Kareline had won three gold medals and nine consecutive world championships, going 12 years without a single loss.

The most successful of all American athletes in 2000 was considered a failure by some. Sprinter/long jumper Marion Jones went to Sydney hoping to win five gold medals, and sometimes outright predicting it. She won five medals, but "only" three were gold, the other two bronze. The fact that she was the first athlete of either sex to win five medals in track and field at a single Olympics was often overlooked.

Perhaps the most unusual gold medal victory went to the U. S. softball team. The women entered the Olympics as heavy favorites, having won 112 games in a row. But they lost three straight in the Olympic tournament, then came back to take the gold bv winning three games in two days.

Leading Medal Winners:

Men				
Athlete	Country	Sport	G-S-B	Total
Alexei Nemov,	RUS	Gymnastics	2-1-3	6
Ian Thorpe,	AUS	Swimming	3-2-0	5
Michael Klim,	AUS	Swimming	2-2-0	4
Gary Hall Jr.,	USA	Swimming	2-1-1	4
Pieter van den Hoogenband,	NED	Swimming	2-0-2	4
Dmitri Sautin,	RUS	Diving	1-1-2	4
Lenny Krayzelburg,	USA	Swimming	3-0-0	3
Florian Rousseau,	FRA	Cycling	2-1-0	3
Massimiliano Rosolino,	ITA	Swimming	1-1-1	3
Matthew Welsh,	AUS	Swimming	0-2-1	3

Women

Athlete	Country	Sport	G-S-B	Total
Marion Jones,	USA	Track	3-0-2	5
Dara Torres,	USA	Swimming	2-0-3	5
Inge de Bruijn,	NED	Swimming	3-1-0	4
Leontien Zijlaard,	NED	Cycling	3-1-0	4
Jenny Thompson,	USA	Swimming	3-0-1	4
Susie O'Neill,	AUS	Swimming	1-3-0	4
Yana Klochkova,	UKR	Swimming	2-1-0	3
Elena Zamolodtchikova,	RUS	Gymnastics	2-1-0	3
Simona Amanar,	ROM	Gymnastics	2-0-1	3
Svetlana Khorkina,	RUS	Gymnastics	1-2-0	3
Liu Xuan,	CHN	Gymnastics	1-0-2	3
Therese Alshammer,	SWE	Swimming	0-2-1	3
Ekaterina Lobazniouk,	RUS	Gymnastics	0-2-1	3
Petria Thomas,	AUS	Swimming	0-2-1	3

Medals by Nation

No.	Nation	G	S	B
1.	United States of America (USA)	40	24	33
2.	Russian Federation (RUS)	32	28	28
3.	People's Republic of China (CHN)	28	16	15
4.	Australia (AUS)	16	25	17
5.	Germany (GER)	13	17	26
6.	France (FRA)	13	14	11
7.	Italy (ITA)	13	8	13
8.	Netherlands (NED)	12	9	4
9.	Cuba (CUB)	11	11	7
10.	Great Britain (GBR)	11	10	7

11.	Romania (ROM)	11	6	9
12.	Korea (KOR)	8	10	10
13.	Hungary (HUN)	8	6	3
14.	Poland (POL)	6	5	3
15.	Japan (JPN)	5	8	5
16.	Bulgaria (BUL)	5	6	2
17.	Greece (GRE)	4	6	3
18.	Sweden (SWE)	4	5	3
19.	Norway (NOR)	4	3	3
20.	Ethiopia (ETH)	4	1	3
21.	Ukraine (UKR)	3	10	10
22.	Kazakhstan (KAZ)	3	4	0
23.	Belarus (BLR)	3	3	11
24.	Canada (CAN)	3	3	8
25.	Spain (ESP)	3	3	5
26.	Turkey (TUR)	3	0	2
27.	Islamic Republic of Iran (IRI)	3	0	1
28.	Czech Republic (CZE)	2	3	3
29.	Kenya (KEN)	2	3	2
30.	Denmark (DEN)	2	3	1
31.	Finland (FIN)	2	1	1
32.	Austria (AUT)	2	1	0
33.	Lithuania (LTU)	2	0	3
34.	Azerbaijan (AZE)	2	0	1
35.	Slovenia (SLO)	2	0	0
36.	Switzerland (SUI)	1	6	2
37.	Indonesia (INA)	1	3	2
38.	Slovakia (SVK)	1	3	1
39.	Mexico (MEX)	1	2	3

40.	Algeria (ALG)	1	1	3
41.	Uzbekistan (UZB)	1	1	2
42.	Yugoslavia (YUG)	1	1	1
43.	Latvia (LAT)	1	1	1
44.	Bahamas (BAH)	1	1	0
45.	New Zealand (NZL)	1	0	3
46.	Thailand (THA)	1	0	2
47.	Estonia (EST)	1	0	2
48.	Croatia (CRO)	1	0	1
49.	Mozambique (MOZ)	1	0	0
50.	Cameroon (CMR)	1	0	0
51.	Colombia (COL)	1	0	0
52.	Brazil (BRA)	0	6	6
53.	Jamaica (JAM)	0	4	3
54.	Nigeria (NGR)	0	3	0
55.	South Africa (RSA)	0	2	3
56.	Belgium (BEL)	0	2	3
57.	Argentina (ARG)	0	2	2
58.	Chinese Taipei (TPE)	0	1	4
59.	Morocco (MAR)	0	1	4
60.	People's Republic of Korea (PRK)	0	1	3
61.	Moldova (MDA)	0	1	1
62.	Saudi Arabia (KSA)	0	1	1
63.	Trinidad and Tobago (TRI)	0	1	1
64.	Ireland (IRL)	0	1	0
65.	Viet Nam (VIE)	0	1	0
66.	Uruguay (URU)	0	1	0
67.	Georgia (GEO)	0	0	6
68.	Costa Rica (CRC)	0	0	2

69.	Portugal (POR)	0	0	2
70.	Qatar (QAT)	0	0	1
71.	Kuwait (KUW)	0	0	1
72.	Kyrgyzstan (KGZ)	0	0	1
73.	Sri Lanka (SRI)	0	0	1
74.	Chile (CHI)	0	0	1
75.	Armenia (ARM)	0	0	1
76.	Barbados (BAR)	0	0	1
77.	Republic of Macedonia (MKD)	0	0	1
78.	Israel (ISR)	0	0	1
79.	Iceland (ISL)	0	0	1
80.	India (IND)	0	0	1

The 2004 Olympics: Athens, Greece

Fast Facts

Host City: Athens, Greece

Opening date: Aug. 13, 2004

Closing date: Aug. 29, 2004

Nations: 201

Athletes: 11,099

Events: 301 events in 28 sports

There had been hopes that Athens would host the 1996 Olympics, marking the centennial of the modern Games. But Atlanta was selected for 1996 and Sydney for the 2000 Olympics. Athens finally got its chance in 2004, eight years late for the centennial celebration. It seemed for a time that Athens would be even later than that. In 2000, the International Olympic Committee seriously considered moving the 2004 games to another country, possibly South Korea, because Athens' preparations were so far behind schedule.

Athens remained the host, though, and everything was ready in time. Well, almost everything. There was no roof on the natatorium, so swimmers struggled with hot sun and high temperatures during afternoon preliminaries. Medal races were fortunately held at night, when the air and water were cooler.

There was praise for the architecture of new and refurbished Olympic venues, for the fountains and reflecting pools that ornamented the areas, for the shimmering Wall of Nations created by Spanish architect Santiago Calatrava, who also designed the new stadium and the Olympic Sport Center. Besides building the obligatory new structures, Athens could serve up tradition as no other host city ever could. The men's and women's shot put competition took place in the stadium of Ancient Olympia.

The Panathinaiko Stadium, where the first modern Olympic Games were held in 1896, was modified to host archery competition and the finish of the marathon. The Karaiskaki Stadium, which had been the velodrome in 1896, was totally renovated to host men's and women's soccer. And the marathon followed the historic route from Marathon to Athens, first run by a military courier named Phidippides in 490 B.C., according to legend.

After Athens was ready, the next perceived problem was terrorism. Despite constant reassurances about all the security measures in place, ticket sales were slow. When the Games officially opened on Aug. 13, fewer than half of the 5.2 million available seats had been sold and, for the first several days, there were thousands of empty seats at the major events.

Then, suddenly, the spectators began to show up. The 70,000-seat stadium was virtually sold out for every night of the track and field competition, and other venues were nearly filled during the final week or so of the Olympics. At the closing ceremony on Aug. 29, IOC President Jacques Rogge proclaimed to the Greek people, "You have won. You have won by brilliantly meeting the tough challenge of holding the games. These were unforgettable, dream games."

In truth, there were some problems, but for the most part they couldn't be blamed on the Athens organizing committee. The biggest controvery arose in gymnastics, where three judges were suspended for a scoring error that gave American Paul Hamm the all-around gold medal that should have gone to Yang Tae-young of South Korea. The International Gymnastics Federation said it couldn't change the result because there was no timely protest. South Korea has filed an appeal with the Court of Arbitation for Sport (CAS).

The CAS had intervened earlier in a controversy over the three-day equstrian event. Judges originally ruled that Bettina Hoy of Germany had made an illegal start, but then changed their decision and awarded Hoy the gold medal. Her score also gave Germany the gold medal in the team event. However, the CAS ruled that the original decision was correct. As a result, Hoy and Germany both dropped into fourth place. Leslie Law of Great Britain was declared the individual winner and France became the winner of the team event.

The only security breach was a bizarre incident that marred the men's marathon, the final competition before the closing ceremony. A defrocked Irish priest with a history of such disturbances burst from the crowd and grabbed Vanderlei de Lima of Brazil, who was leading the race with about three miles to go. De Lima managed to break free, but he kept looking warily over his shoulder for the rest of the race. He finished third and a protest from Brazil's track federation, asking that he be given a share of the gold medal, was rejected. That case, too, may be going to the CAS.

The individual star of the Olympics was unquestionably U. S. swimmer Michael Phelps, who won six gold medals and two bronze. The 19-year-old Phelps can become the all-time leading medal winner in Olympic history by winning four more in 2008.

Another U. S. swimmer, Natalie Coughlin, was the leading medal winner among women athletes. She won five, including two golds. Kayaker Birgit Fischer of Germany quietly moved up the all-time list of medal winners. She won a gold and silver, giving her 12 medals overall, including eight golds. Fischer won her first gold medal in 1980, when she was 18, making her the youngest women ever to win an Olympic kayaking event. With her victory as a member of the four-woman kayaking team, she became the first woman to win Olympic medals 24 years apart.

Track and field didn't really produce a major star, as it often had in the past. Kelly Holmes of Great Britain won the women's 800- and 1500-meter runs and Hicham El Guerrouj of Morocco also won two individual golds, in the men's 1500- and 5000-meter. Marion Jones of the U. S., who had had won five medals at Sydney, qualified for only one individual event, the long jump, where she finished fifth. She also ran a leg of the 4 by 100-meter relay, but a botched baton pass disqualified the American team. Jones was under investigation for possible steroid use and some runners felt she shouldn't have been on the relay team at all, because the entire team could be disqualified if she were suspended later. That, of course, turned out to be moot.

The U. S. Olympic Committee had set a goal of 100 medals and the team exceeded that by three. One of those 103 medals was a bronze for the men's basketball team. The fourth edition of the "Dream Team" was a hastily-assembled melange of players who showed little chemistry or cohesion in losing three games.

Unfortunately, that performance drew much more media attention than the U. S. women's gold medal in basketball. And the U. S. women's soccer team also won gold in an overtime match against Brazil, while the men's team didn't even qualify for the Olympic tournament. China, which will host the 2008 Olympics, was third to the U. S. and Russia in total medal standings, but was a close second in gold medals, with 32 to 35 for the United States.

5

Asian Games

The Asian Games are held for the purpose of developing intercultural knowledge and friendship within Asia. The member countries and regions affiliated to the Olympic Council of Asia participate in this multi-sports event. This World Games is held every four years in between the Olympic Games.

Origin of Asian Games

Unofficial historical data traces the origination of the Asian Games to the Eastern Olympics inaugurated in Manila, the Philippines, in 1913 with 6 member countries of the Philippines, Thailand, China, Japan, Malaysia, and Hong Kong. This bienniel sports meet changed name to the Far East Championship, and continued to be held till 1934, and two years later as the Eastern Championship held in Tokyo in 1934.

From 1913 to 1934, 10 Far East Championships were held in Asia, but the championships stopped because of the outbreak of World War II. After the war a number of Asian countries became independent, their economy and culture developed, and Asian people had an increasing desire to become less isolated from each other and strengthen mutual intercourse. In order to keep abreast of the times, the Indian Prime Minister, Jawahalal Nehru, proposed an Asian sports meet in 1947 at a conference on relations between Asian countries.

In August 1948, during the 14th Olympic Games held in London, India proposed to sports leaders of the Asian teams the idea of having discussions about holding the Asian Games. As a brainchild of Professor Guru Dutt Sondhi, with assistance from Korea, Taiwan, India, the Philippines, Burma and Ceylon, the concept of the Asian Games was formalized at New Delhi in 1949.

A preparatory committee was set up to draft the charter for the Asian Amateur Athletic Federation. In February, 1949, the Asian Amateur Athletic Federation was formally formed, and its name was changed to the Asian Athletic Federation. It was decided to hold the first Asian Games in 1950 in New Dehli, the capital of India. Since then the Asian Games has been regularly held once every four years.

At the General Meeting of the Asian Games Federation in 1982, the participants agreed to the formation of the Olympic Council of Asia. This body has since then been the official governing body of the Asian Games.

The following is a quick listing of the host cities of the previous Games:

1st Asian Games	1951	New Delhi (India)
2nd Asian Games	1954	Manila (Philippines)
3rd Asian Games	1958	Tokyo (Japan)
4th Asian Games	1962	Jakarta (Indonesia)
5th Asian Games	1966	Bangkok (Thailand)
6th Asian Games	1970	Bangkok (Thailand)
7th Asian Games	1974	Teheran (Iran)
8th Asian Games	1978	Bangkok (Thailand)
9th Asian Games	1982	New Delhi (India)

10th Asian Games	1986	Seoul (Korea)
11th Asian Games	1990	Beijing (China)
12th Asian Games	1994	Hiroshima (Japan)
13th Asian Games	1998	Bangkok (Thailand)
14th Asian Games	2002	Bhusan
15th Asian Games	2006	Will be held at Doha

The First Asiad in New Delhi, India

The First Asian Games, originally scheduled for 1950, was postponed until March 1951 because of the delayed preparations. Four hundred and eighty-nine athletes from Afghanistan, Burma, India, Indonesia, Iran, Japan, Nepal, the Philippines, Singapore, SriLanka, and Thailand competed in athletics, aquatics, basketball, cycling, football and weightlifting in the eight-day Games from 4 March 1951 to 12 March 1951.

Korea was unable to participate because of the Korean War. The first gold medalist was N.C. Kok of Singapore who won the 1500-meter freestyle swimming. Winning all four freestyle swimming events, he won four gold medals. Japan placed first with 24 gold medals, 20 silver medals and 14 bronze medals, followed by India which garnered 15 gold, 18 silver and 19 bronze medals. Japan had been barred from the London Olympics for initiating the Pacific War and was not invited to the founding meeting of AGF but was allowed to participate in the First Asian Games.

Details of the 1st Asian Games are given below:

Held at	New Delhi, March 04 to March 11, 1951
Participating Nations	11 countries/NOCs
Participants	500
Sports/Events :	Six

Athletics, Swimming, Football, Cycling, Basketball & Weightlifting

Medals Tally

Rank	Nation	G	S	B	Total
1	Japan	24	20	14	58
2	India	15	18	19	52
3	Iran	8	5	2	15
4	Singapore	4	6	2	12
5	Philippines	3	5	7	15
6	Ceylon	-	1	-	1
7	Indonesia	-	-	5	5
8	Myanmar	-	-	3	3

The Second Asiad in Manila, the Philippines

A total of 1,280 athletes from 18 countries participated in the nine-day Games from 1 May 1954 to 10 May 1954. The 18 participating countries included Cambodia, Hong Kong, Korea, Malaysia, North Borneo and Vietnam. Of the six sports events of the first Asian Games, cycling was dropped and boxing, shooting and wrestling were added to increase the number of sports to eight. Japan won first place garnering 38 gold, 36 silver and 24 bronze medals. The host country, the Philippines, won second place with 14 gold, 14 silver and 17 bronze medals. Participating in Asain Games for the first time, Korea won third place with eight gold, six silver and five bronze medals.

Details of the 2st Asian Games are given below:

Held at	Manila, Philippines May 01 to May 09, 1954
Participating Nations	18

Participants	1,241
Sports/Events	Eight Athletics, Swimming, Soccer,Basketball, Weightlifting, Wrestling, Boxing & Shooting

Medals Tally:

Rank	Nation	G	S	B	Total
1	Japan	38	36	24	98
2	Philippines	14	14	17	45
3	Korea	8	6	5	19
4	Pakistan	4	5	-	9
5	India	4	4	5	14
6	China	2	4	6	12
7	Myanmar	2	-	2	4
8	Israel	2	-	1	3
9	Singapore	1	3	4	8
10	Ceylon	-	1	1	2
11	Indonesia	-	-	3	3
12	Hong Kong	-	-	1	1

The Third Asiad in Tokyo, Japan

The nine-day Third Asian Games were held from 24 May 1958 to 2 June 1958, with participation of 1,820 athletes from 20 countries who competed in 13 different sports consisting of the eight sports of the Second Asiad and tennis, volleyball, table tennis, hockey and cycling. Japan again won top place with 67 gold, 41 silver and 30 bronze medals, followed by the Philippines which won eight gold, 19 silver and 21 bronze medals. Korea dispatched a 156-man delegation to win third place with eight gold, 19 silver and

12 bronze medals. Lee Chang Hun of Korea won the marathon race.

Details of the 3rd Asian Games are given below:

Held at	Tokyo, May 24 to June 01, 1958
Participating Nations	20
Participants	1,692
Sports/Events	13 Athletics, Swimming, Soccer,Basketball, Boxing, Wrestiing,Weightlifting, Shooting, Tennis, Volleyball, Table Tennis, Hockey, and Cycling

Medals Tally

Rank	Nation	G	S	B	Total
1	Japan	67	41	30	138
2	Philippines	8	19	21	48
3	Korea	8	7	12	27
5	China	6	9	10	25
5	Pakistan	6	5	4	15
6	India	5	3	3	11
7	Iran	4	6	6	16
8	Vietnam	2	-	-	2
9	Myanmar	2	-	-	2
10	Singapore	1	1	-	2
11	Ceylon	1	-	-	1
12	Indonesia	-	2	4	6
13	Thailand	-	1	3	4
14	Malaysia	-	-	2	2

15	Israel	-	-	1	1
16	Hong Kong	-	-	1	1

The Fourth Asiad in Jakarta, Indonesia

When the hosting country, Indonesia, opposed the participation of Chinese Taipei and Israel, the noble ideal of peace and friendship of the Asian Games was jeopardized. The IOC said that it would cancel its approval of the Jakarta Asian Games should the host country reject the two countries. The International Amateur Athletic Federation (IAAF) declared that unless the two countries were allowed to participate in the Jakarta Asiad, it would withdraw its approval of the Games and the athletes and their countries who participated would be disqualified as players and IAAF membership.

President of the International Weightlifting Federation (IWF) flew to Jakarta to warn that if the two countries were excluded from the Games the IWF would regard the Games as an unofficial and only a friendship meet. As Indonesia insisted on the exclusion of the two countries, the IWF expelled the Indonesian Weightlifting Federation and decided not to hold the weightlifting event in the Jakarta Asiad.

Without the participation of Chinese Taipei and Israel, 16 countries with 1,460 athletes competed in the 12-day Asian Games from 24 August 1962 to 5 August 1962. The 13 sports of the Games included badminton, which was played for the first time at the Games. Japan won first place with 73 gold, 56 silver and 23 bronze medals, followed by India which collected 10 gold, 13 silver and 10 bronze medals.

Details of the 4th Asian Games are given below:

Held at	Jakarta, Indonesia August 24 to September 04, 1962

Participating Nations	18
Participants	1,527
Sports/Events	13
	Athletics, Swimming, Soccer, Tennis, Basketball, Volleyball, Table Tennis, Cycling, Boxing, Wrestling, Shooting, Hockey, and Badminton

Medals Tally

Rank	Nation	G	S	B	Total
1	Japan	73	56	23	152
2	India	10	13	10	33
3	Indonesia	9	12	27	48
4	Philippines	7	4	16	27
5	Korea	4	4	7	15
6	Pakistan	3	4	4	11
7	Thailand	2	5	5	12
8	Malaysia	2	3	5	10
9	Myanmar	2	1	7	10
11	Singapore	1	-	1	2
12	Ceylon	-	1	2	3
13	Hong Kong	-	-	1	1

The Fifth Asiad in Bangkok, Thailand

Eighteen countries sent over 2,500 athletes and officials to the Fifth Asian Games, held between 9-20 December 1966, to compete in 14 different sports. Chinese Taipei and Israel returned to the Asian Games and Korea dispatched a 275-man delegation to compete in all 14 sports. During this

Games, Korea was chosen to host the Sixth Asian Games in 1970. Japan again was the top winner garnering 78 gold, 53 silver and 33 bronze medals. Korea won second place for the first time in Asian Games with 12 gold, 18 silver and 21 bronze medals. Thailand, the host country, placed third with 12 gold, 14 silver and 11 bronze medals.

Details of the 5th Asian Games are given below:

Held at	Bangkok, Thailand December 09 to December 20, 1966
Participating Nations	18
Participants	2,500
Sports/Events	14 Athletics, Swimming, Soccer,Tennis, Basketball, Volleyball, Table Tennis, Cycling, Boxing, Wrestling, Weightlifting, Shooting, Hockey, and Badminton

Medals Tally:

Rank	Nation	G	S	B	Total
1	Japan	78	53	33	164
2	Korea	12	18	21	51
3	Thailand	12	14	11	37
4	Malaysia	7	5	6	18
5	India	7	4	11	22
6	Indonesia	7	4	10	21
7	Iran	6	8	17	31
8	China	5	9	10	24
9	Israel	3	5	3	11

10	Philippines	2	15	25	42
11	Pakistan	2	4	2	8
12	Myanmar	1	-	4	5
13	Singapore	-	5	7	12
14	Vietnam	-	1	2	3
15	Ceylon	-	-	4	4
16	Hong Kong	-	-	1	1

The Sixth Asiad in Bangkok, Thailand

After Korea gave up hosting rights for the Sixth Asian Games because of domestic reasons, the Sixth Asiad was held in Bangkok, Thailand, with the financial support of Korea and a few other countries, for 12 days beginning 9 December 1970. Over 2,400 athletes from 18 countries participated in the Games which featured 13 sports. Tennis and table tennis were not played and yachting was included for the first time.

Japan won 74 gold, 47 silver and 23 bronze medals to win first place. Korea won second place for the second consecutive Games with 18 gold, 13 silver and 23 bronze medals. Korea's Cho Oh Ryon won the 400-meter and 1500-meter freestyle swimming. Korea also won gold medals in men's high-board diving and women's shot put. Thailand followed Korea with 9 gold, 17 silver and 13 bronze medals.

Details of the 6th Asian Games are given below:

Held at	Bangkok, Thailand
	December 09 to December 20, 1970
Participating Nations	18
Participants	2,500

Sports/Events	13
	Athletics, Swimming, Soccer,Basketball, Volleyball, Cycling, Boxing, Wrestling, Weightlifting,Shooting, Hockey, Badminton and Sailing

Medals Tally:

Rank	Nation	G	S	B	Total
1	Japan	74	47	23	144
2	Korea	18	13	23	54
3	Thailand	9	17	13	39
4	Iran	9	7	7	23
5	India	6	9	10	25
6	Israel	6	6	5	17
7	Malaysia	5	1	7	13
8	Myanmar	3	2	7	12
9	Indonesia	2	5	17	24
10	Ceylon	2	2	-	4
11	Philippines	1	9	12	22
12	China	1	5	12	18
13	Pakistan	1	2	7	10
14	Singapore	-	6	9	15
15	Cambodia	-	2	3	5
16	Vietnam	-	-	2	2

The Seventh Asiad in Tehran, Iran

The expulsion of Chinese Taipei and Israel again haunted the Seventh Asian Games. About 10 months before the Seventh Asiad, the AGF General Assembly on 16 November 1973, expelled Chinese Taipei and admitted the D.P.R.

Korea. Iran, the host country, despite the opposition of Arabic nations, allowed Israeli to participate in Asian Games. Communist bloc nations, such as the People's Republic of China, Mongolia and D.P.R Korea, took part in Asian Games for the first time. Both Korea and D.P.R Korea competed in the Games. Arabic nations, D.P.R. Korea, Pakistan and the People's Republic of China refused to compete in tennis, fencing, basketball and football matches with Israel. Twenty-five countries sent 3,010 athletes to compete in 16 sports at the Seventh Asiad between 1-16 September 1974. Japan, again, won the most medals including 75 gold, 49 silver, and 51 bronze medals. Iran came forward to place second with 36 gold, 28 silver and 17 bronze medals. The People's Republic of China, a new comer, placed third, collecting 33 gold, 45 silver and 28 bronze medals.

Details of the 7th Asian Games are given below:

Held at	Teheran, Iran, September 01 to September 16, 1974
Participating Nations	25
Participants	3,000
Sports/Events	16 Athletics, Swimming, Shooting, Cycling, Weightlifting, Gymnastics, Wrestling, Boxing, Table Tennis, Basketball, Volleyball, Soccer, Tennis, Badminton, Fencing, and Hockey

Medals Tally

Rank	Nation	G	S	B	Total
1	Japan	75	49	51	175
2	Iran	36	28	17	81
3	China	33	45	28	106

The Eight Asiad in Bangkok, Thailand

The Eighth Asian Games originally planned for Islamabad, Pakistan, was held in Bangkok, Thailand, as Pakistan gave up the rights to host the Games because of domestic reasons. Including the Eighth Asiad, Thailand hosted three Asian Games. Israel was expelled from the Asian Games and Syria was readmitted as a member of the Asian Games. United Arab Emirates, Bangladesh, Lebanon, Qatar and Saudi Arabia were newly admitted to Asian Games.

The Bangkok Asian Games Organizing Committee suddenly proposed to use the name of the Republic of Korea rather then Korea. At the last minute, just before the opening ceremony, the Organizing Committee decided to continue to use the name Korea. 3,842 athletes representing 25 countries compete in 19 different sports between 9-20 December 1978. Archery and bowling were new sports and yachting was revived in the Games. Japan ranked first garnering 70 gold, 58 silver and 49 bronze medals. The People's Republic of China followed Japan with 51 gold, 20 silver and 45 bronze medals. Korea won third place, winning 18 gold, 20 silver and 31 bronze medals and D.P.R. Korea placed fourth with 15 gold, 13 silver and 15 bronze medals.

Details of the 8th Asian Games are given below·

Held at	Bangkok, Thailan December 09 to December 20, 1978
Participating Nations	27
Participants	4,000
Sports/Events	19 Athletics, Swimming, Soccer, Tennis, Basketball, Volleyball, Table Tennis, Cycling, Boxing, Wrestling, Weightlifting,

Fencing, Shooting,
Gymnastics, Hockey,
Badminton, Archery,
Bowling and Sailing

Medals Tally

Rank	Nation	G	S	B	Total
1	Japan	70	58	49	177
2	China	51	55	45	151
3	South Korea	18	20	31	69
4	North Korea	15	13	15	43
5	Thailand	11	11	20	42
6	India	11	11	6	28
7	Indonesia	8	7	18	33
8	Pakistan	4	4	9	17
9	Philippines	4	4	6	14
10	Iraq	2	4	6	12
11	Singapore	2	1	4	7
12	Malaysia	2	1	3	6
13	Mongolia	1	3	5	9
14	Lebanon	1	1	-	2
15	Syria	1	-	-	1
16	Myanmar	-	3	3	6
17	Hong Kong	-	2	3	5
18	Sri Lanka	-	-	2	2
19	Kuwait	-	-	1	1

The Ninth Asiad in New Delhi, India

The Ninth Asian Games in New Delhi, 19 November through 4 December 1982, was the first Asian Games under the control of the OCA. The AGF, under whose jurisdiction the first eight Asian Games had been held, dissolved to make way for the OCA. 4,595 athletes representing 33 countries competed in 21 sports. The number of the participating countries was the greatest in Asian Games history. Handball, equestrian sports, rowing and golf were played for the first time in Asian Games history. Fencing and bowling were not included in the 21 events of the Ninth Asiad.

Garnering 61 gold, 51 silver, and 41 bronze medals, the People's Republic of China replaced Japan, which won 57 gold, 52 silver, and 44 bronze medals, as the winner of the first place during the Ninth Asian Games. Korea placed third with 28 gold, 28 silver, and 37 bronze medals, followed by D.P.R. Korea with 17 gold, 19 silver, and 20 bronze medals. Host of the tenth Asiad in 1986 and the 24th Olympiad in 1988, Korea participated in the Ninth Asian Games with a 406-man delegation and an observation team to study the facilities, management and sports events.

Details of the 9th Asian Games are given below:

Held at	New Delhi, India November 19 to December 04, 1982
Participating Nations	33
Participants	4,500
Sports/Events	21 Athletics, Swimming, Soccer, Tennis, Basketball, Volleyball, Table Tennis, Handball, Cycling, Boxing, Wrestling, Weightlifting, Archery, Shooting, Equestrian, Gymnastics, Hockey, Badminton, Canoeing, Sailing , Golf

Medals Tally

Rank	Nation	G	S	B	Total
1	China	61	51	41	153
2	Japan	57	52	44	153
3	South Korea	28	28	37	93
4	North Korea	17	19	20	56
5	India	13	19	25	57
6	Indonesia	4	4	7	15
7	Iran	4	4	4	12
8	Pakistan	3	3	5	11
9	Mongolia	3	3	1	7
10	Philippines	2	3	9	14
11	Iraq	2	3	4	9
12	Thailand	1	5	4	10
13	Kuwait	1	3	3	7
14	Syria	1	1	1	3
15	Malaysia	1	-	3	4
16	Singapore	1	-	2	3
17	Afghanistan	-	1	-	1
18	Lebanon	-	-	1	1
19	Bahrain	-	-	1	1
20	Hong Kong	-	-	1	1
21	Qatar	-	-	1	1
22	Vietnam	-	-	1	1

The Tenth Asiad in Seoul, Korea

The tenth Asian Games was held in Seoul, Korea, from September 20 to October 5, 1986, with 3,345 athletes (755 women) from 27 countries and regions participating. There were 269 events in 25 sports, with judo and taekwondo as newly added sports. 83 Asian records and 3 world records were broken and 2 world records were equalled. Attending the opening ceremony were the Korean president, the Japanese prime minister, the OCA president Sheikh Fahad Al Sabah, the IOC president Juan Antonio Samaranch and officials from various international sports organizations. The tenth Asian Games to be held in Seoul, so sports facilities, stadiums and gymnasiums were all constructed according to the requirements of the Olympic Games.

China sent 385 athletes to participate in 20 sports and won 94 gold medals, holding sway over Asia for the second time. The Indian woman athletic star P.T. Usha won 4 firsts, becoming the biggest winner of gold medals in athletics. Hamada Ahmad from Bahrain defeated his Japanese opponent and Won a gold medal in men 400m. hurdle. Hong Kong bowling player Chen Ju Hong Won the first gold medal for Hong Kong in the history of the Asiad. Chinese gymnast Li Ning won 4 gold medals and silver medals, becoming the biggest winner of medals at the Games. Japanese hammer player Murobushi Shgenobu became champion for the fifth successive time since the sixth Asian Games.

Details of the 10th Asian Games are given below:

Held at	Seoul, Korea September 20 to October 05, 1986
Participating Nations	27
Participants	4,839
Sports/Events	25
	Athletics, Swimming, Archery, Badminton, Basketball, Bowling, Boxing, Cycling, Equestrian, Golf, Fencing, Soccer, Judo, Hockey, Gymnastics, Handball,

Canoeing, Shooting,
Table Tennis, Tennis,
Taekwondo, Volleyball,
Wrestling, Weightlifting and
Yacht Racing

Medals Tally

Rank	Nation	G	S	B	Total
1	China	94	82	46	222
2	South Korea	93	55	76	224
3	Japan	58	76	77	211
4	Iran	6	6	10	22
5	India	5	9	23	37
6	Philippines	4	5	9	18
7	Thailand	3	10	13	26
8	Pakistan	2	3	4	9
9	Indonesia	1	5	4	10
10	Hong Kong	1	1	3	5
11	Qatar	1	-	3	4
12	Lebanon	1	-	1	2
13	Bahrain	1	-	1	2
14	Malaysia	-	5	5	10
15	Iraq	-	5	2	7
16	Jordan	-	3	1	4
17	Kuwait	-	1	7	8
18	Singapore	-	1	4	5
19	Saudi Arabia	-	1	-	1
20	Nepal	-	-	8	8
21	Bangladesh	-	-	1	1
22	Oman	-	-	1	1

The Eleventh Asiad in Beijing, China

The 11th Asian Games was held from September 22 to October 7 in 1990 in Beijing, the capital of China, with the motto "unity, friendship and progress". Participating were 4,655 athletes (1,462 women) from 37 countries and regions. There were 308 events in 27 sports, with softball, sepak takraw, wushu, kabaddi and rowing as newly-added sports, and baseball and soft tennis as demonstration sports.

With the largest number of sports ever seen in the Asiad, the 11th Asian Games was the first large scale international sports meet to be held in the history of China. 7 world records were bettered, 89 Asian records broken, 189 Asian Games records and one world record, 11 Asian records and 20 Asian Games records were equalled.

Details of the 11th Asian Games are given below:

Held at	Beijing, China September 22 to October 07, 1990
Participating Nations	37 (All OCA members except Iraq and Jordan)
Participants	6,122
Sports/Events	27 Athletics, Swimming, Archery, Badminton, Basketball, Boxing, Canoeing, Kabaddi, Cycling, Golf, Fencing, Soccer, Handball, Judo,Gymnastics, Hockey, Canoeing, Sepak Takraw, Shooting, Softball, Table Tennis, Tennis, Volleyball,Weightlifting, Wrestling, Wushu, and Sailing

Medals Tally

Rank	Nation	G	S	B	Total
1	China	183	107	51	341
2	South Korea	54	54	73	181
3	Japan	38	60	76	174
4	North Korea	12	31	39	82
5	Iran	4	6	8	18
6	Pakistan	4	1	7	12
7	Indonesia	3	6	21	30
8	Qatar	3	2	1	6
9	Thailand	2	7	8	17
10	Malaysia	2	2	4	8
11	India	1	8	14	23
12	Mongolia	1	7	9	17
13	Philippines	4	5	9	18
14	Syria	1	-	2	3
15	Oman	1	-	-	1
16	Chinese Taipei	-	10	21	31
17	Hong Kong	-	2	5	7
18	Sri Lanka	-	2	1	3
18	Singapore	-	1	4	5
19	Bangladesh	-	1	-	1
20	Myanmar	-	-	1	1
21	Laos	-	-	1	1
22	Macau	-	-	1	1
21	Nepal	-	-	1	1
22	Saudi Arabia	-	-	1	1

The Twelveth Asiad in Hiroshima, Japan

The 12th Games in Hiroshima, with the participation of 6828 athletes and official from 42 NOCs, including five Central Asian countries newly independent from the former Soviet Union, and featuring 34 sports, broke the Beijing records and became the largest event ever in the history of the Asian Games.

Details of the 12th Asian Games are given below:

Held at	Hiroshima, Japan October 02 to October 16, 1994
Participating Nations	42
Participants	6,824
Sports/Events	34 Athletics, Swimming, Archery, Badminton, Baseball, Basketball, Bowling, Boxing, Canoeing, Cycling, Equestrian, Fencing, Soccer, Golf, Gymnastics, Handball, Hockey, Judo, Kabaddi, Karatedo, Rowing, Modern Pentathlon, Sepak Takraw, Shooting, Softball, Table Tennis, Taekwondo, Tennis, Volleyball, Weightlifting, Wrestling, Wushu, and Sailing

Medals Tally

Rank	Nation	G	S	B	Total
1	China	125	83	58	266
2	Japan	64	75	79	218
3	South Korea	63	56	64	183

4	Kazakhstan	25	26	26	77
5	Uzbekistan	10	11	19	40
6	Iran	9	9	8	26
7	Chinese Taipei	7	12	24	31
8	India	4	3	15	22
9	Malaysia	4	2	13	19
10	Qatar	4	1	15	20
11	Indonesia	3	12	11	26
12	Thailand	3	9	13	25
13	Syria	3	3	1	7
14	Philippines	3	2	8	13
15	Kuwait	3	1	5	9
16	Saudi Arabia	1	3	5	9
17	Turkmenistan	1	3	3	7
18	Mongolia	1	2	6	9
19	Singapore	1	1	5	7
20	Vietnam	1	2	-	3
21	Hong Kong	-	5	7	12
22	Pakistan	-	4	6	10
23	Kyrgyzstan	-	4	5	9
24	Jordan	-	2	2	4
25	U. Arab Emirate	-	1	3	4
26	Macau	-	1	1	2
27	Sri Lanka	-	1	1	2
28	Bangladesh	-	1	-	1
29	Brunei	-	-	2	2
30	Myanmar	-	-	2	2
31	Nepal	-	-	2	2
32	Tajikistan	-	-	2	2

The 13th Asian Games

The 13th Asian Games was held from Dec 6 to Dec 20, 1998 at Bangkok. This is the largest Asian Games to he held in this millennium, with 9,469 athletes and officials from over 41 countries participating. The Games went smoothly without any major problem in the spirit of the motto: Friendship Beyond Frontiers.

Details of the 13th Asian Games are given below:

Held at	Hiroshima, Japan October December 06 to December 20, 1998
Participating Nations	41
Participants	9,699
Sports/Events	36 Athletics, Archery, Badminton, Baseball, Basketball, Billiard, Golf, Bowling, Boxing, Canoeing, Cycling, Equestrian, Fencing, Soccer, Judo, Gymnastics, Handball, Hockey, Kabaddi, Karatedo, Rowing, Rugby, Sepak Takraw, Shooting, Softball, Soft Tennis, Squash, Swimming, Table Tennis, Tennis, Taekwondo, Volleyball, Wrestling, Wushu, Weightlifting and Sailing

Medals Tally

Rank	Nation	G	S	B	Total
1	China	129	78	67	274
2	South Korea	65	46	53	164
3	Japan	52	61	68	181

4	Thailand	24	26	40	90
4	Kazakhstan	24	24	30	78
5	Taipei	19	17	41	77
6	Iran	10	11	13	34
7	North Korea	7	14	12	33
8	India	7	11	17	35
9	Uzbekistan	6	22	12	40
10	Indonesia	6	10	11	27
11	Malaysia	5	10	14	29
12	Hong Kong	5	6	6	17
13	Kuwait	4	6	4	14
14	Sri Lanka	3	0	3	6
15	Pakistan	2	4	9	15
16	Singapore	2	3	9	14
17	Qatar	2	3	3	8
18	Mongolia	2	2	10	14
19	Myanmar	1	6	4	11
20	Philippines	1	5	12	18
21	Vietnam	1	5	11	17
22	Turkmenistan	1	0	1	2
23	Kyrgyzstan	-	3	3	6
24	Jordan	-	3	2	5
25	Syria	-	2	4	6
26	Nepal	-	1	3	4
27	U. Arab Emirate	-	1	1	2
28	Macau	-	1	-	1
29	Bangladesh	-	-	1	1
30	Brunei	-	-	1	1
31	Laos	-	-	1	1
32	Oman	-	-	1	1

14th Asiad in Busan, South Korea

The 14th Asian Games held at Busan (South Korea) from 29th September to 14th October, 2002. Taking more than a third of all gold medals on offer at the Busan Asian Games, world sports power China demonstrated once again it has grown beyond Asia. China was just too strong a competitor for other Asian countries, including the distant runner-up South Korea and third place holder Japan.

Beginning with two fencing golds won on the Sept. 29, the opening day of the 16-day meet, athletes from the world's most populous country swept the board. China's medal haul comprises 150 gold, 84 silver and 74 bronze medals. The feat was no surprise for other participants as the unrivaled athletic power has dominated Asian sports for about two decades. In the previous Bangkok games in 1998, the country also took home more than a third of all golds on offer, 129 of 378, to be exact.

Most participants, and China itself, took it for granted the reigning champion would take the most medals this time too. Finishing first in the medal tally was not the first goal for China. The country had openly stated it would use this year's games to develop stars and better the quality of gold medals in preparation for the 2004 Athens Olympics and the 2008 Olympics on home soil. To that purpose the country picked young athletes, with an average age of 23.3 years. In addition some 80 percent of the athletes have not experienced competing at either Asiad or Olympics level.

Many teenage star athletes were discovered, ncluding female gymnast Zhang Nan, male gymnast Teng Haibin, female weightlifter Liu Chunhong, female shooter Du Li and female swimmer Qi Hui. Considering their youth, they are expected to play a key role in Chinese sports for the next 10 years. In addition to individual events China also succeeded in upgrading its performance in ball sports. While maintaining its traditional edge in basketball and volleyball, the country also made big strides in hockey and handball, posing serious challenges to South Korea which has dominated these sports in the past. China also succeeded in bettering the qualify of its golds. This year's Asiad saw a total of 22 world records with 17 of them set by Chinese athletes. More encouraging is that most of China's new world record holders are in their teens or early twenties. Host South Korea and its rival Japan fought hard for the second spot in the medal standings, but are still far behind China whose gold medals outnumbers their combined total of number one awards. Kazakhstan stood fourth with 20 golds. India and Saudi Arabia stood out in athletics, posing serious challenges to China and Japan.

Details of the 13th Asian Games are given below:

Held at	Busan (South Korea), 29th September to 14th October, 2002
Participating Nations	44
Participants	9782
Sports/Events	38 Archery, Athletics, Badminton, Baseball, Basketball, Billiard & Snooker, Bowling, Boxing, Canoeing, Cycling, Equestrian, Fencing, Soccer, Golf, Gymnastics, Handball, Hockey, Judo, Kabaddi, Karatedo, Rowing, Rugby, Sepaktakraw, Shooting, Softball, soft Tennis, Squash, Swimming, Table Tennis, Taekwondo, Tennis, Volleyball, Weightlifting, Wrestling, Wushu, Modern Pentathlon, Sailing and Body Building

Medals Tally

Rank	Nation	G	S	B	Total
1	China	150	84	74	308
2	Korea	96	80	84	260
3	Japan	44	74	72	190
4	Kazakhstan	20	26	30	76
5	Uzbekistan	15	12	24	51
6	Thailand	14	19	10	43
7	Taipei	10	17	25	52
8	India	10	12	13	35
9	D.P.R. Korea	9	11	13	33
10	Iran	8	14	14	36
11	Saudi Arabia	7	1	1	9
12	Malaysia	6	8	16	30
13	Singapore	5	2	10	17
14	Indonesia	4	7	12	23
15	Vietnam	4	7	7	18
16	Hong Kong	4	6	11	21
17	Qatar	4	5	8	17
18	Philippines	3	7	16	26
19	Bahrain	3	2	2	7
20	Kyrgyzstan	2	4	6	12
21	Kuwait	2	1	5	8
22	Sri Lanka	2	1	3	6
23	Pakistan	1	6	6	13
24	Myanmar	1	5	6	12
25	Turkmenistan	1	2	1	4
26	Mongolia	1	1	12	14

27	Lebanon	1	-	-	1
28	Tajikistan	-	2	4	6
29	Macau	-	2	2	4
30	U.A. E	-	2	1	3
31	Bangladesh	-	1	-	1
32	Syria	-	-	3	3
32	Nepal	-	-	3	3
34	Laos	-	-	2	2
34	Jordan	-	-	2	2
36	Afghanistan	-	-	1	1
36	Yemen	-	-	1	1
36	Brunei	-	-	1	1
36	Palestine	-	-	1	1

14th Asiad in Doha

15th Asian Games will be held at Doha in the year 2006. The State of Qatar and its capital city, Doha, have been selected, after an intense competition with major Asian cities, to host the games from 1st to 15th December, 2006. The Doha Asian Games Organising Committee (DAGOC) and the Qatar National Olympic Committee have shared the responsibilities of organising these meetings.

Around 300 delegates from the 45 member countries of the OCA are expected to attend. Various issues related to the Doha Asian Games will be discussed, and the host of the 2010 Asian Games will be officially revealed.

Member Countries of the Olympic Council of Asia

The present member countries of the Olympic Council of Asia are as follows:

Afghanistan
Bahrain
Bangladesh
Bhutan
Brunei
Cambodia
China
DPR Korea
Hong Kong
India
Indonesia
Iran
Japan
Jordan
Kazakhstan
Korea
Kuwait
Kyrgyzstan
Laos
Lebanon
Macau
Malaysia Maldives
Mongolia
Myanmar
Nepal
Oman
Pakistan
Palestine
Philippines
Qatar
Saudi Arabia
Singapore
Sri Lanka
Syria
Chinese Taipei
Tajikistan
Thailand
Turkmenistan
U. Arab Emirates
Uzbekistan
Vietnam
Yemen

6

Afro Asian Games

Origin of Afro Asian Games

The Afro Asian games were first proposed in 1983, but attempts to hold Afro Asian Games in 1985, 1991, 1999 and 2001 all had fallen through. India, at the very least, should be given credit for their perseverance in bringing the 2003 Afro Asian Games to their beginning.

The first mention of a competition for the combined continents of Africa and Asia was in April of 1983, when Olympic Review stated that Afro Asian Games would be held in New Delhi. In December, 1983, Olympic Review noted that the proposed games venue had been changed to Kuwait and would be held in 1985.

The games were to combine the four best teams in basketball, football and handball, the four best track athletes in each event and the two best boxers in each weight class, from each region, Africa and Asia.

In April 1985 the games were still on but in September they were cancelled, the organizers citing political instability.

In 1989 the idea resurfaced once again with the announcement that New Delhi would host the games in November 1991. Once again nothing came of the plans.

The idea was brought to life again at the end of the and Afro Asian games were to be held in Pune, India in 1999, then

New Delhi in November of 1999. These games were not cancelled but were postponed until November 2001. Preparations were slow however, and this, combined with the terrorist attacks in the United States in September 2001 caused the games to be postponed indefinitely once again.

Egypt had been mentioned as a tentative host for 2005, if the games had been held successfully in 2001, but plans for a second edition have been put on hold until after a first edition is successfully held.

In May of 2002, India proposed holding the Afro Asian Games in Hyderabad, in 2003. Hyderabad was chosen because facilities had recently been upgraded for India's national games.

Ist Afro Asian Games, Hyderabad, India

The Ist ever Afro Asian Games were held in Hyderabad, the Capital of Andhra Pradesh State in India from 24th of October to 1st November, 2003. President OCA presided over the Opening Ceremony of the Ist Afro Asian Games. The games were opened by the Deputy Prime Minister of India Mr. L.K. Advani.

Opening Ceremony

A brilliantly conceptualised display of colour and gaiety marked the grand Opening Ceremony, which got the first-ever Afro Asian Games under way at the GMC Balayogi Stadium in Gachibowli on the outskirts of Hyderabad. The ceremony had all the pomp and grandeur befitting the important occasion, which added a new chapter to the sports history of this city. The whole show was designed to encapsulate the huge variety of culture and traditions of the two continents and it managed to fulfil this demanding task fairly successfully.

To coordinate the various dances, acrobatics and the display of martial arts by such a large number of participants was truly a mind-boggling feat and the organisers deserve praise for putting up the show in such a precise manner. There were no major hitches or glitches and the programme was gone through smoothly, adding to its grandeur. The most breathtaking and remarkable aspect of the show was the fusion of colour, music and lights, which lit up the entire stadium and sent the audience into raptures.

Spotted among the audience were some of the best known personalities of the Hindi and Telugu film industry such as Sanjay Dutt, Chiranjeevi and Balakrishna, while from the world of sports, tennis star Leander Paes and Mohd. Azharuddin were among the more prominent faces.

To top it all, India's hopes of hosting the Commonwealth Games got a boost when Sheikh Al Fahad Ahmed Al Sabah, President of the Olympic Council of Asia, endorsed India's initiative. The visiting VIPs seemed to have been impressed by the organisational ability and commitment towards sports that they witnessed in India and the mood was upbeat during the opening ceremony. In his speech, N. Chandrababu Naidu, Chief Minister of Andhra Pradesh, made it clear that his government was willing and ready to host more such sports extravaganzas, including the Commonwealth Games and the Olympics if given the chance.

The opening ceremony succeeded in showcasing the rich traditions and culture of the host State and the country, and also sent out a message to the world at large that the host was capable of conducting major events in a splendid manner. An unusual aspect of the march past was that the players trooped into the stadium in two groups — Africans and Asians, and not in a countrywise order. The informal manner made the march-past look more like a closing ceremony rather than the inaugural one. One felt that perhaps the move to club the participants into two continentwise groups, instead of the usual practice of each country's team marching separately under its own banner, was due to the fact that there was not enough representation from each country to make up sizeable contingents in the march past. The opening of the centre-stage, which was shaped like a lotus flower, was quite spectacular and the rendition of the Atha Swagatam song by S. P. Balasubramaniam and Usha along with 200 children and 300 Kuchipudi dancers set the right spirit combining the mood of sobriety and gaiety in proper proportions.

When it came to addressing the gathering, one felt the speakers should have restricted themselves to the bare minimum on an occasion like this. The audience became a little restive at this stage and so also the players, some of whom were seen leaving the arena in small groups and this could have been avoided. The Chief Minister Chandrababu Naidu's suggestion to the visitors to try out the taste of Hyderabadi biryani and buy Hyderabad's world famous pearls met with enthusiastic and loud response from the audience.

The honour of lighting the torch was given to Karnam Malleswari, winner of the bronze medal in the Sydney Olympic Games. Triple Olympian hockey player Mukesh Kumar and Malleswari took the torch up to the final point and then Malleswari ascended the stage to set it alight. This was followed by a spectacular display of lights and fireworks, which lit up the surroundings for miles, well beyond the confines of the stadium.

The display of martial arts namely Kalaripayattu, Thangta and Kung Fu was breathtaking. The participants showed their expertise and the movements were superbly done with grace. Also a grand sight was the depiction of the battle of Kalinga by about 1000 participants. The acting out of Mahatma Gandhi's famous Dandi march and the speech on the giant screen by former South African President Nelson Mandela brought to life the philosophy of freedom and equality and the deeds of the freedom fighters of these two countries. Film stars Mahima Choudhary, Simran and Urmila Matondkar regaled the audience with their dances and finally Shankar Mahadevan and others brought the show to an end with the rendition of the theme song.

Results of the Game

A total of 2,000 athletes and officials from almost 75 countries of Asia and Africa participated in the Ist Afro Asian Games held from 24th October to 1st November, 2003.

Two World Records were broken - One in Shooting by Ms. Olga Dovgun from Kazakhstan in 50 M Rifle Prone (Women) who shot 600/600. The second was in Weightlifting by Ms. Sun Dan from China who lifted 277.5 Kgs in over 75 Kgs. in women categories.

China with 25 Gold, 11 Silver and 5 Bronze was placed first in Medals Tally and India with 19 Gold, 32 Silver and 29 bronze was placed second.

Hyderabad hosted the first Afro Asian Games, which saw delegates and dignitaries from over 120 countries representing Asia, Africa and few commonwealth countries. Players from 98 countries take part in eight disciplines namely Athletics, Boxing Football, Hockey, Shooting, Swimming, Tennis, and weightlifting.

The games were held at The GMC Balayogi Athletic Stadium,The Lal Bahadur Stadium,The Shooting Range, Hyderabad Central University,The Acquatics Complex, GMC Balayogi Stadium,The Tennis Complex, Fatehmaidan,The Kotla Vijayabhaskara Reddy Indoor Stadium. The games were being organised by Government of India,Government of Andhra Pradesh,Indian Olympic Association and Afro Asian Games Council.

The games were held over the Indian holiday period of Diwali (analogous in some respect to holding a games over the Christmas Period in North America or Europe) which was criticized by some. In addition, the Muslim period of Ramadan began during the games.

The intent of the Afro Asian Games was to reward the top four finishing teams and individuals from the 2002 Asian Games and the 2003 African Games, and have them meet head to head. In practice this turned out to be quite difficult to achieve.

Stars of the games were Sania Mirza, an Indian junior tennis player ranked in the 400s worldwide, who picked up four gold medals, in women's singles, women's doubles, mixed doubles, and for the women's team competition.

Japanese swimmers picked up numerous medals, Mizuki Wakabayashi with four gold medals, Takamitsu Kojima and Genki Imamura with three each.

China's Sun Dan from China, broke a world record in the women over 75 kilo category by lifting 168.5 kilos in the clean and jerk.

A surprise for Afro Asian Games organizers was the arrival of Namibian champion sprinter Frankie Fredericks, who, it was reported after the African Games, was retiring. Fredericks stated that he had been misunderstood and that he had only said that the Abuja Games were his final African Games, but he is not yet retiring! Frederick's would be 40 years old the next time the African Games are scheduled to roll around in 2007. Fredericks, took the 100 and 200 meter gold medals in Hyderabad, saying that he wanted to support the inaugural games and hoped that other athletes would support future Afro Asian events.

On a continental level, Asia won 82 gold, 80 silver and 88 bronze medals while Africa won 49 gold, 41 silver and 66 bronze medals. On a country basis, China, India, Japan, Nigeria and South Africa led the medals table.

A comparison of India's performance at the 2002 Asian Games and the 2003 Afro Asian Games proves how valuable it is to host a games. In the 2002 Asian Games, with 44 nations and 38 sports, India won 10 gold, 12 silver and 13 bronze medals, or 35 out of a total of 1350 medals awarded at those games about 2.6 percent of the medals.

In the 2003 Afro Asian Games, with just 8 sports, and 406 medals, Indian athletes won 80 total medals, or 19.7 percent.

Closing Ceremony

The closing ceremony, began with a demonstration by jet fighters from the Indian Air Force, then a mixture of African and Asian cultural performances, with singers and dancers from India led by Remo Fernandes, Umoja of South Africa, Imperial State circus of China, Lebanese singer Diana Hadad, and Egyptian singer Hisham Abbas.

The newly established Afro Asian Games council has announced that the next Games will be held in 2007 in Africa, with Nigeria, South Africa and Egypt being considered as hosts. A decision is preliminary scheduled to be made by the Association Of National Olympic Committees of Africa (ANOCA) in the next few months.

Medals Tally

Continent wise Medals Tally

Continent	Gold	Silver	Bronze	Total
Asia	82	80	88	245
Africa	49	51	66	166
Overall Total	131	131	149	411

Country wise Medals Tally

Country	Gold	Silver	Bronze	Total
China	25	11	5	41
India	19	32	29	80
Japan	15	6	2	23
Nigeria	10	12	13	35

South Africa	10	11	15	36
Korea	7	6	11	24
Algeria	7	6	9	22
Uzbekistan	7	2	3	12
Combined Africa	6	4	0	10
Kazakhstan	5	8	6	19
Ethiopia	5	5	3	13
Sudan	3	3	0	6
Iran	2	3	1	6
Kenya	2	0	3	5
Philippines	1	4	10	15
Egypt	1	1	4	6
Seychelles	1	1	2	4
Combined Africa 2	1	1	0	2
Namibia	1	0	2	3
Tanzania	1	0	1	2
Cameroon	1	0	1	2
Vietnam	1	0	0	1
Senegal	0	6	3	9
Thailand	0	2	6	8
Pakistan	0	2	1	3
Indonesia	0	2	1	3
Burkina Faso	0	1	0	1
Qatar	0	1	0	1
Tajikistan	0	1	0	1
Zimbabwe	0	0	5	5
Uganda	0	0	3	3
Sri Lanka	0	0	3	3
Malaysia	0	0	2	2

Chinese Taipei	0	0	2	2
Congo	0	0	1	1
Mongolia	0	0	1	1
Libya	0	0	1	1
Overall Total	131	131	149	411

Sports wise Medals Tally

Sport	Gold	Silver	Bronze	Total
Athletics	42	42	42	126
Swimming	38	38	38	114
Shooting	15	15	15	45
Weightlifting	15	15	15	45
Boxing	11	11	22	44
Tennis	7	7	14	28
Hockey	2	2	2	6
Football	1	1	1	3
Overall Total	131	131	149	411

Closing Ceremony

A grand finale, which comprised a breathtaking display of colour and lights, marked the closing ceremony of the first Afro Asian Games in Hyderabad. The ceremony, which was well co-ordinated, exhibited a variety of cultures. Although there were a few common elements between the opening and closing ceremonies, this aspect could be overlooked for the whole show made a good impact and brought the curtains down in a befitting manner.

The President A.P.J. Abdul Kalam declared the Games closed and several dignitaries and sports administrators were at hand to grace the occasion. They included Suresh Kalmadi, IOA President, Randhir Singh, OCA Secretary General, Alfa Ibrahim Diallo, President of the Associated

National Olympic Committees of Africa, Vikram Verma, Union Minister for Sports and of course the man whose initiative made everything possible N. Chandrababu Naidu, Chief Minister of Andhra Pradesh.

The CM drew a round of applause when he made a fervent plea for India to make a strong bid to host the Olympics and said that Hyderabad was ready to be the venue for this mega event. But all said and done, one felt that the speeches could have been restricted to the minimum on such an occasion.

The fireworks display was truly remarkable and lit up the night sky. Anchor Yukta Mukhi, former beauty queen did a commendable job and the cultural segments were interesting, particularly the acrobatics by the State circus of China. The songs rendered by singers such as Diana Haddad and Hisham Abbas brought the ambience of the deserts to the city of Hyderabad. India's own singers such as Hariharan and Remo Fernandes provided the Indian touch to the programme and regaled the audience. But the surprising aspect was the paltry number of sportspersons who were available to take part in the closing march past.

Generally at the closing ceremony of an event such as this, the march past on the final day will find the sportspersons in a relaxed mood after having gone through all the stress and tension of the sports tournaments. The participants have a chance to relax and mingle with each other and interact with the spectators. The festive atmosphere, usually witnessed during the closing ceremonies, provided a feeling of emotional bonding and friendship. So it was surprising to see just a handful of sportspersons trooping into the stadium and marching past the dais. Many of the participants had already left the venue it was learnt and this was the reason behind the poor turn out. This was something, which could have been avoided with a better planning.

Another aspect that disappointed many sports lovers was the mismanagement of the issuing of complimentary passes and tickets for the closing ceremony. Hundreds of genuine ticket holders were refused entry into the stadium by securitymen manning the gates. The reason being that the stadium was already full and there was no more space to accommodate the ticket holders. Many of them had come from faraway places but had to return home disappointed. To add injury to insult some were roughed up by the securitymen. They left the venue with bitter feelings that they had been cheated of their money. They had come with the hope of viewing the closing finale of what was one of the most magnificent sports events ever held in Hyderabad but their hopes were dashed. This was the major blemish to an otherwise well-conceived ending to a thrilling sports extravaganza.

Grand Moments of the Game

It is now futile to examine whether the country deserved such an expensive inaugural Afro Asian Games. What must be assessed dispassionately is the efficacy of the venture and the degree of sporting excellence displayed during those eventful days in Hyderabad. Even assuming that the contests were mediocre and lacked world class fare, the fact that India cornered as many as 80 medals, more than what the super power of the region, China, could aggregate must be acknowledged.

China did top the gold medal tally with 25, but India picked up 19 with 32 silver and 29 bronze. Statistically speaking, as many as 35 countries from the two continents figured on the medal board, and India's second place on it makes the effort noteworthy. True, the big names were missing in some disciplines like soccer, athletics and shooting, but these aberrations should not cloud what the Indians had achieved, nor be dismissed as worthless. The golds, in men's and women's hockey, testified the level of competence. While the men prevailed over Pakistan twice in a space of four days to take the top honours, the women outclassed two major powers, South Korea and South Africa.

In the individual events, stars who were expected to strike it rich performed with a measure of credit. Anju George, Neelam Jaswant Singh in athletics and Anjali Bhagwat in shooting are worthy of being named as outstanding in the meet. Competition in athletics acquired a trace of class with the participation of Frankie Fredericks of Namibia and a few world level stars in long distance running from Ethiopia. The Chinese women lifters enhanced the stature of the competition what with San Dan breaking the world record in an event in which the home team's star performer, Karnam Malleswari, was missing, after taking part in the opening ceremony.

Viewed from a larger perspective of globalisation and the role of India as an all round developing power, the inaugural Afro Asian Games can be categorised as pathbreaking. Indisputably, the hiccups before the Games became a reality were far too many, genuine and created, more often the latter. Conceived as an instrument to strengthen the bonds between two large continents sometime in the late Eighties, it was difficult to convince many in the power hierarchy over the need for such a venture. Initially, it did look as though the chief proponent of the idea, the Indian Olympic Association, mishandled the whole project by making far too many commitments to crystallise the concept. But looking back, one should not flinch from paying a tribute to the persistence, patience and pragmatism of Suresh Kalmadi as head of the IOA.

Several hurdles had to be crossed and so many power brokers had to be silenced before he struck a rapport with the Chief Minister of Andhra Pradesh, Chandrababu Naidu, whose wholesome support ensured the creation of a magnificent infrastructure for the Games. No effort was spared by the Government to get the venues ready. The hockey administration headed by the FIH President, Els van Breda Vriesmann, was amazed by the fact that two artificial pitches were laid in less than three weeks time.

The optimism expressed by Suresh Kalmadi that the launch of the Afro Asian Games is a sure sign of framing a long chain to make sport a vibrant social, economic and political plank in the two continents is certainly not misplaced. He was not tired of citing the fact that it was India that gave shape to the dream of sportsmen and women through the first Asian Games in New Delhi in 1951 and how this idea caught the imagination of the youth to the point of staging as many as 14 successive Asiads without a break. One hopes that the fire lit in Hyderabad is kept burning in future with Africa taking up the gigantic task of hosting the second edition in 2007.

When the project was put up for approval, the International Olympic Committee, headed by the then President, Juan Antonio Samaranch, applauded it as a major promotional exercise. The present administration is unlikely to have any other opinion. But the delegates representing Asia and Africa in the IOC should endeavour to exercise their influence to get the event a greater recognition in future. After all, the two continents represent more than a majority of the global population thirsting for better conditions of living and dreaming of courting excellence using sport as the medium.

Whatever be the initial misgivings, the Afro Asian Games mirrored the fact that India has the wherewithal and expertise to stage a mega event with eclat.

India's Achievement in Afro Asian Games

Amidst the general mediocrity that various disciplines presented in the Afro Asian Games, athletics salvaged some pride for the Indian Olympic Association (IOA) and the host State with a few big names making it to Hyderabad. Of course it could have been a world-class fare had all the top stars made it. But then such an eventuality was never really on, despite the projections, promises and claims.

The very fact that Indians were able to win five gold medals in such a championship should tell its own tale. This is not to take any credit away from those who won the gold medals, discus thrower Anil Kumar and shot putter Shakti Singh in the men's section, and long jumper Anju George, discus thrower Neelam J. Singh and heptathlete J. J. Shobha in the women's section. At least in the case of Neelam, she can claim with some pride and satisfaction that she had recorded a season best of 61.94m to claim the gold in a field that included all those who mattered from either continent.

Though the same could not have been said of the other events where the Indians gained gold and lesser medals, they can as well counter that it was not their fault that the big names stayed away from this meet. The world-class fare many people talked about came only in a few events; in a majority of the events the performance levels were below our own National records. The oft-repeated argument that the Indians would be stretched to give off their best in such a competition did not manifest itself into personal bests, leave alone National records. Any talk thus of Indian athletics having benefited from this meet will be totally misplaced. So, too, any attempt to paint this meet as next only in magnitude, importance and standards to the Olympics. That will be laughable.

Thin fields and empty lanes, not to speak of the absence of a large majority of the champions from either continent, projected a disappointing picture, no matter that the officials kept parroting the jingle, 'the cream of Asia v the cream of Africa.' A total of 23 Asian Games champions and 12 All-Africa Games champions, apart from eight world champions from Africa besides innumerable other medal winners from both continents were missing. And yet they kept talking about this 'cream v cream' business.

It was a wrongly timed meet and it was indeed a wonder that some of the world-class athletes such as Frankie Fredericks, Shingo Suetsugu, Tirunesh Dibaba, Meseret Defar, Silesh Sihine, Hailu Mekonnen and

Gebregziabher Gebremariam competed in Hyderabad. Obviously, extra efforts were made to get at least some of them if not all.

Fredericks for one praised the initiative taken by India and said that it was a "powerful concept" and in future such meets could even challenge the World championships. The 36-year-old Namibian was the star attraction in a meet starved of big names. Despite arriving at 6 a.m. on the day of his event, the 200m, the former World champion gave a classic display, winning in an Indian all-comers' record of 20.57 seconds from Kazakh Gennadiy Chernovol and Senegalese Oumar Loum.

Nigerians Deji Aliu and Uchenna Emedolu were conspicuous by their absence, but the shorter sprint title still went to a Nigerian all right. Nineteen-year-old Olufasuba Olusoji clocked a personal best of 10.15s to launch himself into top-flight international levels. Team-mate Tamunosiki Atorudibo was second, leaving Japanese Suetsugu, the 200m bronze medallist at the Paris World championships, with the bronze. Suetsugu, like Fredericks, was a late arrival in the Andhra capital.

The track events, thanks to the Ethiopians and Nigerians, generally provided a decent fare, barring the 3000m steeplechase where you had the rare sight of a Kenyan (John Kemboi) clocking 8:56.43 to win a title and another Kenyan (Joel Kiptanui Chelimo) timing 9:24.08 to be pushed to the bronze status by an Indian, Arun D'Souza. Men from the land of Kip Keino and Moses Kiptanui are not expected to clock such timings, forgetting for a moment the defeat of Chelimo to the Indian. D'Souza's 9:05.97 was well below his best of 8:50.92. Incidentally, Kemboi's timing in Hyderabad was his personal best.

Talking of personal bests and all-comers' records, Olusoji's 10.15s for the 100m, Kenyan Ezra Sambu's 45.03s for the 400m, Ethiopian Hailu Mekonnen's 13:49.08 for the 5000m, Ethiopian Sileshi Sihine's 27:48.40 for the 10,000m, and Kazakh Yevgeniy Melshenko's 49.66s for the 400m hurdles were the best recorded on Indian soil. So, too, Hardus Pienaar's javelin mark of 84.50m, a personal best for the South African, and Chinese woman hammer thrower Liu Yinghui's 68.03m.

There were four National records in all. Sudanese Todd Matthews Jouda timed 13.68s to win the 110m hurdles gold in a National record time, Aissata Soulama of Burkina Faso clocked a 57.99 for the fourth place in the women's 400m hurdles, Sri Lankan Gallage Geetha Nandan timed 52:58.80 for another National mark while finishing fourth in the women's 10,000m walk and the Thai women's team timed 43.90s for the bronze in the shorter relay. Nineteen-year-old Cameroonian, Delphine Atangana had a National junior record of 23.37s while winning the women's 200m.

The closest that any Indian came to a personal best was in the heptathlon where Shobha's 5884 was just four points shy of her best recorded at the same venue in the last National Games.

"In championships you go for the gold, not for personal bests," remarked discus thrower Anil Kumar. He is of course right. The 60.68 was his season's best. More importantly it was his best in an international competition. Anil himself would readily admit, however, that he won in an ordinary field. Two men who beat him at the last Asian Games and Asian championships, Chinese Wu Tao and Iranian Abbas Samimi were not there. South African Frantz Kruger, who would have been the overwhelming favourite, with a season best of 66.70m (personal best 70.32m) was also not in the field. The All-Africa Games champion, 19-year-old Egyptian, Omar Al-Ghazali finished third with 59.77m.

Shakti Singh also had a season best of 19.05m in shot put, off his sixth and last attempt. The veteran has found a new-found enthusiasm in competitions after doing his coach's course at the NIS, Patiala. Asian Games champion Bahadur Singh could manage only the fourth place behind

South African Burger Lambrechts and Navpreet Singh. Lambrechts had an 18.97, Navpreet 18.81 and Bahadur 18.68. The only man in the field who had crossed 20 metres this season, Nigerian Chima Uguwu finished fifth with 18.42. Asian champion Saad Bilal Mubarak of Qatar was absent, while South African Janus Roberts, a 20-metre-plus putter this season was also missing.

Neelam J. Singh had her revenge. She was beaten by Chinese Li Yanfeng at the Asian championships in Manila, but the Hoshiarpur woman struck form in Hyderabad with a 61.94m that could not be surpassed either by Li Yanfeng or by her better-rated team-mate Song Aimin, world-ranked 11. Incidentally, going into this competition, Song Aimin had the best mark in Asia and Africa this season, a 65.33m.

Anju George talked about the break in training, thanks to the innumerable felicitations following her World championships bronze and the rain-interrupted preparations at Bangalore, as possible reasons for her below-par 6.53. That it was a clear 23cm ahead of the rest was another matter. Anju looked the favourite right through the build-up for this meet and she did not disappoint. Maybe a better field might have brought out the best from this Kerala woman who has stirred a new interest and brought a new vibrancy to Indian athletics in the post-Paris phase.

For the record, it must, however, be mentioned here that the top Chinese this season, Guan Yingnan (6.72m), was not in the field. Another Chinese, Liang Shuyan, though entered and present, pulled out at the last moment. Asian champion Anastasiya Zhuravlyeva was allowed only as a 'guest' competitor since Asia had filled in its quota. Japanese Maho Hanaoka (second in Busan Asian Games) and Kumiko Ikeda as well as Kazakh Yelena Kashcheyeva (third in Asian Games) were also not in the fray.

Anju and husband Bobby George have talked about sticking to their Bangalore base for the next season, meaning their association with world record holder Mike Powell might have is as good as ended. Athens is the goal for all the athletes who are either sure of their qualification or are within the range. One such athlete is high jumper Bobby Aloysius. Her 1.88 and the silver were satisfying efforts for one who had found the switch from a faulty Fosbury technique to the correct one, under coach Denis Doyle, a tough one. Kazakh Marina Aitova (nee Korzhova) was the winner, on a countback. She had shared the silver at the Busan Asian Games with Bobby, at 1.88.

Three other Indian silvers in the women's section came through Saraswati Saha (200m), Gurmeet Kaur (javelin) and Jasmine Kaur (10,000m walk). Saraswati's 23.43 was a good effort in only her first competition over 200m this season, while Gurmeet, though well below her best, should also have some satisfaction that she has come back into the limelight after a long gap. Jasmine as well as male walker Sitaram Basat, who also won a silver, brought coach Harmana Ram plenty of joy.

There was a fine effort from the men's 4x100m relay team as well. A bronze at this level, after more than two decades of emptiness at the Asian level, is something to be proud of. The foursome of Thirunanadurai, Sandeep Sarkaria, Piyush Kumar and Sanjay Ghosh, were indeed thrilled that they won the medal ahead of Thailand.

The other relay teams disappointed, however. With a few African mixed teams being fielded, the relays lost much of the relevance in the overall context. Disappointment was also in store for Sunita Rani, coming back into top-level competition for the first time after the doping scandal at the Busan Asian Games. She looked drained totally as she tried to match the rest in the 1500m, eventually finishing fourth behind team-mate Madhuri Singh in 4:22.60. She said she was trying herself out after an injury and she was aiming for the Olympics next year. One thing is clear; Sunita is no longer the athlete who took the continent by storm at Busan.

7

Commonwealth Games

Origin of Commonwealth Games

The first Commonwealth Games were held in 1930 in Hamilton, Ontario, Canada. Bobby Robinson, a major influence within athletics in Canada at the time, finally implemented the event that had been talked about amongst Commonwealth nations for over thirty years. Eleven countries with 400 athletes in total participated in the first Commonwealth Games. $30,000 was provided by the City of Hamilton to these nations to help cover travelling costs. Since then, the Games have been conducted every four years except for 1942 and 1946, due to World War II.

From 1930 to 1950 the Games were known as the British Empire Games, then the British Empire and Commonwealth Games until 1962. From 1966 to 1974 they took on the title of British Commonwealth Games and from 1978 onwards they have been known as simply the Commonwealth Games. A governor-general represents her in the country.

While other Games around the globe have been founded on geographic or climatic factors such as the Asian, Pan Am, African Games and Winter Olympics, the Commonwealth Games has been founded on history. Unique characteristics of the Commonwealth Games include being the only Games which shares a common language.

All athletes and officials can converse with each other in English, creating an atmosphere that has led to the Commonwealth Games being long known as the "Friendly Games".

The bonds of the Commonwealth Games help to encourage and support the pursuit of health and fitness in each of the member countries and provide an inspiration for youth to strive for excellence.

1930 British Empire Games

The city of Hamilton proved a gracious first host of the Commonwealth Games movement and is as important to it as Athens is to the Olympics. Then called the British Empire Games, the sociological, cultural and political makeup of the Commonwealth Movement has altered substantially since 1930.

The inaugural Games was utilitarian and very down to earth, proving that more doesn't necessarily mean better. The athletes' village was the Prince of Wales School next to the Civic Stadium, where the competitors slept two dozen to a classroom. Despite missing some basic comforts, the participants were unanimous in their praise for the Games and Hamilton's hospitality.

Eleven countries sent a total of about 400 athletes to the Hamilton Games. Women competed in only the swimming events. The participant nations were Australia, Bermuda, British Guiana, Canada, England, Northern Ireland, Newfoundland, New Zealand, Scotland, South Africa and Wales.

The Hamilton Games featured six sports: track and field, boxing, lawn bowls, rowing, swimming and diving, and wrestling and ran at a cost of $97,973.00.

Results by Country

Country	Gold	Silver	Bronze	Total
Australia	3	4	1	8
Bermuda	-	-	-	-
Canada	20	15	19	54
England	25	23	13	61
Guyana	-	1	1	2
New Zealand	3	4	2	9
Newfoundland	-	-	-	-
Northern Ireland	-	1	-	1
Scotland	2	3	5	10
South Africa	6	4	7	17
Wales	-	2	1	3
Total Medals	59	57	49	165

1934 British Empire Games

Sixteen nations sent a total of about 500 competitors to the London Games. In addition to the 11 nations that had competed at the 1930 Hamilton Games, making their debut at the London Games were Hong Kong, India, Jamaica, Zimbabwe (Rhodesia) and Trinidad. This was also to be the last time that Newfoundland took independent of Canada.

Six sports were featured in the Games – athletics, boxing, cycling, lawn bowls, swimming and diving, and wrestling. A highlight of the 1934 Games was the inclusion of events for women in athletics, with careful consideration given not to include events that were considered 'too exhaustive'. The running events were restricted to the short sprints and a shortened 4 x 220 yard relay instead of the 4 x 440 yard realy as per the men's program. Nevertheless this was a breakthrough for women in sport that would one day lead to full recognition and programming for women's athletics on the international stage.

The athletes oath was read by the captain for the England Athletics team, R.L. Howland as follows:

"We declare that we are loyal subjects of His Majesty the King, Emporer, and will take part in the British Empire Games in the spirit of true sportsmanship, recognising the rules which govern them and desirous of participating in them for the honour of our Empire and the Glory of Sport."

Originally scheduled for Johannesburg, South Africa, the II Games were hosted by London, in order to avoid a political crisis over South Africa's 'Apartheid' policy and its implications on visiting Commonwealth athletes and officials.

Results by Country

Country	Gold	Silver	Bronze	Total
Australia	8	4	2	14
Bermuda	-	-	-	-
Canada	17	25	9	51
England	29	20	24	73
Guyana	1	-	-	1
India	-	-	1	1
Jamaica	-	1	1	2
New Zealand	1	-	2	3
Newfoundland	-	-	-	-
Northern Ireland	-	1	2	3
Scotland	5	4	17	26
South Africa	7	10	5	22
Trinidad & Tobago	-	-	-	-
Wales	-	3	3	6

Zimbabwe	-	-	2	2
Total Medals	68	68	68	204

1938 British Empire Games

Held in the southern hemisphere for the first time, the III Games opening ceremony took place at the famed Sydney Cricket Ground in front of 40,000 spectators who were keen to see Australia and New Zealand excel against England in particular.

Fifteen nations participated down under at the Sydney Games involving a total of 466 athletes and 43 officials. New participants included Fiji and Ceylon.

Seven sports were featured in the Sydney Games – track and field, boxing, cycling, lawn bowls, rowing, swimming and diving, and wrestling.

Results by Country

Country	Gold	Silver	Bronze	Total
Australia	25	19	22	66
Bermuda	-	-	-	-
Canada	13	16	15	44
England	15	15	10	40
Fiji	-	-	-	-
Guyana	-	1	-	1
India	-	-	-	-
New Zealand	5	7	13	25
Northern Ireland	-	-	-	-
Scotland	-	2	3	5
South Africa	10	10	6	26
Sri Lanka	1	-	-	1

Trinidad & Tobago	-	-	-	-
Wales	2	1	-	3
Zimbabwe	-	-	2	2
Total Medals	71	71	71	213

1950 British Empire Games

World War II interrupted the staging of the British Empire Games scheduled for 1942 and 1946, however the enthusiasm from within the British Empire to continue what was started in 1930 was still strong enough for interest to be shown in their revival.

Awarded to New Zealand, the IV Games were held at the nation's largest city, Auckland. New Zealand had never been the focus of so much sporting attention and the hosts responded in a most magnificent and hospitable manner.

The opening ceremony at Eden Park was attended by 40,000 spectators, whilst nearly 250,000 people attended the Auckland Games, paying out a total of £89,435 as event spectators.

The atmosphere of the Opening Ceremony is best described by this paragraph from the Official Record of the Games:

> "The entrance of the gladiators in the days of ancient Athens and ancient Rome could not have been more impressive than was that Parade at Eden Park on the afternoon of February 4, 1950. As one, the crowd stitted by the majesty of the colourful scene, wonderful too in its simplicity, rose to its feet to remain standing throughout the ceremony, cheering to the echo as the parade passed on its way around the stadium..."

Twelve countries sent a total of 495 male and 95 female competitors to Auckland. Newly formed Malaysia and Nigeria made their first appearance. Nine sports featured at the Auckland Games – track and field, boxing, cycling, fencing, lawn bowls, rowing, swimming and diving, weightlifting and wrestling.

Results by Country

Country	Gold	Silver	Bronze	Total
Australia	34	27	19	80
Canada	8	9	13	30
England	19	16	13	48
Fiji	1	2	2	5
Malaya	2	1	1	4
New Zealand	10	22	22	54
Nigeria	-	1	-	1
Scotland	5	3	2	10
South Africa	8	4	8	20
Sri Lanka	1	2	-	3
Wales	-	1	-	1
Zimbabwe	-	1	-	1
Total Medals	88	89	80	257

1954 British Empire & Commonwealth Games

The awarding of the Games to Vancouver, was the culmination of two years of very hard work by an enterprising group of Civic leaders spearheaded by then Mayor, Charles E. Thompson. Vancouver then proceeded to set new standards in organisation and presentation of not only Commonwealth Games but all multi-sport Games of the times.

The athletes oath was taken by the captain of the Canadian team, Mr Bill Parnell, which for the first time would reflect the involvement of Commonwealth nations, outside of the British Empire.

The Fifth (V) Games, placed Vancouver on a world stage and featured memorable sporting moments as well as outstanding entertainment, technical innovation and cultural events. The 'Miracle Mile', as it became dubbed, saw both the gold medallist, Roger Bannister of England, and silver medallist, John Landy of Australia, run sub-four minute races in an event that was televised live across the globe for the first time.

Some 24 nations sent a total of 662 athletes and 127 officials to the Vancouver Games. This was a 'qantum leap' in size for the Commonwealth Games and represented the most significant increase in (100%) for any Commonwealth Games.

Nations winning medals at the Games included England, Australia, South Africa, Canada, New Zealand, Scotland, Trinidad, Northern Ireland, (Zimbabwe)North and South Rhodesia, Nigeria, Pakistan, Wales, Jamaica, Hong Kong, Uganda, Barbados and British Guiana.

Results by Country

Country	Gold	Silver	Bronze	Total
Australia	21	11	17	49
Bahamas	-	-	-	-
Barbados	-	1	-	1
Bermuda	-	-	-	-
Canada	9	21	14	44
England	23	24	20	67
Fiji	-	-	-	-
Ghana	-	-	-	-
Guyana	-	-	1	1

Hong Kong	-	1	-	1
India	-	-	-	-
Jamaica	1	-	-	1
Kenya	-	-	-	-
New Zealand	7	7	5	19
Nigeria	1	3	3	7
Northern Ireland	2	1	-	3
Pakistan	1	3	2	6
Scotland	6	2	5	13
South Africa	16	6	14	36
Trinidad & Tobago	2	2	-	4
Uganda	-	1	-	1
Wales	1	1	5	7
Zambia	-	-	1	1
Zimbabwe	3	6	3	12
Total Medals	93	90	90	273

1958 British Empire & Commonwealth Games

The VI Games marked the largest sporting event ever held in Wales and it was the smallest Country ever to host a British Empire and Commonwealth Games. Cardiff had to wait 12 years longer than originally scheduled to become host of the Games, as the 1946 event was cancelled because of World War II.

"The triumph of Wales and Cardiff in staging the Sixth British Empire and Commonwealth Games is now history - and history that will ring down the years to come".

England's famed middle distance runners, Roger Bannister and Chris Chattaway, were handed the honour of taking the Queen's Baton from Buckingham Palace on the first stage of its journey to Wales.

The Cardiff Games were to be South Africa's last until their post-apartheid return to the Games in 1994. A number of objections against South Africa took place in Cardiff because their team had been selected on the basis of race and colour rather than ability. South Africa subsequently withdrew from the Commonwealth in 1961 for 30 years.

Thirty-five nations sent a total of 1,130 athletes and 228 officials to the Cardiff Games and 23 countries and dependencies won medals, including, for the first time, Singapore, Ghana, Kenya and the Isle of Man.

Nine sports were featured in the Cardiff Games – athletics, boxing, cycling, fencing, lawn bowls, rowing, swimming and diving, weightlifting and wrestling.

Results by Country

Country	Gold	Silver	Bronze	Total
Australia	27	22	17	66
Bahamas	1	1	-	2
Barbados	1	1	-	2
Canada	1	10	16	27
Dominica	-	-	-	-
England	29	22	29	80
Fiji	-	-	-	-
Ghana	-	-	1	1
Gilbraltar	-	-	-	-
Guyana	-	1	-	1
Hong Kong	-	-	-	-
India	2	1	-	3
Isle of Man	-	-	1	1
Jamaica	4	2	1	7
Jersey	-	-	-	-

Kenya	-	-	2	2
Malaya	-	2	-	2
Malta	-	-	-	-
Mauritius	-	-	-	-
New Zealand	4	6	9	19
Nigeria	-	1	1	2
Northern Ireland	1	1	3	5
Pakistan	3	5	2	10
Sabah	-	-	-	-
Sarawak	-	-	-	-
Scotland	5	5	3	13
Sierra Leone	-	-	-	-
Singapore	2	-	-	2
South Africa	13	10	8	31
Sri Lanka	-	-	-	-
St. Vincent & Grenadines	-	-	-	-
Trinidad & Tobago	-	-	1	1
Uganda	-	1	-	1
Wales	1	3	7	11
Zimbabwe	-	-	3	3
Total Medals	94	94	104	292

1962 British Empire & Commonwealth Games

The VII Commonwealth Games are remembered for its "heat, dust and glory". The day before the Perth Games opened the temperature was an expected 80 degrees Fahrenheit, but the heat was measured at 105 degrees at the opening ceremony in the new Perry Lakes Stadium the following day and such extremes persisted throughout the Games' duration. In the previous 65 years, only 10 100 degree plus days had been recorded in Perth. Australian soldiers were pressed into action, ferrying water to competing athletes.

James Coote of the London Daily Telegraph describes:

> "The VIIth Commonwealth Games have proved that it is possible for an area as basically devoid of sports interest as Perth to stage the second most important sports meeting in the World - and stage it successfully. Perth has shown that these Games will continue for years to come"

Thirty-five countries sent a total of 1,041 athletes and officials to Perth. Jersey was amongst the medal winners for the first time, whilst British Honduras, Dominica, Papua New Guinea and St Lucia all made their inaugural Games appearances. Aden also competed by special invitation. Sabah, Sarawak and Malaya competed for the last time before taking part in 1966 under the Malaysian flag.

Nine sports were featured at the Perth Games – athletics, boxing, cycling, fencing, lawn bowls, rowing, swimming and diving, weightlifting and wrestling.

For Perth, the staging of the Commonwealth Games provided it with a springboard for phenominal development in sport and recreation, centered around the sports facilities that were built for the Games. These facilities have catered not only for elite sport but provided much needed opportunity for the development of organised recreational sport as well as a focus for Australia's first University degree Program in Physical Education.

Results by Country

Country	Gold	Silver	Bronze	Total
Aden	-	-	-	-
Australia	38	36	31	105

Bahamas	-	1	-	1
Barbados	-	-	1	1
Belize	-	-	-	-
Canada	4	12	15	31
Dominica	-	-	-	-
England	29	22	27	78
Fiji	-	-	2	2
Ghana	3	5	1	9
Gilbraltar	-	-	-	-
Guyana	-	-	1	1
Hong Kong	-	-	-	-
Isle of Man	-	-	-	-
Jamaica	3	1	1	5
Jersey	-	-	1	1
Kenya	2	2	1	5
Malaya	-	-	1	1
Malta	-	-	-	-
Mauritius	-	-	-	-
New Zealand	10	12	10	32
Northern Ireland	-	-	1	1
Pakistan	8	1	-	9
Papua New Guinea	-	-	1	1
Sabah	-	-	-	-
Sarawak	-	-	-	-
Scotland	4	7	3	14
Singapore	2	-	-	2
Sri Lanka	-	-	-	-
St. Lucia	-	-	-	-
Tanzania	-	-	-	-

Trinidad & Tobago	-	-	2	2
Uganda	1	1	4	6
Wales	-	2	4	6
Zimbabwe	-	2	5	7
Total Medals	104	104	112	320

1966 British Empire & Commonwealth Games

With the British Empire formally ended, the Kingston Games became the VIII British Commonwealth Games. There was a worry amongst the larger nations that Jamaica's infrastructure would not enable a successful Games delivery – but this proved to be largely unfounded. Controversially, also, the event programme was altered for the first time since 1950 with lawn bowls and rowing dropped and replaced with badminton and shooting instead.

Thirty-four nations (including Aden and Saudi Arabia) competed in the Kingston Games sending a total of 1,316 athletes and officials.

The nine sports featured in the Kingston Games were athletics, badminton, boxing, cycling, fencing, shooting, swimming and diving, weightlifting and wrestling.

Results by Country

Country	Gold	Silver	Bronze	Total
Aden	-	-	-	-
Antigua & Barbuda	-	-	-	-
Australia	23	28	22	73
Bahamas	-	1	-	1
Barbados	-	-	1	1
Belize	-	-	-	-
Bermuda	-	1	-	1

Canada	14	20	23	57
England	33	24	23	80
Fiji	-	-	-	-
Ghana	5	2	2	9
Gilbraltar	-	-	-	-
Guyana	-	1	-	1
India	3	4	3	10
Isle of Man	1	-	-	1
Jamaica	-	4	8	12
Jersey	-	-	-	-
Kenya	4	1	3	8
Malaysia	2	2	1	5
Mauritius	-	-	-	-
New Zealand	8	5	13	26
Nigeria	3	4	3	10
Northern Ireland	1	3	3	7
Pakistan	4	1	4	9
Papua New Guinea	-	1	-	1
Saudi Arabia	-	-	-	-
Scotland	1	4	4	9
Sierra Leone	-	-	-	-
Singapore	-	-	-	-
Sri Lanka	-	-	-	-
St. Vincent & Grenadines	-	-	-	-
Tanzania	-	-	-	-
Trinidad & Tobago	5	2	2	9
Uganda	-	-	3	3
Wales	3	2	2	7
Total Medals	110	110	120	340

1970 British Commonwealth Games

The IX Games from the 16th to the 25th of July, 1970 in Edinburgh will be remembered for a number of firsts. It was the first time that metric distances and electronic photo-finish technology were employed at the Games and also the first time that HM Queen Elizabeth II attended in her capacity as Head of the Commonwealth. Scots will further remember the Games for the Stewart brothers Ian (gold) and Peter (4th) in the 5000 metres and Lachie Stewart (no relation) who took gold in the 10000 metres.

Forty-two nations sent a total of nearly 1,750 athletes and officials to the first Edinburgh Games. New medal winning nations included Tanzania, Malawi and St Vincent.

Ten sports were featured in the Games – athletics, badminton, boxing, cycling, fencing, lawn bowls, shooting, swimming and diving, weightlifting and wrestling.

Results by Country

Country	Gold	Silver	Bronze	Total
Antigua & Barbuda	-	-	-	-
Australia	36	24	22	82
Bahamas	-	-	-	-
Barbados	-	1	-	1
Bermuda	-	-	-	-
Canada	18	24	24	66
Dominica	-	-	-	-
England	27	25	32	84
Fiji	-	-	1	1
Ghana	2	3	2	7
Gilbraltar	-	-	-	-
Grenada	-	-	-	-

Guernsey	-	-	-	-
Guyana	-	-	1	1
Hong Kong	1	-	-	1
India	5	3	4	12
Isle of Man	-	-	1	1
Jamaica	4	2	1	7
Jersey	-	-	-	-
Kenya	5	3	6	14
Malawi	-	-	1	1
Malaysia	1	1	1	3
Malta	-	-	-	-
Mauritius	-	-	-	-
New Zealand	2	6	6	14
Nigeria	2	-	-	2
Northern Ireland	3	1	5	9
Pakistan	4	3	3	10
Papua New Guinea	-	-	-	-
Scotland	6	8	11	25
Sierra Leone	-	-	-	-
Singapore	-	1	1	2
Sri Lanka	-	-	-	-
St. Lucia	-	-	-	-
St. Vincent & Grenadines	-	-	1	1
Swaziland	-	-	-	-
Tanzania	-	1	-	1
The Gambia	-	-	1	1
Trinidad & Tobago	-	4	3	7
Uganda	3	3	1	7
Wales	2	6	4	12
Zambia	-	2	2	4
Total Medals	121	121	134	376

1974 British Commonwealth Games

Following the massacre of Israeli athletes at the 1972 Munich Olympics, the X Games at Christchurch was the first multi-sport event to place the safety of participants and spectators as its uppermost requirement. Security guards surrounded the athlete's village and there was an exceptionally high-profile police presence. Even so, Christchurch enchanted the watching world as a city of beautiful churches and gardens.

On the running track, Jamaica's Don Quarrie successfully defended both his 1970 100m and 200m gold medals. Quarrie was to go on to win the 1978 100m as well.

Only 22 countries succeeded in winning medals from the total haul of 374 medals on offer, but first time winners included Western Samoa, Lesotho and Swaziland.

Nine sports were featured in the Christchurch Games – athletics, badminton, boxing, cycling, lawn bowls, shooting, swimming and diving, weightlifting and wrestling.

Results by Country

Country	Gold	Silver	Bronze	Total
Australia	29	28	25	82
Barbados	-	-	-	-
Bermuda	-	-	-	-
Botswana	-	-	-	-
Canada	25	19	18	62
Cook Islands	-	-	-	-
England	28	31	21	80
Fiji	-	-	-	-
Ghana	1	3	5	9
Gilbraltar	-	-	-	-
Grenada	-	-	-	-

Guernsey	-	-	-	-
Hong Kong	-	-	-	-
India	4	8	3	15
Isle of Man	-	-	-	-
Jamaica	2	1	-	3
Jersey	-	-	-	-
Kenya	7	2	9	18
Lesotho	-	-	-	-
Malawi	-	-	-	-
Malaysia	1	-	3	4
Mauritius	-	-	-	-
New Zealand	9	8	18	35
Nigeria	3	3	4	10
Northern Ireland	3	1	2	6
Papua New Guinea	-	-	-	-
Samoa	-	1	1	2
Scotland	3	5	11	19
Singapore	-	-	1	1
St.Vincent & Grenadines	1	-	-	1
Swaziland	-	-	1	1
Tanzania	1	-	1	2
The Gambia	-	-	-	-
Tonga	-	-	-	-
Trinidad&Tobago	-	1	1	2
Uganda	2	4	3	9
Wales	1	5	4	10
Zambia	1	1	1	3
Total Medals	121	121	132	374

1978 British Commonwealth Games

The XI Games was the first to bear the current day name of the Commonwealth Games. Whilst Edmonton had won the right to host the Games with an audacious vision presented six years earlier to the Commonwealth Games Federation General Assembly, the organisers had to walk a careful tightrope in the immediate run up to the Edmonton Games to ensure that there was no repeat of the African nations boycott of the 1976 Montreal Olympics caused by a New Zealand rugby tour of South Africa.

Forty-six countries sent a total of 1,405 athletes and 504 officials to the Edmonton Games. As host nation, Canada also topped the medal table for the first time.

Ten sports were featured at the Edmonton Games – athletics, badminton, boxing, cycling, gymnastics, lawn bowls, shooting, swimming and diving, weightlifting and wrestling.

Results by Country

Country	Gold	Silver	Bronze	Total
Antigua & Barbuda	-	-	-	-
Australia	24	33	27	84
Bahamas	-	1	-	1
Bangladesh	-	-	-	-
Barbados	-	-	-	-
Belize	-	-	-	-
Bermuda	-	-	-	-
Canada	45	31	33	109
Cayman Islands	-	-	-	-
Cyprus	-	-	-	-
England	27	28	32	87

Fiji	-	-	-	-
Ghana	1	1	1	3
Gilbraltar	-	-	-	-
Grenada	-	-	-	-
Guernsey	-	-	-	-
Guyana	1	1	1	3
Hong Kong	2	-	-	2
India	5	4	6	15
Isle of Man	-	-	1	1
Jamaica	2	2	3	7
Jersey	-	-	-	-
Kenya	7	6	5	18
Lesotho	-	-	-	-
Malawi	-	-	-	-
Malaysia	1	2	1	4
Mauritius	-	-	-	-
New Zealand	5	6	9	20
Northern Ireland	2	1	2	5
Papua New Guinea	-	1	-	1
Samoa	-	-	3	3
Scotland	3	6	5	14
Sierra Leone	-	-	-	-
Singapore	-	-	-	-
Sri Lanka	-	-	-	-
St. Kitts	-	-	-	-
St. Lucia	-	-	-	-
St. Vincent & Grenadines	-	-	-	-
Swaziland	-	-	-	-
Tanzania	1	1	-	2

The Gambia	-	-	-	-
Trinidad & Tobago	-	2	2	4
Turks & Caicos Islands	-	-	-	-
Wales	2	1	5	8
Zambia	-	2	2	4
Zimbabwe	-	-	-	-
Total Medals	128	129	138	395

1982 Commonwealth Games

The Brisbane Games are still hailed as one of the very best. Everything went so well from the moment Matilda, a 13-metre mechanical kangaroo, helped out with the opening ceremonies. Once again, a boycott was avoided and the sun shone throughout the duration of the XII Games.

Forty-six nations participated in the Brisbane Games with a new record total of 1,583 athletes and 571 officials. As hosts, Australia headed the medal table leading the way ahead of England, Canada, Scotland and New Zealand respectively.

The men's 200m gold was shared by England's Mike McFarlane and Scotland's Allan Wells, with judges unable to separate the pair at the winning post.

Nine sports featured at the Brisbane Games – athletics, badminton, boxing, cycling, lawn bowls, shooting, swimming and diving, weightlifting and wrestling.

Results by Country

Country	Gold	Silver	Bronze	Total
Australia	39	39	29	107
Bahamas	2	2	2	6
Barbados	-	-	-	-

Bermuda	-	-	1	1
Botswana	-	-	-	-
Canada	26	23	33	82
Cayman Islands	-	-	-	-
Cyprus	-	-	-	-
England	38	38	32	108
Fiji	1	-	-	1
Ghana	-	-	-	-
Gilbraltar	-	-	-	-
Guernsey	-	1	1	2
Guyana	-	-	-	-
Hong Kong	1	-	-	1
India	5	8	3	16
Isle of Man	-	-	-	-
Jamaica	2	1	1	4
Kenya	4	2	4	10
Malawi	-	-	-	-
Malaysia	1	-	1	2
Malta	-	-	-	-
Mauritius	-	-	-	-
New Zealand	5	8	13	26
Nigeria	5	-	8	13
Northern Ireland	-	3	3	6
Papua New Guinea	-	-	-	-
Samoa	-	-	-	-
Scotland	8	6	12	26
Singapore	-	-	1	1
Solomon Islands	-	-	-	-
St. Helena	-	-	-	-

Swaziland	-	-	1	1
Tanzania	1	2	2	5
The Gambia	-	-	-	-
Tonga	-	-	-	-
Trinidad & Tobago	-	-	-	-
Uganda	-	3	-	3
Vanuatu	-	-	-	-
Wales	4	4	1	9
Zambia	-	1	5	6
Zimbabwe	1	-	-	1
Total Medals	143	141	153	437

1986 Commonwealth Games

After nearly two decades successfully averting political stay-aways and protests because of apartheid and sanction-busting sports tours to South Africa, the XIII Games, the second to be staged at Edinburgh, was to become known as "the Boycott Games". Sadly, despite there being so many fond memories of the Scottish hospitality offered in 1970, 32 Commonwealth nations decided that they could not attend, because of their opposition to apartheid in sports.

Twenty-six nations did attend the second Edinburgh Games and sent a total of 1,662 athletes and 461 officials. Ten sports were featured at the second Edinburgh Games – athletics, aquatics, badminton, boxing, cycling, lawn bowls, rowing, shooting, weightlifting and wrestling.

Results by Country

Country	Gold	Silver	Bronze	Total
Australia	40	46	35	121
Botswana	-	-	1	1

Canada	51	35	31	117
Cook Islands	-	-	-	-
England	52	43	49	144
Fiji	-	-	-	-
Gilbraltar	-	-	-	-
Guernsey	-	2	-	2
Hong Kong	-	1	2	3
Isle of Man	1	-	-	1
Jersey	-	-	1	1
Lesotho	-	-	-	-
Malawi	-	-	2	2
New Zealand	8	16	14	38
Northern Ireland	2	4	9	15
Scotland	3	12	18	33
Singapore	-	-	1	1
Swaziland	-	1	-	1
Vanuatu	-	-	-	-
Wales	6	5	11	22
Total Medals	163	165	174	502

1990 Commonwealth Games

The XIV Commonwealth Games, the third to be hosted by New Zealand and Auckland's second, witnessed a fantastic opening ceremony comprising a magnificent and moving portrayal of the forces that led to the formation of New Zealand society and culture.

Thankfully, the perennially threatened boycott gave way to a new positive spirit of co-operation far more in keeping with the image of "The Friendly Games" and a new record of 54 nations participated in the second Auckland Games.

Twenty-nine of the competing nations succeeded in winning medals from a total of 639 medals available. Australia headed the medals table with New Zealand claiming fourth place behind England and Canada.

Ten sports featured in the second Auckland Games – athletics, aquatics, badminton, boxing, cycling, gymnastics, judo, lawn bowls, shooting and weightlifting.

Results by Country

Country	Gold	Silver	Bronze	Total
Australia	52	54	55	161
Bahamas	-	-	2	2
Bangladesh	1	-	1	2
Barbados	-	-	-	-
Bermuda	1	-	-	1
Botswana	-	-	-	-
British Virgin Islands	-	-	-	-
Brunei Darussalam	-	-	-	-
Canada	36	42	37	115
Cayman Islands	-	-	-	-
Cook Islands	-	-	-	-
Cyprus	1	1	-	2
England	47	40	42	129
Falkland Islands	-	-	-	-
Ghana	-	2	-	2
Guernsey	1	-	-	1
Guyana	-	-	1	1
Hong Kong	1	1	3	5
India	13	8	11	32
Isle of Man	-	-	-	-
Jamaica	2	-	2	4

Jersey	1	-	1	2
Kenya	6	9	3	18
Lesotho	-	-	-	-
Malawi	-	-	-	-
Malaysia	2	2	-	4
Maldives	-	-	-	-
Malta	-	-	1	1
Mauritius	-	-	-	-
Nauru	1	2	-	3
New Zealand	17	14	27	58
Nigeria	5	13	7	25
Norfolk Island	-	-	-	-
Northern Ireland	1	3	5	9
Pakistan	-	-	-	-
Papua New Guinea	1	-	-	1
Samoa	-	-	2	2
Scotland	5	7	10	22
Seychelles	-	-	-	-
Sierra Leone	-	-	-	-
Solomon Islands	-	-	-	-
Sri Lanka	-	-	-	-
St. Kitts	-	-	-	-
Swaziland	-	-	-	-
Tanzania	-	1	2	3
The Gambia	-	-	-	-
Tonga	-	-	-	-
Trinidad & Tobago	-	-	-	-
Uganda	2	-	2	4
Vanuatu	-	-	-	-
Wales	10	3	12	25
Zambia	-	-	3	3

Zimbabwe		2	1	3
Total Medals	206	204	230	640

1994 Commonwealth Games

Following the successful Victoria delegation to the Commonwealth Games Federation in 1988, the XV Games were held in Canada for the fourth time. The end of apartheid in the early part of the decade also heralded the return of South Africa to the Commonwealth Games and ensured that the era of threatened boycotts was over. Both the opening and closing ceremonies were held at Victoria's Centennial Stadium, which had undergone a superb refit in honour of the Games.

Sixty-three nations sent a total of nearly 2,450 athletes and 892 officials as the Commonwealth Games burgeoned at Victoria. Once again, Australia headed the medals table whilst the hosts, Canada, pushed England into third place. Nigeria marked its arrival as a Commonwealth sporting force by picking up more gold medals than both New Zealand and India. Hong Kong said farewell to the Games with the territory becoming a special administrative region of the People's Republic of China in 1997.

Ten sports were featured at the Victoria Games – athletics, aquatics, badminton, boxing, cycling, gymnastics, lawn bowls, shooting, weightlifting and wrestling.

Results by Country

Country	Gold	Silver	Bronze	Total
Antigua & Barbuda	-	-	-	-
Australia	87	52	43	182
Bahamas	-	-	-	-
Bangladesh	-	-	-	-
Barbados	-	-	-	-

Belize	-	-	-	-
Bermuda	-	-	1	1
Botswana	-	-	1	1
British Virgin Islands	-	-	-	-
Brunei Darussalam	-	-	-	-
Canada	40	42	46	128
Cyprus	2	1	2	5
Dominica	-	-	-	-
England	31	45	49	125
Falkland Islands	-	-	-	-
Ghana	-	-	1	1
Guernsey	-	-	1	1
Guyana	-	-	-	-
Hong Kong	-	-	4	4
India	6	11	7	24
Isle of Man	-	-	-	-
Jamaica	2	4	2	8
Jersey	-	-	-	-
Kenya	7	4	8	19
Lesotho	-	-	-	-
Malawi	-	-	-	-
Malaysia	2	3	2	7
Maldives	-	-	-	-
Malta	-	-	-	-
Mauritius	-	-	-	-
Montserrat	-	-	-	-
Namibia	1	-	1	2
Nauru	3	-	-	3
NewZealand	5	16	20	41
Nigeria	11	13	13	37

Norfolk Island	-	-	1	1
Northern Ireland	5	2	3	10
Pakistan	-	-	3	3
Papua New Guinea	-	1	-	1
Samoa	-	1	-	1
Scotland	6	3	11	20
Seychelles	-	-	1	1
Sierra Leone	-	-	-	-
Singapore	-	-	-	-
South Africa	2	4	5	11
Sri Lanka	1	2	-	3
St. Kitts	-	-	-	-
St. Lucia	-	-	-	-
St. Vincent& Grenadines	-	-	-	-
Swaziland	-	-	-	-
Tanzania	-	-	1	1
The Gambia	-	-	-	-
Tonga	-	-	1	1
Trinidad&Tobago	-	-	2	2
Uganda	-	-	2	2
Vanuatu	-	-	-	-
Wales	5	8	6	19
Zambia	1	1	2	4
Zimbabwe	-	3	3	6
Total Medals	217	216	242	675

1998 Commonwealth Games

For the first time in its 68-year history, the Commonwealth Games were held in Asia. The XVI Games, held in Kuala

Lumpur were also the first Games to feature team sports - an overwhelming success that added large numbers to both participators and TV audience numbers.

A new record of 70 countries sent a total of 5,250 athletes and officials to the Kuala Lumpur Games. The top five countries in the medal standing were Australia, England, Canada, Malaysia and South Africa. Nauru also achieved an impressive haul of three gold medals.

Fifteen sports were featured in the Kuala Lumpur Games – aquatics, athletics, badminton, boxing, cricket, cycling, gymnastics, hockey, netball, lawn bowls, rugby 7s, shooting, tenpin bowling, weightlifting and wrestling.

Results by Country

Country	Gold	Silver	Bronze	Total
Anguilla	-	-	-	-
Antigua & Barbuda	-	-	-	-
Australia	80	61	57	198
Bahamas	1	1	-	2
Barbados	1	-	2	3
Belize	-	-	-	-
Bermuda	-	1	-	1
Botswana	-	-	-	-
British Virgin Islands	-	-	-	-
Cameroon	-	3	3	6
Canada	30	31	38	99
Cook Islands	-	-	-	-
Cyprus	1	1	1	3
Dominica	-	-	-	-
England	36	47	53	136
Falkland Islands	-	-	-	-

Fiji	-	1	-	1
Ghana	1	1	3	5
Grenada	-	-	-	-
India	7	10	8	25
Isle of Man	-	1	-	1
Jamaica	4	2	-	6
Kenya	7	5	4	16
Lesotho	1	-	-	1
Malawi	-	-	-	-
Malaysia	10	14	12	36
Maldives	-	-	-	-
Malta	-	-	-	-
Mauritius	1	1	2	4
Montserrat	-	-	-	-
Mozambique	1	1	-	2
Namibia	-	2	1	3
Nauru	3	-	-	3
New Zealand	8	6	20	34
Norfolk Island	-	-	-	-
Northern Ireland	2	1	2	5
Pakistan	-	1	-	1
Papua New Guinea	-	-	1	1
Samoa	-	-	-	-
Scotland	3	2	7	12
Seychelles	-	2	-	2
Sierra Leone	-	-	-	-
Singapore	-	-	-	-
Solomon Islands	-	-	-	-
South Africa	9	11	14	34

Sri Lanka	-	1	1	2
St. Kitts	-	-	-	-
St. Lucia	-	-	-	-
St. Vincent & The Grenadines	-	-	-	-
Swaziland	-	-	-	-
Tanzania	1	1	1	3
The Gambia	-	-	-	-
Tonga	-	-	-	-
Trinidad & Tobago	1	1	1	3
Turks & Caicos Islands	-	-	-	-
Uganda	-	-	1	1
Vanuatu	-	-	-	-
Wales	3	4	8	15
Zambia	-	-	1	1
Zimbabwe	2	-	3	5
Total Medals	213	213	244	670

2002 Commonwealth Games

The city of Manchester is the capital of the North West and is the commercial, educational and cultural focus for this vibrant region of England. As well as having a population of over 400,000, 60 per cent of the population of Britain, more than 33 million people, live within a two hour drive of Manchester. Manchester is an international destination for conferences and exhibitions with more than 200,000 bed spaces within one hour's drive of the city centre.

The XVII Commonwealth Games was a world-class event and the most significant multi-sport event to be held in Great Britain since the Olympics of 1948. It was the largest in the history of the Commonwealth Games with participating athletes from 72 nations competing in 14 individual sports and three team sports from 25 July - 4 August 2002.

The sports contested were:Aquatics, Athletics, Badminton, Boxing, Cycling, Gymnastics, Hockey, Judo, Lawn Bowls, Netball, Rugby 7s, Shooting, Squash, Table Tennis, Triathlon, Weightlifting and Wrestling.

Results by Country

Country	Gold	Silver	Bronze	Total
Anguilla	-	-	-	-
Antigua & Barbuda	-	-	-	-
Australia	82	62	63	207
Bahamas	4	-	4	8
Bangladesh	1	-	-	1
Barbados	-	-	1	1
Belize	-	-	-	-
Bermuda	-	-	-	-
Botswana	-	2	1	3
British Virgin Islands	-	-	-	-
Cameroon	9	1	2	12
Canada	31	41	44	116
Cayman Islands	-	-	1	1
Cook Islands	-	-	-	-
Cyprus	2	1	1	4
Dominica	-	-	-	-
England	54	51	60	165
Fiji	1	1	1	3
Ghana	-	-	1	1
Gilbraltar	-	-	-	-
Grenada	-	-	-	-

Guernsey	-	-	-	-
Guyana	1	-	-	1
India	30	22	17	69
Isle of Man	-	-	-	-
Jamaica	4	6	7	17
Jersey	-	-	-	-
Kenya	4	8	4	16
Kiribati	-	-	-	-
Lesotho	-	-	1	1
Malawi	-	-	-	-
Malaysia	7	9	18	34
Maldives	-	-	-	-
Malta	-	-	1	1
Mauritius	-	-	1	1
Montserrat	-	-	-	-
Mozambique	1	-	-	1
Namibia	1	-	4	5
Nauru	2	5	8	15
New Zealand	11	13	21	45
Nigeria	5	3	11	19
Niue	-	-	-	-
Norfolk Island	-	-	-	-
Northern Ireland	2	2	1	5
Pakistan	1	3	4	8
Papua New Guinea	-	-	-	-
Samoa	-	1	2	3
Scotland	6	8	16	30
Seychelles	-	-	-	-
Sierra Leone	-	-	-	-

Singapore	4	2	7	13
Solomon Islands	-	-	-	-
South Africa	9	20	17	46
Sri Lanka	-	-	-	-
St. Kitts	1	-	-	1
St. Lucia	-	-	1	1
St. Vincent & Grenadines	-	-	-	-
Swaziland	-	-	-	-
Tanzania	1	-	1	2
The Gambia	-	-	-	-
Tonga	-	-	-	-
Trinidad & Tobago	-	1	-	1
Turks & Caicos Islands	-	-	-	-
Uganda	-	2	-	2
Vanuatu	-	-	-	-
ales	6	13	12	31
Zambia	1	1	1	3
Zimbabwe	1	1	-	2
Total Medals	282	279	334	895

2006 Commonwealth Games

The Australian city of Melbourne, will host the Commonwealth Games in 2006. Melbourne was the location for the 1956 Olympic Games, and 50 years on will host a Commonwealth Games.

Melbourne is the capital of the State of Victoria and the second largest city in Australia with a population of nearly 3,500,000 people. The city is a multicultural one, known for its arts, culture, parks and gardens, restaurants and sport.

The Melbourne Games will have one village which will house both the athletes and team officials, located within three kilometres of the city centre. The majority of the sports venues are located along the Yarra River within the city precinct and are of world class standard. The Opening Ceremony and Athletics competition will be held at the Melbourne Cricket Ground, one of the world's largest and most outstanding outdoor sporting grounds. It seats approximately 100,000 spectators.

The Sports that will be contested are: Aquatics, Athletics, Badminton, Basketball, Bowls, Boxing, Cycling, Gymnastics, Hockey, Netball, Rugby 7s, Shooting, Squash, Table Tennis, Triathlon and Weightlifting. To get the latest on preparations for the Games follow the link opposite to the official Games website for Melbourne 2006.

2010 Commonwealth Games

The city of New Delhi, home to 13.8 million people, will host the Commonwealth Games in 2010. This will be the first time India has hosted the Games and only the second time the event has been held in Asia.

Delhi is the capital city of India and is rich in culture and history. It stands on the western end of the Gangetic Plain and is bordered by the states of Uttar Pradesh and Haryana. There are two main districts of the city, Old Delhi the capital of Muslim India between the mid 17th and late 19th centuries with its historic sites, mosques and monuments and New Delhi, the imperial city created by the British Raj with its imposing government buildings and tree lined avenues.

The proposed dates for the Games are Saturday 23 October to Wednesday 3 November 2010 inclusive of the Opening and Closing Ceremonies. Weather wise the city experiences an October mean temperature minimum 17.2

degrees centigrade and maximum 31.3 degrees centigrade with humidity ranging from 31 to 78% for the October and November months.

The Delhi Games Village is to be constructed as a low rise medium development on a 40 acre site in the heart of the capital with a possible capacity for 8,500 athletes and officials. Existing and new stadia will be used to house the following sports: Aquatics, Athletics, Badminton, Bowls, Boxing, Cycling, EAD Events, Gymnastics, Hockey, Netball, Rugby 7s, Shooting, Squash, Table Tennis and Weightlifting.

Delhi won the right to host the 2010 Games by defeating the Canadian city of Hamilton by 46 votes to 22 at the CGF General Assembly held in Montego Bay in November.2003.

To get the latest on preparations for the Games follow the link on the left to the official Games website for Delhi 2010 as well as clicking on the links below to read the Delhi and Hamilton Bid documents and CGF Bid Evaluation Report.

8

Paralympic Games

The Paralympic Games are an official equivalent of the Olympics for athletes with physical disabilities. This includes mobility disabilities, amputees, visual disabilities and those with Cerebral Palsy. Sir Ludwig Guttmann organized a sports competition in 1948 which became known as the Stoke Mandeville Games, involving World War II veterans with spinal cord injuries; in 1952 competitors from the Netherlands took part in the competition, giving an international notion to the movement. The first Olympic Style games for athletes with a disability were held in Rome in 1960 which became the Paralympic Games. The first Winter Paralympics were held in Örnsköldsvik, Sweden in 1976.

The Games are now always held alongside the Olympic Games as of June 19, 2001 when an agreement was signed between the International Olympic Committee (IOC) and the International Paralympic Committee (IPC) securing this practice for the future. The IPC logo denotes three Tae-Geuks, one in red, blue and green. The three Tae-Geuks symbolise the most significant components of the human being: Mind, Body, Spirit. "Mind, Body, Spirit" was adopted as the IPC motto.

The next Paralympic Games are going to be held in Athens, Greece from 17th to 28th September 2004. These will be the 12th Paralympic Summer Games. Four thousand athletes will participate, representing 145 countries in nineteen sports. A record number of broadcasters will be present to cover the Athens 2004 Paralympics, though the events will not be broadcast in the United States. Previous Paralympics have also suffered from limited broadcast and sponsorship.

The name derives from the Greek "para" ("beside" or "alongside"), and has nothing do do with paralysis or paraplegia.

Summer Games

1960 Summer Paralympic Games

The 1960 Summer Paralympic Games were the first Paralympics. They were held in Rome, Italy with the Olympics. The only disability included in this paralympics was spinal cord injury.

Games of the I Paralympics

Nations participating	23
Athletes participating	400
Events	57 in 8 sports
Opening ceremonies	September 18, 1960
Closing ceremonies	September 25, 1960
Officially opened by	Camillo Giardina

Medals Tally

Rank	Country	Gold	Silver	Bronze	Total
1	United States	29	7	7	43
2	Great Britain	19	16	18	53
3	France	15	1	3	19
4	Australia	11	4	1	16
5	Rhodesia	10	1	2	13
6	Belgium	8	1	0	9
7	Ireland	4	0	0	4

8	German Federal Republic	3	6	9	18
9	Italy	2	29	25	56
10	Austria	2	9	10	21
11	Netherlands	2	6	0	8
12	Malta	2	4	3	9
13	Switzerland	2	4	0	6
14	Norway	1	4	4	9
15	Israel	1	2	2	5
16	Finland	1	0	0	1
17	Argentina	0	3	2	5

1964 Summer Paralympics

The 1964 Summer Paralympics were the 2nd Paralympic Games to be held. They were held in Tokyo, Japan.

Games of the II Paralympics

Nations participating	21
Athletes participating	375
Events	144 in 9 sports
Opening ceremonies	November 3, 1964
Closing ceremonies	November 12, 1964

Medals Tally

Rank	Country	Gold	Silver	Bronze	Total
1	United States	50	41	31	122
2	Great Britain	18	23	19	60
3	Italy	14	15	24	53
4	Australia	11	11	8	30
5	Rhodesia	10	5	2	17
6	South Africa	8	8	3	19

7	Israel	7	3	10	20
8	Argentina	6	15	16	37
9	Germany	5	2	3	10
10	Netherlands	4	6	3	13
11	France	4	2	4	10
12	Austria	4	1	4	9
13	Japan	1	5	3	9
14	Belgium	1	0	2	3
15	Switzerland	0	1	0	1
16	Malta	0	0	2	2
17	Sweden	0	0	1	1

1968 Summer Paralympics

The 1968 Summer Paralympics were the third Paralympic Games to be held. They were originally planned to be held alongside the Summer Olympics in Mexico City, but in 1966, the Mexican government decided against it, due to difficulties. The Israeli government then offered to host the games in Tel Aviv.

Games of the III Paralympics

Nations participating	29
Athletes participating	750
Events	181 in 10 sports
Opening ceremonies	November 4, 1968
Closing ceremonies	November 13, 1968
Officially opened by	Yigal Allon

Medals Tally

Rank	Country	Gold	Silver	Bronze	Total
1	United States	33	27	39	99
2	Great Britain	27	21	20	68

3	Israel	17	21	25	63
4	Australia	15	16	7	38
5	France	14	9	9	32
6	Italy	13	10	15	38
7	German Federal Republic	12	12	11	35
8	Netherlands	12	4	4	20
9	Argentina	11	10	10	31
10	South Africa	9	10	7	26
11	Canada	6	6	7	19
12	Rhodesia	5	8	7	20
13	Norway	5	3	1	9
14	Jamaica	3	1	1	5
15	Austria	2	6	11	19
16	Japan	2	2	8	12
17	Sweden	1	6	4	11
18	Ireland	1	5	5	11
19	New Zealand	1	2	1	4
20	Spain	0	4	0	4
21	Belgium	0	3	3	6
22	Switzerland	0	2	6	8

1972 Summer Paralympics

The 1972 Summer Paralympics were the fourth Paralympic Games to be held. They were held in Heidelberg, Germany.

Games of the IV Paralympics

Nations participating	41
Athletes participating	1,004
Events	187 in 10 sports

Opening ceremonies	August 2, 1972
Officially opened by	Dr. Gustav Heinemann

Medals Tally

Rank	Country	Gold	Silver	Bronze	Total
1	Germany	28	15	24	67
2	United States	17	28	28	73
3	South Africa	16	12	13	41
4	Great Britain	15	15	20	50
5	Netherlands	14	13	11	38
6	Poland	14	12	7	33
7	France	10	8	12	30
8	Israel	9	10	9	28
9	Italy	8	3	5	16
10	Jamaica	8	3	4	15
11	Australia	6	9	10	25
12	Canada	6	6	8	20
13	Austria	6	6	5	17
14	Sweden	5	5	5	15
15	Japan	4	5	3	12
16	Rhodesia	3	5	4	12
17	New Zealand	3	3	3	9
18	Switzerland	3	2	3	8
19	Korea	3	2	1	6
20	Argentina	2	5	3	10
21	Ireland	2	4	2	8
22	Norway	1	5	5	11
23	Belgium	1	2	2	5
24	Yugoslavia	1	1	2	4
25	India	1	0	0	1

26	Kenya	1	0	0	1
27	Spain	0	4	1	5
28	Finland	0	2	2	4
29	Hong Kong	0	1	1	2
30	Hungary	0	0	1	1
31	Russia	0	0	1	1

1976 Summer Paralympics

The 1976 Summer Paralympics were the fifth Paralympic Games to be held. They were held in Toronto, in the province of Ontario, Canada.

The Paralympics in Canada and Toronto

1976 was the first time Canada has hosted the Paralympics, subsequently Canada will host the 2010 Winter Paralympics in Vancouver. Coincidentally, Montreal hosted the 1976 Summer Olympics. Toronto has in later years failed to win the Summer Olympics and Paralympics. Losing the bid for the 2008 Summer Olympics (2008 Summer Paralympics) was seen as being a boost to the Vancouver 2010 Winter Olympics bid.

Games of the V Paralympics

Athletes participating	1,657 (1,404 men, 253 women)
Events	447 in 13 sports
Opening ceremonies	August 3, 1976
Closing ceremonies	August 11, 1976

Medals Tally

Rank	Country	Gold	Silver	Bronze	Total
1	United States	66	44	45	155
2	Netherlands	45	25	14	84

3	Israel	39	13	16	68
4	Germany	37	33	26	96
5	Great Britain	29	29	36	94
6	Canada	25	26	26	77
7	Poland	24	17	12	53
8	France	23	22	14	59
9	Sweden	22	27	25	74
10	Austria	18	16	17	51
11	Australia	16	18	8	42
12	Mexico	16	14	9	39
13	Finland	12	20	18	50
14	Japan	10	6	3	19
15	Switzerland	9	12	10	31
16	Norway	9	6	4	19
17	South Africa	7	9	12	28
18	Belgium	7	7	8	22
19	New Zealand	7	1	5	13
20	Egypt	5	2	1	8
21	Ireland	4	10	6	20
22	Spain	4	6	2	12
23	Argentina	3	4	6	13
24	Denmark	3	0	3	6
25	Italy	2	5	11	18
26	Indonesia	2	1	4	7
27	Korea	1	2	1	4
28	Burma	1	1	1	3
29	Peru	1	0	2	3
30	Hong Kong	0	1	2	3
31	Brazil	0	1	0	1
32	Guatemala	0	0	1	1

1980 Summer Paralympics

The 1980 Summer Paralympics were the sixth Paralympic Games to be held. They were held in Arnhem, Netherlands.

Games of the VI Paralympics

Nations participating	42
Athletes participating	1,973
Events	489 in 12 sports
Opening ceremonies	June 21, 1980
Officially opened by	Princess Margriet

Medals Tally

Rank	Country	Gold	Silver	Bronze	Total
1	United States	62	58	54	174
2	Germany	61	47	41	149
3	Canada	53	27	31	111
4	Poland	51	51	47	149
5	Great Britain	43	29	20	92
6	Netherlands	32	27	33	92
7	Sweden	25	35	24	84
8	France	25	23	24	72
9	Mexico	20	16	4	40
10	Israel	12	18	11	41
11	Norway	11	11	7	29
12	Belgium	11	9	13	33
13	Austria	9	12	4	25
14	Switzerland	9	10	9	28
15	Australia	8	19	18	45
16	Japan	8	10	6	24

17	Finland	6	15	12	33
18	Italy	6	4	9	19
19	New Zealand	5	6	5	16
20	Jamaica	5	6	4	15
21	Egypt	4	7	3	14
22	Argentina	4	4	6	14
23	Yugoslavia	3	5	9	17
24	Denmark	3	4	6	13
25	Ireland	2	2	10	14
26	Kuwait	2	2	1	5
27	Iceland	2	0	1	3
28	Spain	1	14	9	24
29	Korea	1	2	1	4
30	Kenya	1	2	0	3
31	India	1	1	0	2
32	Indonesia	1	0	4	5
33	Colombia	1	0	1	2
34	Sudan	1	0	0	1
35	Zimbabwe	0	7	4	11
36	Bahamas	0	1	2	3
37	Hong Kong	0	0	2	2
38	Czechoslovakia	0	0	1	1
39	Greece	0	0	1	1
40	Malta	0	0	1	1

1984 Summer Paralympics

The 1984 Summer Paralympics were the seventh Paralympic Games to be held. They were held in Stoke Mandeville, United Kingdom (wheelchair athletes) and New York, United States of America (cerebral palsy, visually impaired, amputee and les autres).

Games of the VII Paralympics

New York celebration

Nations participating	45
Athletes participating	1,800
Events	~300 in 15 sports
Opening ceremonies	June 17, 1984
Closing ceremonies	June 30, 1984
Officially opened by	Ronald Reagan

Stoke Mandeville celebration

Nations participating	41
Athletes participating	1,100
Events	~300 in 10 sports
Opening ceremonies	July 22, 1984
Closing ceremonies	August 1, 1984
Officially opened by	HRH Prince Charles

Medals Tally

Rank	Country	Gold	Silver	Bronze	Total
1	United States	101	91	84	276
2	Great Britain	75	80	85	240
3	Sweden	51	30	22	103
4	Canada	48	52	49	149
5	Germany	44	42	29	115
6	Netherlands	44	40	17	101
7	France	37	39	23	99
8	Australia	29	38	26	93
9	Norway	22	24	20	66
10	Denmark	22	6	11	39
11	Spain	21	8	12	41

12	Poland	20	15	13	48
13	Finland	15	10	17	42
14	Ireland	13	11	20	44
15	Hungary	12	12	3	27
16	Belgium	9	11	6	26
17	Yugoslavia	7	9	8	24
18	Austria	5	13	7	25
19	Switzerland	5	2	2	9
20	Portugal	4	2	7	13
21	Italy	3	7	6	16
22	Japan	3	2	5	10
23	China	2	12	8	22
24	Israel	2	6	7	15
25	New Zealand	2	3	1	6
26	Egypt	2	0	3	5
27	Trinidad and Tobago	2	0	1	3
28	Luxembourg	1	4	1	6
29	Brazil	1	3	2	6
30	Burkina Faso	1	1	2	4
31	Mexico	0	3	3	6
32	Iceland	0	2	6	8
33	German Democratic Republic	0	2	1	3
34	India	0	2	1	3
35	Indonesia	0	1	1	2
36	Zimbabwe	0	1	0	1
37	Hong Kong	0	0	1	1
38	Korea	0	0	1	1

1988 Summer Paralympics

The 1988 Summer Paralympics were the first Paralympics, for 24 years, that were held along side the Olympics. They took place in Seoul, South Korea.

Games of the VIII Paralympics

Nations participating	61
Athletes participating	3,053
Events	729 in 16 sports
Opening ceremonies	October 15, 1988
Closing ceremonies	October 24, 1988
Officially opened by	Roh Tae-Woo

Medals Tally

Rank	Country	Gold	Silver	Bronze	Total
1	United States	92	91	85	268
2	Germany	77	64	48	189
3	Great Britain	62	66	51	179
4	Canada	54	42	57	153
5	France	45	48	49	142
6	Sweden	42	38	22	102
7	Korea	40	35	19	94
8	Netherlands	30	23	29	82
9	Denmark	25	18	22	65
10	Australia	23	34	37	94
11	Poland	22	25	34	81
12	Russia	21	19	15	55
13	Spain	18	13	12	43
14	China	17	17	9	43

15	Italy	16	15	27	58
16	Japan	16	12	17	45
17	Belgium	15	17	9	41
18	Israel	15	13	15	43
19	Ireland	13	13	18	44
20	Austria	13	7	15	35
21	Switzerland	12	12	10	34
22	Finland	11	23	15	49
23	Norway	11	11	13	35
24	Mexico	8	9	6	23
25	Brazil	4	9	14	27
26	Kuwait	4	6	8	18
27	Yugoslavia	4	4	11	19
28	Iran	4	1	3	8
29	Portugal	3	4	5	12
30	New Zealand	2	4	11	17
31	Iceland	2	2	8	12
32	Bulgaria	2	1	0	3
33	Jamaica	1	4	3	8
34	Faroe Islands	1	3	3	7
35	Egypt	1	2	3	6
36	Puerto Rico	1	2	0	3
37	Bahrain	1	1	1	3
38	Guatemala	1	0	0	1
39	Argentina	0	7	2	9
40	Hungary	0	4	7	11
41	Kenya	0	4	1	5
42	Hong Kong	0	2	7	9
43	Greece	0	1	3	4

44	Indonesia	0	1	0	1
45	Czec and Esl Federal Republic	0	1	0	1
46	Thailand	0	1	0	1
47	Tunisia	0	0	2	2
48	Malta	0	0	1	1

1992 Summer Paralympics

The 1992 Summer Paralympics were the ninth Paralympic Games to be held. They were held in Barcelona, Spain.

Games of the IX Paralympics

Nations participating	82
Athletes participating	3,020
Events	487 in 15 sports
Opening ceremonies	September 3, 1992
Closing ceremonies	September 14, 1992

Medals Tally

Rank	Country	Gold	Silver	Bronze	Total
1	United States	76	51	48	175
2	Germany	60	50	60	170
3	Great Britain	40	46	41	127
4	France	36	35	33	104
5	Spain	34	31	42	107
6	Canada	28	21	26	75
7	Australia	24	27	25	76
8	Unified Team	17	14	15	46
9	Netherlands	13	15	11	39

10	Norway	13	12	7	32
11	Denmark	12	22	12	46
12	China	11	7	7	25
13	Korea	10	14	18	42
14	Italy	10	7	18	35
15	Finland	8	6	11	25
16	Poland	7	10	7	24
17	Japan	7	8	15	30
18	Switzerland	6	16	12	34
19	Sweden	5	22	8	35
20	Austria	5	4	13	22
21	Belgium	5	4	6	15
22	Egypt	5	4	4	13
23	New Zealand	5	1	0	6
24	Czec and Esl Fed.R.	4	3	6	13
25	Hungary	4	3	4	11
26	Ind.Paralympians	4	3	1	8
27	South Africa	4	1	3	8
28	Hong Kong	3	4	4	11
29	Cuba	3	3	3	9
30	Portugal	3	3	1	7
31	Iceland	3	2	12	17
32	Brazil	3	0	4	7
33	Israel	2	4	5	11
34	Slovenia	2	0	1	3
35	Nigeria	2	0	0	2
36	Kuwait	1	3	1	5
37	Iran	1	2	1	4
38	Bulgaria	1	2	0	3

39	Panama	1	2	0	3
40	Argentina	1	1	0	2
41	Kenya	1	0	1	2
42	Lithuania	0	4	3	7
43	Ireland	0	3	3	6
44	Estonia	0	2	1	3
45	Greece	0	2	1	3
46	Mexico	0	1	10	11
47	Jamaica	0	1	2	3
47	Malaysia	0	1	2	3
49	Faroe Islands	0	1	0	1
50	Bahrain	0	0	1	1
51	Chinese Taipei	0	0	1	1
52	Croatia	0	0	1	1
53	Iraq	0	0	1	1
54	Thailand	0	0	1	1
55	Venezuela	0	0	1	1

1996 Summer Paralympics

The 1996 Paralympic Games in Atlanta, USA were the first Paralympics to get mass media sponsorship.

Games of the X Paralympics

Nations participating	103
Athletes participating	3,195(2,415 men, 780 women)
Events	508 in 20 sports
Opening ceremonies	October 15, 1996
Closing ceremonies	October 26, 1996
Officially opened by	Al Gore

Medals Tally

Rank	Country	Gold	Silver	Bronze	Total
1	United States	46	46	65	157
2	Australia	42	37	27	106
3	Germany	40	58	51	14
4	Great Britain	39	42	41	122
5	Spain	39	31	36	106
6	France	35	29	31	95
7	Canada	24	21	24	69
8	Netherlands	17	11	17	45
9	China	16	13	10	39
10	Japan	14	10	12	36
11	Poland	13	2	8	35
12	South Korea	13	2	15	30
13	Sweden	12	14	10	36
14	Italy	11	20	15	46
15	South Africa	10	8	10	28
16	Russia	9	7	11	27
17	Norway	9	7	4	20
18	Switzerland	9	6	6	21
19	New Zealand	9	6	3	18
20	Iran	9	5	3	17
21	Egypt	8	11	11	30
22	Belgium	8	10	7	25
23	Cuba	8	3	0	11
24	Denmark	7	17	17	41
25	Austria	6	6	10	22
26	Portugal	6	4	4	14
27	Hong Kong	5	5	5	15

28	Iceland	5	4	5	14
29	Hungary	5	2	3	10
30	Finland	4	5	4	13
31	Mexico	3	5	4	12
32	Estonia	3	4	2	9
33	Belarus	3	3	7	13
34	Lithuania	3	2	6	11
35	Nigeria	3	2	3	8
36	Czech Republic	2	7	1	10
37	Brazil	2	6	13	21
38	Argentina	2	5	2	9
39	Slovakia	2	4	5	11
40	Algeria	2	2	3	7
41	Yugoslavia	2	2	0	4
42	Côte d'Ivoire	2	0	0	2
42	Panama	2	0	0	2
44	Ukraine	1	4	2	7
45	Ireland	1	3	6	10
46	Greece	1	1	3	5
47	Kuwait	1	1	1	3
48	Kenya	1	1	0	2
49	Chinese Taipei	1	0	2	3
50	Dominican Rep.	1	0	0	1
50	Peru	1	0	0	1
52	Israel	0	4	5	9
53	Slovenia	0	2	3	5
54	Tunisia	0	2	0	2
55	Bulgaria	0	1	1	2
56	Jordan	0	1	0	1

57	Moldova	0	0	2	2
57	Thailand	0	0	2	2
59	Jamaica	0	0	1	1
59	Uruguay	0	0	1	1

2000 Summer Paralympics

Games of the XI Paralympics

Nations participating	127
Athletes participating	3,843(2,867 men, 979 women)
Events	551 in 20 sports
Opening ceremonies	October 18, 2000
Closing ceremonies	October 29, 2000
Officially opened by	William Deane
Lit the Torch	Louise Sauvage

Medals Tally

Rank	Country	Gold	Silver	Bronze	Total
1	Australia	63	39	47	149
2	Great Britain	41	43	47	131
3	Spain	39	30	38	107
4	Canada	38	33	25	96
5	United States	36	39	34	109
6	China	34	22	17	73
7	France	30	28	28	86
8	Poland	19	22	12	53
9	South Korea	18	7	7	32
10	Germany	15	42	38	95
11	Czech Republic	15	15	13	43
12	Japan	13	17	11	41

13	South Africa	13	12	13	38
14	Russia	12	11	12	35
15	Netherlands	12	9	9	30
16	Iran	12	4	7	23
17	Mexico	10	12	12	34
18	Italy	9	8	10	27
19	Denmark	8	8	14	30
20	Switzerland	8	4	8	20
21	Hong Kong	8	3	7	18
22	Nigeria	7	1	5	13
23	Egypt	6	11	11	28
24	Brazil	6	10	6	22
25	New Zealand	6	8	4	18
26	Portugal	6	5	4	15
27	Tunisia	6	4	1	11
28	Belarus	5	8	10	23
29	Sweden	5	6	10	21
30	Thailand	5	4	2	11
31	Ireland	5	3	1	9
32	Hungary	4	5	14	23
33	Greece	4	4	3	11
34	Cuba	4	2	2	8
35	Ukraine	3	20	14	37
36	Slovakia	3	5	5	13
37	Israel	3	2	1	6
38	Algeria	3	0	0	3
39	Austria	2	7	6	15
40	Norway	2	6	7	15
41	Iceland	2	0	2	4

42	Belgium	1	4	4	9
43	Finland	1	3	6	10
44	Chinese Taipei	1	2	4	7
45	Estonia	1	1	3	5
46	Kenya	1	1	2	4
47	Azerbaijan	1	1	0	2
47	Peru	1	1	0	2
47	Azerbaijan	1	1	0	2
49	Côte d'Ivoire	1	0	1	2
50	Bulgaria	1	0	0	1
50	Jordan	1	0	0	1
50	Zimbabwe	1	0	0	1
53	Faroe Islands	0	3	1	4
53	United Arab Emirates	0	3	1	4
55	Argentina	0	2	3	5
56	Slovenia	0	2	2	4
57	Lithuania	0	2	1	3
58	Kuwait	0	1	4	5
59	Bahrain	0	1	1	2
59	Panama	0	1	1	2
61	Bosnia and Herzegovina	0	1	0	1
61	Yugoslavia	0	1	0	1
63	Latvia	0	0	3	3
64	Libya	0	0	1	1
64.	Palestine	0	0	1	1
64	Philippines	0	0	1	1
64	Puerto Rico	0	0	1	1
64	Venezuela	0	0	1	1

2004 Summer Paralympics

The 2004 Summer Paralympic Games, the twelfth Paralympics, were held in Athens, Greece from September 17 to 28. The Paralympic Summer Games are the second-largest sporting event in the world, after the Summer Olympic games. An estimated 4,000 athletes took part, with ages ranging from 11 to 66.

The 800 m Women's Wheelchair Race and 1500 m Men's Wheelchair Race were the first competitions held for the 2004 Summer Paralympics, and also occurred during the 2004 Summer Olympics as demonstration sports. These races are now open to able-bodied people. See Wheelchair racing at the 2004 Summer Olympics for more details.

Athletes with learning difficulties are excluded from the games due to the difficulties in testing for and classifying these disabilities. The exclusion was introduced after the 2000 Summer Paralympics in Sydney, the first games with events exclusively for people with learning difficulties, after it was found that the majority of the Spanish basketball team were not disabled. The IPC has said that the exclusion will continue until there are sufficient tests for the disabilities and a way to measure the effect they have on a sport. Exhibition matches for these categories will still continue in basketball and table tennis. There is a separate games designed particularly for athletes with learning difficulties called the Special Olympics.

Medals Tally

Rank	Country	Gold	Silver	Bronze	Total
1	China	63	46	32	141
2	Great Britain	35	30	29	94
3	Canada	28	19	25	72
4	United States	27	22	39	88
5	Australia	26	38	36	100
6	Ukraine	24	12	19	55

7	Spain	20	27	24	71
8	Germany	19	28	32	79
9	France	18	26	30	74
10	Japan	17	15	20	52

Opening Ceremony

The opening ceremony for the 2004 Summer Paralympics took place on September 17, 2004. The show started with children passing on knowledge and raising their lights to the sky. This was a reference to Hippocrates, who transferred knowledge to the children. A 26 meters tall olive tree symbolising life stood in the middle of the arena. The opening ceremony also featured a performance with human drama, with light and with music, in an allegory about obstacles and limits.

The Parade of Delegations was accompanied by music of French composers Yves Stepping and Jean Christophe. The music told the legend of Hephaestos, god of fire and son of Zeus and Hera. An athlete from Turkmenistan propelled himself around the stadium by doing somersaults. Greece, the home team, received a strong cheer. After that, fireworks erupted at the stadium. There were 150 local support staff involved and 400 volunteers. The children were from ages 8 to 17, coming from Australia, France, Spain, Greece and Germany.

The Games were officially declared opened by Greek president Costis Stephanopoulos and Phil Craven, the president of the International Paralympic Committee. They were accompanied by the head of the organizing committee Gianna Angelopoulos–Daskalaki. Gianna Angelopolous told the athletes and the audience: "The Olympic flame illuminates athletes. Many of you will leave Athens with medals, but all of you will leave as champions." Phil Craven quoted Democritus in his speech: "Two thousand years ago, Democritus said 'To win oneself is the first and best of all victories.' This holds true for all athletes, but especially for Paralympians. Recognising and cultivating your unique abilities and mastering challenges - you set standards and give expression for many people, young and old, around the world." The Olympic flame was lit by Greek athlete Georgios Toptsis.

Closing Ceremony

The closing ceremony for the 2004 Summer Paralympics took place on September 28, 2004. The traditional cultural dislay was removed from the ceremony as a mark of respect for the deaths of 37 teenagers and 4 teachers from Farkadona, travelling to Athens, whose bus collided with a lorry near the town of Kamena Vourla. "The Athens Olympics Organising Committee [ATHOC] has decided to cancel the closing ceremony of the 12th Paralympics as initially planned and scheduled because of the tragic accident that cost the life of pupils," it was announced in a statement. "The artistic and entertainment part of the ceremony will not take place." Flags were flown at half mast and a minute's silence was observed.

In contrast with the formal nature of the operning ceremony, the athletes entered the stadium for the final time as a collective. The flag of the International Paralymic Committee was then officially handed over to the 2008 hosts, Beijing. A procession of young people then made their way to join the athletes in the centre of the stadium carrying paper lanterns, before the Paralympic flame was extinguished, the final moment of the Paralympic Games.

Sports played in 2004 Paralympic Games ,with results

The 2004 Paralympic Games included 19 sports. New categories for these games were five-a-side blind football, sitting volleyball for women, and Quads wheelchair tennis. The sports played were:

— Archery

— Athletics (including Wheelchair Racing)

— Boccia (see Boccia for details of this sport)

— Cycling
— Equestrian
— Football (5-a-side)
— Football (7-a-side)
— Goalball (see Goalball for details of this sport)
— Judo
— Powerlifting
— Sailing
— Shooting
— Swimming
— Table Tennis
— Volleyball (Sitting)
— Wheelchair Basketball
— Wheelchair Fencing
— Wheelchair Rugby
— Wheelchair Tennis

Nations

Athletes from 136 nations competed in the Athens Paralympics.

2008 Summer Paralympics

The 2008 Summer Paralympic Games will be the thirteenth Paralympics and they will be held in Beijing, China.

Winter Paralympics

1976 Winter Paralympics

The 1976 Winter Paralympic Games were the first winter Paralympics. They were held in Örnsköldsvik, Sweden. The disabilities included in this paralympics were blindness and amputees. Fourteen countries took part with 250+ athletes.

Medals Tally

Rank	Country	Gold	Silver	Bronze	Total
1	West Germany	9	12	6	27
2	Switzerland	9	1	1	11
3	Finland	8	7	7	22
4	Sweden	6	7	7	20
5	Austria	5	16	14	35
6	Norway	5	3	2	10
7.	Czechoslovakia	3	0	0	3
8	France	2	0	3	5
9	Canada	1	0	2	3

1980 Winter Paralympics

The 1980 Winter Paralympic Games were the second winter Paralympics and they were held in Geilo, Norway.

1984 Winter Paralympics

The 1984 Winter Paralympic Games were the third winter Paralympics and they were held in Innsbruck, Austria.

1988 Winter Paralympics

The 1988 Winter Paralympic Games were the fourth winter Paralympics and they were held in Innsbruck, Austria. These were the last Winter Paralympics to be held separately from the Winter Olympics, the next cycle, in 1992, the Olympics and Paralympics were held together.

1992 Winter Paralympics

The 1992 Winter Paralympics were the first winter Paralympics to be held along side the Olympics.

1994 Winter Paralympics

Games of the XVII Winter Olympiad

Nations participating	31
Athletes participating	512
Events	5 sports
Opening ceremonies	March 10, 1994
Closing ceremonies	March 19, 1994
Officially opened by	His Majesty King Harald V
Lit the Flame	Cato Zahl Pedersen

Medals Tally

Rank	Country	Gold	Silver	Bronze	Total
1	Norway	29	22	13	64
2	Germany	25	21	18	64
3	United States	24	12	7	43
4	France	14	6	11	31
5	Russia	10	12	8	30
6	Austria	7	16	12	35
7	Finland	7	6	11	24
8	Sweden	3	3	2	8
9	Australia	3	2	4	9
10	New Zealand	3	0	3	6
11	Switzerland	2	9	5	16
12	Poland	2	3	5	10
13	Spain	1	6	3	10
14	Canada	1	2	5	8
15	Netherlands	1	0	3	4
16	Denmark	1	0	2	3
17	Italy	0	7	6	13

18	Japan	0	3	3	6
19	Slovakia	0	3	2	5
20	Great Britain	0	0	5	5
21	Belgium	0	0	1	1
21	Czech Republic	0	0	1	1
21	Estonia	0	0	1	1
21	Liechtenstein	0	0	1	1

1998 Winter Paralympics

The Seventh Winter Paralympics were held alongside the Winter Olympics in Nagano, Japan.

Games of the VII Winter Paralympics

Nations participating	32
Athletes participating	571
Opening ceremonies	March 5, 1998
Closing ceremonies	March ??, 1998
Officially opened by	Crown Prince Naruhito
Athlete's Oath	Yonoe Ryuei
Lit the Flame	Maruyama Naoya

Medals Tally

Rank	Country	Gold	Silver	Bronze	Total
1	Norway	18	9	13	40
2	Germany	14	17	13	44
3	United States	13	8	13	34
4	Japan	12	16	13	41
5	Russia	12	10	9	31
6	Switzerland	10	5	8	23
7	Spain	8	0	0	8

8	Austria	7	16	11	34
9	Finland	7	5	7	19
10	France	5	9	8	22
11	New Zealand	4	1	1	6
12	Italy	3	4	3	10
13	Czech Republic	3	3	1	7
14	Ukraine	3	2	4	9
15	Canada	1	9	5	15
16	Australia	1	0	1	2
16	Denmark	1	0	1	2
18	Slovakia	0	6	4	10
19	Sweden	0	1	5	6
20	Netherlands	0	1	1	2
21	Poland	0	0	2	2

2002 Winter Paralympics

The 2002 Olympic Winter Games, including the 2002 Winter Paralympics, were held in Salt Lake City, Utah, United States.

Opening ceremonies held:	March 7, 2002
Closing ceremonies held:	March 16, 2002
Number of nations participating:	36
Number of athletes participating:	416
Persons who lit the Torch:	Muffy Davis and Chris Waddel

Medals Tally

Rank	Country	Gold	Silver	Bronze	Total
1	Germany	17	1	15	33
2	United States	10	22	11	43

3	Norway	10	3	6	19
4	Austria	9	10	10	29
5	Russia	7	9	5	21
6	Canada	6	4	5	15
7	Switzerland	6	4	2	12
8	Australia	6	1	0	7
9	Finland	4	1	3	8
10	New Zealand	4	0	2	6
11	Italy	3	3	3	9
12	Spain	3	3	2	10
13	France	2	11	6	19
14	Czech Republic	2	1	2	5
15	Netherlands	1	3	0	4
16	Belarus	1	1	0	2
17	Poland	1	0	2	3
18	Ukraine	0	6	6	12
19	Sweden	0	6	3	9
20	Slovakia	0	3	6	9
21	South Korea	0	1	0	1
22	Japan	0	0	3	3

2006 Winter Paralympics

The 2006 Winter Paralympic Games will be the ninth winter Paralympics and they will be held in Turin, Italy.